Relocation: A Practical Guide

CELEBRATING
150
YEARS

JORDANS

Relocation: A Practical Guide

Dr Rob George
University of Oxford and Harcourt Chambers

Frances Judd QC
Harcourt Chambers

Damian Garrido
Harcourt Chambers

Anna Worwood
Manches LLP

ƒ **Family Law**

Published by Family Law
A publishing imprint of Jordan Publishing Limited
21 St Thomas Street
Bristol BS1 6JS

Whilst the publishers and the author have taken every care in preparing the material included in this work, any statements made as to the legal or other implications of particular transactions are made in good faith purely for general guidance and cannot be regarded as a substitute for professional advice. Consequently, no liability can be accepted for loss or expense incurred as a result of relying in particular circumstances on statements made in this work.

Crown Copyright material is reproduced with kind permission of the Controller of Her Majesty's Stationery Office.

British Library Cataloguing-in-Publication Data

A catalogue record for this book is available from the British Library.

ISBN 978 1 84661 504 7

Typeset by Letterpart Ltd, Caterham on the Hill, Surrey CR3 5XL

Printed in Great Britain by CPI Antony Rowe, Chippenham and Eastbourne

FOREWORD

When I was asked some time ago to write a foreword to this book, then only under construction, I readily agreed. Knowing the authors, I was confident that it would make a valuable contribution to the field of family law. The finished book has surpassed my high expectations of it.

The authors set out to reach a diverse audience including lawyers, parents who want to relocate with their child or who want to oppose a relocation, and other professionals involved in the legal process. This is a tall order but they have succeeded in fulfilling it.

The law and practice relating to relocation applications, international and internal, is plainly and comprehensively explained. There is critical discussion of the state of the law and consideration of how it is developing or may develop. Contained in appendices are extracts from important source material of various kinds including the Children Act 1989, the Family Procedure Rules 2010 and significant decided cases.

What will make the book invaluable to many readers is the down to earth practical advice that punctuates it. It will assist lawyers and parents alike in what to do from the earliest stage when a move is contemplated to the moment when, if it comes to that, the judge determines the relocation application and even thereafter.

Any judge who has ever tried a relocation case, particularly one involving international boundaries, knows how difficult it is to resolve such a dispute without there being fundamental damage to some or all members of the family involved. Often no one has done anything wrong. They simply have the misfortune that one parent wants to move with the children to live somewhere else a long way away, for reasons which seem good ones. There are no winners and there is frequently a great deal of sadness all round.

Perhaps one of this book's greatest contributions will therefore turn out to be in enabling parents to look constructively at their plans for their children and to avoid litigation about where, geographically, they are going to live. How sensible it is to point out, as the authors do, that one needs to have an eye to the future before becoming embroiled in an issue of this kind, asking oneself what life will be like after the case is over and what the impact of litigation on the family finances may be. What wise advice it is to suggest that parents talk to each other at an early stage and that they listen to what their children have to say, taking care to keep the right side of the fine line that has to be walked when deciding how and when to broach the subject of a move with them. If the book succeeds in helping parents to reflect upon whether their decision to seek to relocate or to oppose a relocation has been taken carefully and after all the options have been properly weighed, it will have achieved a great deal.

Jill Black
Rt Hon Lady Justice Black
May 2013

INTRODUCTION

We decided to write this book following a CPD seminar in Reading at which two of us (DG and RG) gave a joint presentation on international relocation law in the wake of *K v K (Relocation: Shared Care Arrangement)*.[1] Chatting with family solicitors and barristers after the talk, we were told more than once that it would be useful to have a handbook on relocation law. The combination of complex law, specific procedural issues, and the relative infrequency with which the cases arose in most lawyers' daily practice meant that many practitioners found relocation cases hard, and they wanted a book that brought all the information that they needed together in one place. That is what we have attempted to write.

Most of the time, 'relocation' is taken to mean international cases where one parent is seeking to remove their child or children permanently from the jurisdiction. However, because relocation within the United Kingdom is becoming an increasingly important issue, we have addressed both international and internal (or domestic) relocation here.

This book's main intended audience is family solicitors and barristers, as well as others who need to know about the law and practice of relocation disputes such as Cafcass officers and independent social workers. We also hope that the book will be useful for parents who do not have a lawyer, whether just in the early stages of their relocation dispute before they have sought legal advice, or all the way through if they proceed without legal representation.

To those parents and other family members who read this book, we would say that we know from experience how deeply upsetting and fraught most relocation cases are, both for the parents and for the children. Our focus here is on the legal issues relating to relocation disputes, but we have kept well in mind how serious these cases are, and how much the consequences of the decision, either way, affect the children, parents and wider family members involved.

For the most part, *Relocation: A Practical Guide* is focused on practical issues relevant to the process of bringing or defending a relocation case, but we start off with two background chapters. The first is about the context of relocation cases, and the second is an overview of the law itself. Some readers will not have need of those opening chapters, but that discussion, of course, forms an important part of the background against which the rest of the book should be understood.

---

[1] *K v K (Relocation: Shared Care Arrangement)* [2011] EWCA Civ 793, [2012] 2 FLR 880; see **Appendix 3.3**.

We have also included reasonably lengthy appendices in which we lay out relevant statutory provisions, extracts from cases and other materials (including key Practice Directions and sample C100 and C2 forms) that we think will be useful to practitioners. The cases that we have extracted are, we think, the most useful for understanding the law itself; but inevitably they do not address all the issues that might arise in a relocation case, and we do not suggest that they are the only authorities that would be needed in many cases. When we refer in the text to a case, statute, Practice Direction or other material that is found in an appendix, we point to the relevant appendix in a footnote. We also cross-refer between chapters when an issue is dealt with more fully elsewhere so as to minimise the extent to which we repeat ourselves.

The body of the book (chapters 3 through 8) focuses on practicalities. Four of the chapters (3, 4, 5 and 6) are in pairs, which look at pre-court and then court issues from the perspective of applicants and respondents in turn. We imagine that most readers will look at both 'sides' of the pairings, but in order to make each chapter free-standing there is inevitably some repetition between the chapters.

Insofar as possible, we have endeavoured to make sure that the law as stated in this book is accurate as of 28 February 2013. However, the law is constantly changing, and no reliance should be placed on the law as stated here.

We have all been involved in the writing of the entirety of this book, but the primary division of responsibility has meant that RG focused on Chapters 1, 2 and 8, as well as Appendices 1 through 4; FJQC focused on Chapters 6, 7 and 8; DG focused on Chapters 5 and 6, along with Appendix 6; and AW focused on Chapters 3 and 4, along with Appendix 5. We are grateful to our Research Assistant, Dan Cashman, who did an excellent job of double-checking our references and suggesting improvements of both style and substance.

Finally, we would like to offer our thanks to the Rt Hon Lady Justice Black for graciously agreeing to write the foreword to this book.

Dr Rob George
Frances Judd QC
Damian Garrido
Anna Worwood
28 February 2013

BIOGRAPHICAL DETAILS

Dr Rob George is a British Academy Postdoctoral Fellow in Law at University College, Oxford, and an Associate Member of Harcourt Chambers. He researches primarily on relocation law, and frequently advises on relocation cases, including the recent application for permission to appeal *Re F (Permission to Relocate)* [2012] EWCA Civ 1364, [2012] 3 FCR 443 to the Supreme Court. Recent publications include *Ideas and Debates in Family Law* (Hart Publishing, 2012), 'Reviewing Relocation?' [2012] *Child and Family Law Quarterly* 110, and 'The International Relocation Debate' [2012] *Journal of Social Welfare and Family Law* 141. His next book, *Relocation Disputes: Law and Practice in England and New Zealand* (Hart Publishing) will be published in autumn 2013.

Frances Judd QC is Head of Chambers at Harcourt Chambers, and also sits as a Deputy High Court Judge and as a Recorder. She practices exclusively in family law, and frequently takes relocation cases at first instance and on appeal, including the reported cases of *Re L (Internal Relocation: Shared Residence Order)* [2009] EWCA Civ 20, [2009] 1 FLR 1157 and *Re F and H (Children: Relocation)* [2007] EWCA Civ 692, [2008] 2 FLR 1667. Most recently, she was leading counsel for the father in the application for permission to appeal *Re F (Permission to Relocate)* [2012] EWCA Civ 1364, [2012] 3 FCR 443 to the Supreme Court.

Damian Garrido is a Barrister at Harcourt Chambers with 20 years of experience in family law, and also a Recorder hearing children and family applications in the County Court. He is recognised as a leading family law specialist, having been described in the Legal 500 as 'excellent and tenacious'. He is frequently instructed in cases involving international elements, including relocation disputes, and regularly lectures to the legal profession on family law issues.

Anna Worwood is a Partner in the Family Law department of Manches LLP. She is ranked as a Leading Individual by Chambers and Partners 2012 for her work in family law, particularly cases involving children. She has an international practice and is highly experienced in relocation law, including the reported cases of *Re C (Permission to Remove from Jurisdiction)* [2003] EWHC 596 (Fam), [2003] 1 FLR 1066 and *Re D (Leave to Remove: Shared Residence)* [2006] EWHC 1794 (Fam), [2006] *Family Law* 1006. She is a Fellow of the International Academy of Matrimonial Lawyers (IAML).

CONTENTS

Appendix 2
Extracts from Key Practice Directions

Appendix 3
Extracts from Key International Relocation Cases

Appendix 4
Extracts from Key Internal Relocation Cases

TABLE OF CASES

References are to paragraph numbers.

TABLE OF STATUTES

References are to paragraph numbers.

TABLE OF STATUTORY INSTRUMENTS

References are to paragraph numbers.

TABLE OF EUROPEAN AND INTERNATIONAL LEGISLATION

References are to paragraph numbers.

Chapter 1

WHAT IS RELOCATION?

1.1   Relocation cases are disputes between two parents of a child which arise when one of them intends to move with the child to a new geographic location – a new town or city or, more commonly in terms of cases where the courts get involved, a new country – and the other parent objects to the child moving. Relocation cases are amongst the most fraught parenting disputes, with high stakes for both sides and little room for compromise. Sometimes a relocation case arises as the final stage of a protracted series of disputes between the parents, but other times the relocation case is the first time that otherwise amicable and co-operative parents find themselves in serious conflict.

1.2   Relocation cases are also difficult for legal advisers. The usual approach that family lawyers adopt, seeking compromise and agreement,[1] faces particular challenges in the relocation context because of the binary nature of the dispute. Either the child moves to a new place or she stays where she is and, while there is some scope to negotiate possible ongoing contact or maintenance arrangements if a move goes ahead, it is hard to negotiate about the question of whether the move itself should happen or not.

1.3   Alongside that issue, relocation law itself is quite complicated and requires a great deal of attention to detail in order for pitfalls to be avoided, not least because the law on relocation is quite different for proposed international moves and for proposed moves within the United Kingdom. However, most family lawyers do not do enough relocation cases to be immediately familiar with all those legal complexities. It is hard to know how many relocation cases receive legal advice from solicitors or barristers each year, but many family lawyers do just one or two cases a year, if that.

---

[1]   See, eg, J Eekelaar, M Maclean and S Beinart, *Family Lawyers: The Divorce Work of Solicitors* (Oxford, Hart Publishing, 2000); M Maclean and J Eekelaar, *Family Law Advocacy: How Barristers Help the Victims of Family Failure* (Oxford, Hart Publishing, 2009).

Helpful Hint:

Throughout this book, we refer to relocation cases in two broad categories:[2]

- **International relocation**: cases where the proposed relocation destination is outside the borders of the United Kingdom

- **Internal relocation**: cases where the proposed relocation destination is within the borders of the United Kingdom (also known sometimes as 'domestic relocation')

1.4   Because of the legal and factual difficulty of relocation disputes, and because most family lawyers are only 'occasional' users of relocation law, we have prepared this text to be a practical guidebook. While we have mainly written the book with solicitors and barristers as our intended audience, we envisage that the book may be used by parents involved (or potentially involved) in relocation cases, as well as other professionals involved in the legal process.

1.5   As the book goes on, we progress, step by step, through the entire process of a relocation case. We start with questions that a parent should ask him- or herself and practical things that should be done before starting any formal process at all, including the practicalities of preparing to bring or oppose an application, ways of resolving any potential dispute without needing lawyers or courts, and advice on when to get legal advice. We then work through the process of applying for and opposing a relocation, looking separately at relocation within the United Kingdom and international relocation. Finally we consider when and how to consider appealing a relocation decision.

1.6   At the end of this book, we include extracts from a number of key relocation cases (amongst other materials). While we refer to those cases in the text and occasionally quote short passages from them, they are important in general and we refer frequently to the appendices so that the sections upon which we are relying can be seen in context.

1.7   This opening chapter is designed to introduce the key themes and issues which arise in relocation cases. Readers who are familiar with the issues raised by relocation cases may choose, at this point, to move on to Chapter 2, where we talk in more detail about relocation law itself. Alternatively, readers who are also reasonably familiar with the law may choose, instead, to move on to Chapter 3, where we begin discussing the practicalities of a relocation case. But, for those who want to start at the beginning, this is the place.

---

[2]   We take these from the Children Act 1989, s 13(1)(b) and the Child Abduction Act 1984, s 1(1), which draw a distinction between moves within the United Kingdom and those beyond. Moves to Scotland or Northern Ireland do have potential complications which do not arise for moves within England and Wales, which we discuss in **2.69** *et seq*.

> **Helpful Hint:**
>
> Throughout this book, we use the following terminology:[3]
>
> - **Applicant**: the person seeking to relocate
>
> - **Respondent**: the person opposing the relocation

THE CONTEXT OF RELOCATION DISPUTES

1.8 Relocation cases are usually disputes about whether a parent or other main carer should be allowed to take their child to live in a new location as his or her main home.[4] That question sounds simple enough, but relocation disputes are widely recognised as being amongst the most difficult cases that the family courts face.

1.9 One of the reasons why relocation cases are so complex is that they interconnect with many other issues.[5] This section addresses: the factual context of relocation disputes; the broader legal context in which relocation law is placed; the connection between relocation and other parenting issues; and the possible gender dimension of relocation cases.

Factual context

1.10 It is, of course, true that many parents move house following separation, whether over long or short distances.[6] Sometimes such moves are necessitated by finances, since the parent cannot afford to continue living in the previous location without the additional resources that came from their former partner.[7] Other moves are prompted by new jobs, family support, or the desire for a fresh start.

---

[3] We recognise, of course, that on paper the person seeking to relocate will not always formally be the applicant, and that the person opposing the relocation will not always formally be the respondent, especially in an internal relocation case. We have decided to use this terminology to avoid stereotyped references to 'mother' and 'father', or inelegant phrases like 'the parent seeking to relocate'. We do, however, use female pronouns in relation to applicants, and male pronouns in relation to respondents, primarily as a way of making our meaning grammatically clear.

[4] Sometimes there is dispute over temporary moves, where the case usually arises because of the respondent's worry that the applicant will not return with the child, or his worry about the child's well-being while away; see **Chapter 7**.

[5] For a useful summary, see R George, 'The International Relocation Debate' [2012] *Journal of Social Welfare and Family Law* 141, pp 142–145 (upon which this section draws) and a preliminary document prepared by the Permanent Bureau of the Hague Conference on Private International Law, *Preliminary Note on International Family Relocation*, Preliminary Document No 11 of January 2012, online at www.hcch.net/upload/wop/abduct2012pd11e.pdf.

[6] For reasons why relocation cases arise, see **1.13** *et seq*.

[7] In a longitudinal study in Virginia, USA, divorced woman moved four times in the first six

1.11 The vast majority of relocation cases are disputes between the two parents of a child, and usually it is the mother who is the applicant (seeking to relocate) and the father who is the respondent (opposing the relocation) – but neither of these characteristics is inevitable. Applications are sometimes brought by fathers or by other family members with whom the child is living, most commonly grandparents. In those cases, the respondent may be the mother or, in the case of grandparent applicants, either parent (or even both).[8]

1.12 Relocation cases can arise at any time once the parents' relationship starts to come to an end. Some cases follow immediately from the separation, and indeed the relocation question can be incorporated fully into initial questions about residence and contact arrangements.[9] Other relocation cases arise years after the separation. In some of those cases, the relocation case is the first time that otherwise amicable parents have found themselves in serious dispute about their children. In other cases, perhaps more commonly, the relocation issue is the culmination of an ongoing series of disputes,[10] and indeed can be an attempt by the applicant parent to put an end to the conflict by physically moving herself and the child away.

1.13 Relocation cases arise for many different reasons, but there are five main factual patterns that can be seen. While these patterns are common, it is important to note that research with parents involved in relocation cases reveals that parents who seek to relocate often have 'multiple, complex and multi-layered … reasons for the decision',[11] so these patterns should be understood as trends which overlap, not as isolated 'categories'.

1.14 The first, and perhaps most common, fact pattern is the *going home* case. These are cases where the applicant is originally from somewhere else and is now seeking to return. The applicant was originally from Australia or Singapore or Norway and now, with the relationship with the other parent

---

months after separation, on average; but, for poor women, the average was seven times: see M Hetherington and J Kelly, *For Better or For Worse: Divorce Reconsidered* (New York, Norton, 2001), p 88.

8   Such a case would likely arise where grandparents had taken on the main care of a child because of some factor which prevented one or both parents from doing so.

9   It is in part for this reason that s 13(3) of the Children Act 1989 envisages that leave to remove the child from the jurisdiction can be granted as part of a residence order; see **Appendix 1.1**.

10   For Australian research showing that many relocation cases are part of an ongoing story of litigation, see R Kaspiew, J Behrens and B Smyth, 'Relocation Disputes in Separated Families Prior to the 2006 Reforms: An Empirical Study' (2011) 86 *Family Matters* 72. Similarly, a New Zealand study of 100 families who had been involved in a relocation issue found that 'a relocation "dispute" is not a discrete, one-time-only event, but is instead illustrative of an ongoing process of family post-separation transition(s)': N Taylor, M Gollop and M Henaghan, *Relocation Following Parental Separation: The Welfare and Best Interests of Children* (Dunedin, Centre for Research on Children and Families, 2010), p 92.

11   N Taylor, M Gollop and M Henaghan, *Relocation Following Parental Separation: The Welfare and Best Interests of Children* (Dunedin, Centre for Research on Children and Families, 2010), p 26, discussing Australian research by R Kaspiew, J Behrens and B Smyth, 'Relocation Disputes in Separated Families Prior to the 2006 Reforms: An Empirical Study' (2011) 86 *Family Matters* 72.

having ended, she wants to go back. Usually, though not always, the applicant in a *going home* case has family in the relocation destination. It is also not uncommon for the respondent to have originally come from the proposed relocation destination as well, though whether this has any real effect on individual cases is hard to know.

1.15 The second fact pattern involves a *specific opportunity*, where the applicant is looking to move somewhere new for a particular reason that is specific to the present moment. Perhaps she works for a company that is offering a promotion if she goes to the New York office; perhaps she is doing research that can only be done if she moves to South Africa.

1.16 Third is the *new partner* case. The applicant has met a new partner and he, for one reason or another, is the main driver for the relocation application. Often it is the new partner wanting to return to his original home (where there is obvious overlap with the *going home* case) or, indeed, he may already be in the relocation destination and the applicant is seeking to join him. Alternatively, the new partner may have a job offer or some other reason for wanting to move (where there is overlap with the *specific opportunity* case).

1.17 Fourth, there is the *lifestyle* case. The applicant parent is seeking to move somewhere new because she thinks that, in general, that location will offer a better quality of life, or better life chances, for her and/or her child than staying where she is at the moment. These cases are distinguished from *going home* cases because the applicant usually has only limited (or even no) previous connection with the proposed destination – and if the applicant has a new partner, he too has no particular connection with the proposed destination. Similarly, *lifestyle* cases are distinguished from *specific opportunity* cases because, although the applicant may in fact have obtained an offer of employment or something like that before bringing a *lifestyle* case, the decision to move came first, and the job offer followed; in a *specific opportunity* case, the applicant was not thinking about moving until the opportunity presented itself.

1.18 Finally, there is the occasional case where the applicant's main motivation is to get herself or the child away from respondent, which we might call the *get away* case. In general, the law looks very poorly on such cases,[12] but there are no hard-and-fast rules. If the respondent represents a serious and objective risk to the child or to the other parent, then it may be appropriate for the applicant to rely on this as a basis for seeking relocation;[13] however, cases where it is legitimate to raise such issues are a tiny exception, and most cases fall into one of the other categories.

---

[12] See **2.34–2.35**.
[13] See, for example, a county court case discussed briefly in R George, 'Relocation Research: Early Ideas from Ten County Court Cases' [2012] *Family Law* 700: the father had criminal convictions for child pornography offences and was considered an ongoing risk to the child. The judge thought that the mother was acting responsibly in seeking to move away from the father and granted her permission to relocate, ordering indirect contact to take place after the move was complete.

1.19   While it is possible to categorise cases in this rough-and-ready way, there are two important things to bear in mind. First, no two cases are the same. Just because two applicants are both 'going home' does not mean that their cases will develop in the same way, nor that they will eventually reach the same conclusion.

1.20   Second, there is no legal difference whatsoever based on any of these categories.[14] As Charles J once said, the judge's job is 'to consider the facts and competing considerations in this case and [he] should not decide it by reference to the class or subclass of case into which it could be said to fall'.[15]

1.21   However, that is not to say that the applicant parent's reasons for wanting to relocate are not relevant. Quite the contrary. As the Court of Appeal has stressed, '[t]he applicant's explanation for fundamental relocation is the core of every case'.[16] In legal terms, that starts with a preliminary question about whether the application is 'genuine' or not[17] – in other words, about whether the applicant has a *real* reason for seeking to relocate, rather than a ruse or an excuse to get the child away from the other parent for no good reason.

1.22   But that check of the applicant's good faith is just the start. Much of the case will turn on why the applicant seeks to relocate. However, assuming good faith, one 'type' of reason is not inherently better than any other, and every case in any category must be prepared carefully and seriously if it is not to fall down for inadequate justification.

1.23   In terms of respondents to relocation applications, there is generally less variation in terms of the reasons for opposing the relocation. Almost invariably, the core of the respondent's case is that the proposed move would have a serious and detrimental impact on the child's relationship with him and other family members in the original location. Occasionally, this main reason is supplemented with other concerns, such as that the move has been inadequately planned and would therefore raise too many uncertainties for the child's upbringing, or that the child has particular needs (usually medical or educational), which would not be properly met in the proposed destination.

Legal context

1.24   The detail of relocation law is addressed in Chapter 2. The purpose of this section is to say a little about the general legal context within which relocation decisions are made.

---

14   *Re B (Leave to Remove: Impact of Refusal)* [2004] EWCA Civ 956, [2005] 2 FLR 239 at [16]–[17].
15   *Re C (Permission to Remove from Jurisdiction)* [2003] EWHC 596 (Fam), [2003] 1 FLR 1066 at [24(2)].
16   *Re B (Leave to Remove: Impact of Refusal)* [2004] EWCA Civ 956, [2005] 2 FLR 239 at [17].
17   *Payne v Payne* [2001] EWCA Civ 166, [2001] 1 FLR 1052 at [40(a)]; see **Appendix 3.1**.

1.25 Relocation disputes are part of private child law, the guiding principle in all cases being the welfare of each individual child concerned in his or her individual circumstances.[18] That does not mean that the rights or welfare of other people (the parents and other family members involved) are not relevant – they are, but the court's question is how those matters will affect the child, both directly and indirectly.[19]

1.26 Within the general principle that the child's welfare is paramount, relocation law has a number of complexities. One complication is that the legal guidance which applies to a relocation dispute varies depending on whether the proposed relocation destination is within the United Kingdom or not, though even within those two broad categories there are many factual variations which require the guidance to be modified to a greater or lesser extent.

1.27 Regardless of these complications, which we discuss in Chapter 2, any decision about relocation (whether international or internal) should be made with the assistance of the welfare checklist.[20] The well-known list includes a number of factors to which the court should have particular regard in assessing a child's welfare, namely:

(a) the ascertainable wishes and feelings of the child concerned (considered in the light of his age and understanding);

(b) his physical, emotional and educational needs;

(c) the likely effect on him of any change in his circumstances;

(d) his age, sex, background and any characteristics of his which the court considers relevant;

(e) any harm which he has suffered or is at risk of suffering;

(f) how capable each of his parents, and any other person in relation to whom the court considers the question to be relevant, is of meeting his needs;

(g) the range of powers available to the court under this Act in the proceedings in question.

Relocation and other parenting issues

1.28 The main connection between relocation cases and other areas of child law is about children's residence and contact arrangements,[21] underpinned by 'parental responsibility', which is the legal responsibility for children's

---

[18]   Children Act 1989, s 1(1); see **Appendix 1.1**.
[19]   *J v C* [1970] AC 668 (HL).
[20]   Children Act 1989, s 1(3); see **Appendix 1.1**.
[21]   Children Act 1989, s 8; see **Appendix 1.1**.

upbringing.[22] In some ways, the law in these areas leads social trends, and in other ways the law reflects, or tries to keep up with, social changes which are taking place anyway.

1.29 The main change in the social background which is of significance to relocation law over the last 25 years has been the increasing involvement of both parents in their children's upbringing after separation. In the earlier stages of this trend, the law in England and Wales was towards the front of this development, with specific provisions about parents retaining equal parental responsibility after separation introduced in the Children Act 1989.[23]

1.30 More recently, though, England and Wales has generally resisted a trend of legislatures around the western world to introduce provisions specifically relating to shared time, or shared care, for children after parental separation.[24] While the government has explored the possibility of amending the law a number of times,[25] the law currently states simply that in each case the court should do what is best for the particular child. The courts' initial hostility to shared residence orders has been replaced with an approach whereby shared residence can be ordered whenever that label is an accurate reflection of the child's living arrangements.[26]

1.31 While the law itself has not changed much in terms of the way that children's upbringing is arranged, family practices have been shifting within the existing legal framework. In the years since the Court of Appeal made clear that a shared residence order is not 'exceptional' and may be made whenever that label is an accurate reflection of the child's life,[27] those orders have become increasingly common. It is certainly our experience that increasing numbers of parents are sharing the care of their children, whether in equal or unequal proportions, after separation, such that the children are spending lots of time with each parent regardless of the label attached to the court order (if there is any such order).

1.32 It is clear that a court order can be called 'shared residence' even when the child's time is divided in substantially unequal proportions between each parent.[28] Given this, it is generally thought that the label given to a child's care

---

[22]   Children Act 1989, s 2.

[23]   Children Act 1989, s 2.

[24]   See, for example, the Family Law Act 1975 (Australia), s 65DAA; Code Civil (France), Art 373-2-9.

[25]   The Adoption and Children Act 2006 resulted from one such consideration. At time of writing, the Children and Families Bill 2013 was before Parliament; clause 11 provided that, in private law proceedings, the court is 'to presume, unless the contrary is shown, that involvement of [each] parent in the life of the child concerned will further the child's welfare'.

[26]   See, eg, *D v D (Shared Residence)* [2001] 1 FLR 495 (CA); *Re W (Shared Residence Order)* [2009] EWCA Civ 370, [2009] 2 FLR 436.

[27]   See *D v D (Shared Residence Order)* [2001] 1 FLR 495 (CA).

[28]   See, eg, *T v T (Shared Residence)* [2010] EWCA Civ 1366, [2011] 1 FCR 267 at [26]. In *Re A (Temporary Removal from Jurisdiction)* [2004] EWCA Civ 1587, [2005] 1 FLR 639, the mother

arrangements are of little relevance to relocation law;[29] however, the effect of truly shared care arrangements on relocation law is not entirely clear, as we discuss in the next chapter.[30] What is clear, though, is that as social patterns change such that increasingly both parents remain closely involved in their children's day-to-day care after separation, the arguments of respondent parents opposed to relocation will likely carry increasing weight.

Relocation and gender

1.33 As noted earlier,[31] the majority of relocation applications are brought by mothers, which some scholars have noted raises possible gender questions for relocation law.[32] On its face, relocation law is, like all of child law, gender neutral. In fact, the law says nothing about restricting the free movement of either parent: it is only the child whose residence arrangements are within the court's jurisdiction.[33]

1.34 However, in practice this rule affects resident parents more than non-resident parents because, as a matter of fact, few resident parents choose to relocate without their children if the children's relocation is prohibited by the court.[34] Of course, if a non-resident parent wishes to continue having frequent contact with his children, he too cannot relocate.[35] However, the position is not entirely equal, because regardless of the importance of the child's relationship with the non-resident parent, that parent cannot be compelled to stay if he chooses to leave,[36] whereas as a question of fact (though not of law) the resident parent can usually be so compelled.

---

was allowed to relocate to South Africa with the child for two years, but a shared residence order was made for the duration of the trip with the father who remained in England.

[29] *Re L (Internal Relocation: Shared Residence Order)* [2009] EWCA Civ 20, [2009] 1 FLR 1157 at [36] (see **Appendix 4.2**); *K v K (Relocation: Shared Care Arrangement)* [2011] EWCA Civ 793, [2012] 2 FLR 880 at [57] and [144] (see **Appendix 3.3**).

[30] See **2.22** *et seq*.

[31] See **1.11**.

[32] See, eg, S Boyd, 'Gendering the Best Interests Principle: Custody, Access and Relocation in a Mobile Society' in H Niman and G Sadvari (eds), *Family Law: 'The Best Interests of the Child'* (Ottawa, Law Soc of Upper Canada, 2000); J Behrens, 'U v U: The High Court on Relocation' *Melbourne University Law Review* 572.

[33] See **Chapter 2**.

[34] While applicants do not often choose to move without their child if the relocation is refused, it does happen. In a New Zealand study of 100 families, seven applicants moved without their children after relocation was refused by the court, and five parents who moved within New Zealand without permission did not return with their children when the court ordered the children back to the original location: N Taylor, M Gollop and M Henaghan, *Relocation Following Parental Separation: The Welfare and Best Interests of Children* (Dunedin, Centre for Research on Children and Families, 2010), p 93. NB this study is qualitative, asking about people's experiences, and is not based on a representative sample; consequently, these findings cannot be generalised to the population in general.

[35] P Parkinson, 'Freedom of Movement in an Era of Shared Parenting: The Differences in Judicial Approaches to Relocation' (2008) 36 *Federal Law Review* 145.

[36] Contact orders cannot be made or enforced against an unwilling parent, and the government specifically rejected the idea of introducing a power to require a parent to have contact against

DEBATES ABOUT RELOCATION LAW

1.35 For the most part, this book is not intended as a place to engage in debate about the merits or otherwise of the approaches to relocation disputes adopted by the courts of England and Wales. However, we think that it is important to understand that there are serious and ongoing discussions, in this country and internationally, about how relocation disputes should be resolved, and so we aim here to give a flavour of those discussions.[37]

1.36 In this section, we discuss briefly two of the criticisms that are made of the current law, but these represent just some of the main academic views. It may also be noted that relocation law has been subjected to criticism by campaign groups, including a dedicated online group called the Relocation Campaign;[38] it is fair to say that, so far, this campaign has had little impact in terms of effecting change to the law. On the other hand, though, and importantly, there are those in this jurisdiction and abroad who support the existing approach here.[39]

1.37 One line of criticism, made most clearly by Mary Hayes, suggests that the guidance given by the Court of Appeal in relocation cases is overly directive and, indeed, goes so far as to constrain trial judges in the exercise of their discretionary jurisdiction under the welfare principle.[40] Those who take this view think that relocation decisions should be made with less guidance as to how the child's welfare will best be met. Hayes also reads the Court of Appeal judgments in the early 2000s as being unduly interventionist, though whether that assessment remains true more recently is unclear given an apparent retreat by the appeal court in the last few years.[41]

---

his will: see *Re L, V, M and H (Contact: Domestic Violence)* [2000] 2 FLR 334 (CA) at 364; N Lowe and G Douglas, *Bromley's Family Law* (10th edn, Oxford, Oxford University Press, 2007), pp 521 and 572–573.

[37] In addition to the materials cited in this section, see R George, *Relocation Disputes: Law and Practice in England and New Zealand* (Oxford, Hart Publishing, 2013); R George, 'Reviewing Relocation?' [2012] *Child and Family Law Quarterly* 110; S Gilmore, 'The *Payne* Saga: Precedent and Family Law Cases' [2011] *Family Law* 970; R George, 'Re L (Internal Relocation: Shared Residence Order) [2009] EWCA Civ 20, [2009] 1 FLR 1157' (casenote) [2010] *Journal of Social Welfare and Family Law* 71; F Judd QC and R George, 'International Relocation: Do We Stand Alone?' [2010] *Family Law* 63; C Renton, 'Rethinking Relocation' [2010] *New Law Journal* 958; M Freeman, 'Relocation: The Reunite Research' (London, Reunite, 2009); C Geekie QC, 'Relocation and Shared Residence: One Route or Two?' [2008] *Family Law* 446.

[38] See www.relocationcampaign.co.uk.

[39] See, eg, M Henaghan, 'Relocation Cases: The Rhetoric and the Reality of a Child's Best Interests: A View from the Bottom of the World' [2011] *Child and Family Law Quarterly* 226; L Young, 'Resolving Relocation Disputes: The "Interventionist" Approach in Australia' [2011] *Child and Family Law Quarterly* 203; P Pressdee, 'Relocation, Relocation, Relocation: Rigorous Scrutiny Revisited' [2008] *Family Law* 220; G Brasse, 'The *Payne* Threshold: Leaving the Jurisdiction' [2005] *Family Law* 780.

[40] M Hayes, 'Relocation Cases: Is the Court of Appeal Applying the Correct Principles?' [2006] *Child and Family Law Quarterly* 351.

[41] In January 2010, two of the authors suggested that this shift might have been caused by the warning from the House of Lords in *Re J (Return to Foreign Jurisdiction: Convention Rights)*

1.38 A second criticism, made most powerfully by Jonathan Herring and Rachel Taylor, uses relocation law as an example of the failure of family law in general to grasp the significance of the Human Rights Act 1998 for the way that cases are approached.[42] While Herring and Taylor suggest that a human rights approach would likely not make a significant difference to the outcomes of most relocation cases, they think that the analytical rigour that such an approach offers would be superior to a welfare approach, and at the same time would avoid the problems that Hayes identifies.[43]

1.39 These debates about the best way to approach relocation disputes are, in fact, part of a wider global discussion about this issue.[44] There are many approaches taken to relocation cases around the world, even though most of those approaches are based around versions of the welfare principle.[45] While it is hard to be sure how these different approaches compare in terms of case outcomes, there is at least some evidence to suggest that there are real differences.[46]

1.40 Given these variations, there has been some movement at the international level over the last few years to consider harmonising international relocation law. Those discussions led to a preliminary document with a lengthy list of factors to consider in a relocation application, in the form of the Washington Declaration on International Family Relocation 2010; but further progress stalled after a meeting at The Hague in January 2012 saw little support for more work on the project.[47] Any thought that these ideas could or should be incorporated into domestic law were, therefore, put on hold.[48]

1.41 It now seems that the Council of Europe may be resuming thoughts about international work in this area. A Preparatory Meeting held in January 2013 entrusted the European Committee on Legal Co-operation with the task of drafting, during 2013, a legal instrument on parental dispute resolution in the exercise of parental responsibilities, focused on the relocation of children (including consideration of factors to be taken into account and procedures to

---

[2005] UKHL 40, [2005] 2 FLR 802 at [12] that the Court of Appeal must not interfere with discretionary decisions without adequate justification: F Judd QC and R George, 'International Relocation: Do We Stand Alone?' [2010] *Family Law* 63. See also **8.2–8.4**.

[42] J Herring and R Taylor, 'Relocating Relocation' [2006] *Child and Family Law Quarterly* 517; see also R George, *Ideas and Debates in Family Law* (Oxford, Hart Publishing, 2012), Ch 2.

[43] Subsequent European Court of Human Rights cases may call for some reassessment of the apparent difference between welfare and rights analyses: see, eg, *YC v United Kingdom* (Application No 4547/10) [2012] 2 FLR 332 (ECtHR).

[44] See generally R George, 'The International Relocation Debate' [2012] *Journal of Social Welfare and Family Law* 141.

[45] See A Worwood, 'International Relocation – The Debate' [2005] *Family Law* 621.

[46] For a comparison of English and New Zealand approaches to three hypothetical cases, based on interviews with practising lawyers and judges in the two countries, see R George, 'Practitioners' Views on Children's Welfare in Relocation Disputes: Comparing Approaches in England and New Zealand' [2011] *Child and Family Law Quarterly* 178.

[47] R George, 'The International Relocation Debate' [2012] *Journal of Social Welfare and Family Law* 141, pp 148–150.

[48] See *Re H (Leave to Remove)* [2010] EWCA Civ 915, [2010] 2 FLR 1875 at [26].

be followed).[49] This work shows the international interest in relocation law, but it must be understood that any changes to the law in England and Wales stemming from such deliberations are likely to be several years off.

CONCLUSIONS

1.40   The aim of this chapter was simply to 'set the scene' and give some of the contextual background that will help those who work on relocation cases. We move in the next chapter to an overview of relocation law, providing the essential legal basis for those working on relocation disputes. Once that is done, we begin our step-by-step analysis of the practice of relocation cases.

---

[49]   See Council of Europe, *Prevention and Resolution of Parental Disputes (Relocation of Children)*, (The Hague, Document CDCJ(2013)1, 10 January 2013).

Chapter 2

RELOCATION LAW

2.1   There is only one legal principle applicable to relocation disputes,[1] namely that the welfare of the child concerned is the paramount consideration.[2] Within this broad principle, the courts have laid down guidance about how relocation cases should be approached, and it is important that those involved in relocation cases understand both what the guidance means and how it applies to individual cases.

2.2   This chapter starts with a short discussion about the meaning of guidance in family law cases, and then moves to address the law itself. Because the guidance varies depending on whether the proposed relocation destination is within the United Kingdom or abroad, we divide our discussion of the law in the same way, starting with international cases and then turning to internal ones.

GUIDANCE IN FAMILY LAW CASES

2.3   It has been said that much of the controversy about relocation law in England and Wales[3] stems from inadequate attention having been paid to the difference between legal principles and guidance.[4] In short,[5] a principle of law is something which must be followed by a judge, whereas guidance is intended to help the judge to understand and follow a principle correctly.[6] According to Thorpe LJ,[7] guidance can be seen as a judicial equivalent of the statutory welfare checklist.[8]

2.4   It follows that this chapter is about judicial guidance, intended to inform an analysis of the child's welfare. However, although the welfare principle is the only legal principle applicable to relocation cases:[9]

---

[1]   *K v K (Relocation: Shared Care Arrangement)* [2011] EWCA Civ 793, [2012] 2 FLR 880 (hereafter, *K v K*) at [39], [86] and [141]; see **Appendix 3.3**.

[2]   Children Act 1989, s 1(1); see **Appendix 1.1**.

[3]   See **1.35–1.41**.

[4]   *K v K* at [86].

[5]   See further S Gilmore, 'The *Payne* Saga: Precedent and Family Law Cases' [2011] *Family Law* 970; R George, 'Reviewing Relocation?' [2012] *Child and Family Law Quarterly* 110, pp 115–120.

[6]   *K v K* at [40].

[7]   Ibid.

[8]   Children Act 1989, s 1(3); see **Appendix 1.1**.

[9]   *K v K* at [142]; see **Appendix 3.3**.

'that does not mean that everything else – the valuable guidance – can be ignored. It must be heeded ... but as guidance not as rigid principle or so as to dictate a particular outcome in a sphere of law where the facts of individual cases are so infinitely variable.'

2.5   That means that the elements identified in the guidance as being important questions or factors to consider should be approached in an organic manner determined by the case, and not recited in an 'unduly mechanistic' way.[10] As was explained in *K v K*:[11]

'Guidance of the kind provided in *[appellate relocation cases]* is, of course, very valuable both in ensuring that judges identify what are likely to be the most important factors to be taken into account and the weight that should generally be attached to them. It also plays a valuable role in promoting consistency in decision-making. However, the circumstances in which these difficult decisions have to be made vary infinitely and the judge in each case must be free to weigh up the individual factors and make whatever decision he or she considers to be in the best interests of the child.'

2.6   Another way of putting the point would be to say that 'the questions asked by [the relocation guidance] are genuine questions, rather than loaded ones'.[12] For example, authorities say that, especially in international relocation cases, the impact of refusing the application is likely to be an important consideration.[13] What this means is that the judge must assess the impact of refusal on the applicant and its consequent effect on the child, but neither of those points is pre-determined by the guidance.[14] The judge might find that the impact will be minimal, or that its effect on the child is outweighed by other factors.[15]

INTERNATIONAL RELOCATION LAW

2.7   Where a residence order is in force with respect to a child,[16] there is an automatic prohibition on removing that child from the United Kingdom for a period of more than one calendar month unless everyone with parental responsibility gives written consent or unless the court gives permission.[17]

---

[10]   *K v K* at [87].
[11]   *K v K* at [86]; see **Appendix 3.3**.
[12]   R George, 'Reviewing Relocation?' [2012] *Child and Family Law Quarterly* 110, p 119.
[13]   See, eg, *Payne v Payne* [2001] EWCA Civ 166, [2001] 1 FLR 1052 at [41]; see **Appendix 3.1**.
[14]   *K v K* at [84] (see **Appendix 3.3**); *J v S (Leave to Remove)* [2010] EWHC 2098 (Fam), [2011] 1 FLR 1694 at [81] (see **Appendix 3.2**).
[15]   For examples where this has happened, see, eg, *Re W (Relocation: Contact)* [2009] EWCA Civ 160, [2009] All ER (D) 120 (May) (appeal against the trial judge's refusal of the relocation application dismissed); *Re AR (A Child: Relocation)* [2010] EWHC 1346 (Fam), [2010] 2 FLR 1577 (relocation refused); *Re C (Children)* [2012] EWCA Civ 203 (permission to appeal the trial judge's refusal of the relocation application refused).
[16]   Children Act 1989, s 8; see **Appendix 1.1**.
[17]   Children Act 1989, s 13(1)(b); see **Appendix 1.1**.

2.8   However, regardless of whether there is a residence order or not, it is strongly inadvisable to relocate without written agreement from all those with parental responsibility or, failing that, court permission. The same is true even if the other parent does not have parental responsibility for the child. In both cases, the reason is that interference with a parent's 'rights of custody' (which need not include daily care or control of the child) is child abduction.[18] The consequences of parental child abduction can include orders that the child be summarily returned,[19] or even criminal charges.[20] At the very least, the stress and hassle of dealing with a potential child abduction case, which usually starts with the police arriving at the front door, is something that most parents prefer to avoid, even if in the end it turns out that the relocation was not an abduction.

2.9   If the parent seeking to relocate cannot obtain written consent for the relocation from all those with parental responsibility for the child, then court permission is required. If a residence order is in force, this permission should be sought as an application under s 13 of the Children Act 1989; where there is no residence order, the application should be either for a specific issue order or for a residence order with leave attached,[21] both under s 8.[22] In practical terms, there is no difference between these two applications, since it is clear that the welfare checklist should be employed either way (even though it is technically mandatory[23] only under the s 8 route).[24]

The principal guidance: *Payne v Payne*

2.10   The leading case on international relocation is *Payne v Payne*.[25] *Payne* has a long pedigree,[26] though its interpretation in the years since it was decided has shifted a little. We extract significant portions of the leading judgments of Thorpe LJ and Dame Elizabeth Butler-Sloss P in **Appendix 3.1**, but some key passages are worth laying out here.

---

[18] See generally N Lowe, M Everall QC and M Nicholls, *International Movement of Children: Law Practice and Procedure* (Bristol, Jordan Publishing, 2004).

[19] Hague Convention on the Civil Aspects of International Child Abduction 1980; within the EU, Council Regulation (EC) 2201/2003 takes precedence over the Hague Convention, but is to similar effect.

[20] Child Abduction Act 1984, s 1.

[21] Children Act 1989, s 13(3); see **Appendix 1.1**.

[22] For an argument that this two-approach system is based on a misreading of the Children Act 1989, and that all applications should be made under s 8, see R George, 'Changing Names, Changing Places: Reconsidering Section 13 of the Children Act 1989' [2008] *Family Law* 1121.

[23] Children Act 1989, s 1(4).

[24] *Re B (Change of Surname)* [1996] 1 FLR 791 (CA).

[25] *Payne v Payne* [2001] EWCA Civ 166, [2001] 1 FLR 1052 (hereafter, *Payne*); see **Appendix 3.1**.

[26] See, eg, *Poel v Poel* [1970] 1 WLR 1469 (CA); *Chamberlain v de la Mare* (1983) 4 FLR 434 (CA); *Re F (A Ward) (Leave to Remove Ward Out of Jurisdiction)* [1988] 2 FLR 116 (CA); *M v M (Removal from Jurisdiction)* [1993] 1 FCR 5 (CA). On the history, see R Taylor, 'Poels Apart: Fixed Principles and Shifting Values in Relocation Law' in S Gilmore, J Herring and R Probert (eds) *Landmark Cases in Family Law* (Oxford, Hart Publishing, 2011); R George, *Relocation Disputes: Law and Practice in England and New Zealand* (Oxford, Hart Publishing, 2013), Ch 2.

2.11   While Thorpe LJ gave the first judgment in *Payne*, it has been said on high authority that the President's judgment must not only be included in any consideration of relocation law,[27] but indeed that it is 'the best summary of the approach which judges are required to take to these difficult decisions'.[28] After reviewing the previous authorities, the President said this:

> '[85] In summary I would suggest that the following considerations should be in the forefront of the mind of a judge trying one of these difficult cases. They are not and could not be exclusive of the other important matters which arise in the individual case to be decided. All the relevant factors need to be considered, including the points I make below, so far as they are relevant, and weighed in the balance. The points I make are obvious but in view of the arguments presented to us in this case, it may be worthwhile to repeat them:[29]
>
> (a)   The welfare of the child is always paramount.
> (b)   There is no presumption created by s 13(1)(b) [of the Children Act 1989] in favour of the applicant parent.
> (c)   The reasonable proposals of the parent with a residence order wishing to live abroad carry great weight.
> (d)   Consequently the proposals have to be scrutinised with care and the court needs to be satisfied that there is a genuine motivation for the move and not the intention to bring contact between the child and the other parent to an end.
> (e)   The effect upon the applicant parent and the new family of the child of a refusal of leave is very important.
> (f)   The effect upon the child of the denial of contact with the other parent and in some cases his family is very important.
> (g)   The opportunity for continuing contact between the child and the parent left behind may be very significant.
>
> [86] All the above observations have been made on the premise that the question of residence is not a live issue. If, however, there is a real dispute as to which parent should be granted a residence order, and the decision as to which parent is the more suitable is finely balanced, the future plans of each parent for the child are clearly relevant. If one parent intends to set up home in another country and remove the child from school, surroundings and the other parent and his family, it may in some cases be an important factor to weigh in the balance. But in a case where the decision as to residence is clear as the judge in this case clearly thought it was, the plans for removal from the jurisdiction would not be likely to be significant in the decision over residence.'

2.12   Thorpe LJ, concerned to ensure that relocation cases were not granted without adequate consideration being given to effects either way of the decision, suggested a 'discipline' for judges to follow when considering a relocation application. His Lordship later amended para (c) of the discipline

---

[27]   See, eg, *K v K* at [143]; see **Appendix 3.3**.
[28]   *Re D (Leave to Remove: Appeal)* [2010] EWCA Civ 50, [2010] 2 FLR 1605 at [18].
[29]   *Payne* at [85]–[86]; see **Appendix 3.1**.

slightly,[30] and we offer it here as amended. It is also important to remember that 'para [41] is as much a part of the discipline as if it had been expressed in para [40](c)'.[31]

> '[40] ... [I]f the regard which the court pays to the reasonable proposals of the primary carer were elevated into a legal presumption then there would be an obvious risk of the breach of the respondent's rights not only under Art 8 but also his rights under Art 6 to a fair trial. To guard against the risk of too perfunctory an investigation resulting from too ready an assumption that the mother's proposals are necessarily compatible with the child's welfare I would suggest the following discipline as a prelude to conclusion:
>
> (a) Pose the question: is the mother's application genuine in the sense that it is not motivated by some selfish desire to exclude the father from the child's life? Then ask is the mother's application realistic, by which I mean founded on practical proposals both well researched and investigated? If the application fails either of these tests refusal will inevitably follow.
>
> (b) If however the application passes these tests then there must be a careful appraisal of the father's opposition: is it motivated by genuine concern for the future of the child's welfare or is it driven by some ulterior motive? What would be the extent of the detriment to him and his future relationship with the child were the application granted? To what extent would that be offset by extension of the child's relationships with the maternal family and homeland?
>
> (c) What would be the impact on the mother, either as the single parent or as a new wife, of a refusal of her realistic proposal? [Where the mother cares for the child or proposes to care for the child within a new family, the impact of refusal on the new family and on the stepfather or prospective stepfather must also be carefully calculated.]
>
> (d) The outcome of the second and third appraisals must then be brought into an overriding review of the child's welfare as the paramount consideration, directed by the statutory checklist insofar as appropriate.
>
> [41] In suggesting such a discipline I would not wish to be thought to have diminished the importance that this court has consistently attached to the emotional and psychological well-being of the primary carer. In any evaluation of the welfare of the child as the paramount consideration great weight must be given to this factor.'[32]

2.13 This guidance, as seen, is designed to help judges to determine the outcome which best promotes the child's welfare. In addition to the *Payne* guidance, it is often helpful to give express consideration to those elements from the welfare checklist which are especially relevant (though it is not essential for judges to go through the welfare checklist step by step in their judgments).[33] While every case is different, the checklist factors which are most commonly at the fore in a relocation case are:

---

[30] *Re B (Removal from Jurisdiction), Re S (Removal from Jurisdiction)* [2003] EWCA Civ 1149, [2003] 2 FLR 1043 at [11].

[31] *Re B (Leave to Remove: Impact of Refusal)* [2004] EWCA Civ 956, [2005] 2 FLR 239 at [14].

[32] *Payne* at [40]–[41]; see **Appendix 3.1**.

[33] Children Act 1989, s 1(3); see **Appendix 1.1**.

(a)   the ascertainable wishes and feelings of the child concerned (considered in
       the light of his age and understanding);

(c)   the likely effect on [the child] of any change in his circumstances;

(f)   how capable each of [the child's] parents, and any other person in relation
       to whom the court considers the question to be relevant, is of meeting his
       needs.

2.14   The guidance applicable to international relocation applications has been
stable and consistent since *Payne*, with the Court of Appeal rejecting calls to
review the guidance,[34] and leave to appeal beyond the Court of Appeal being
refused a number of times.[35] However, it is widely thought that the 'rigour' with
which trial judges approach relocation applications has tightened up over the
last few years,[36] meaning that applicant parents now face more of a challenge
than perhaps once they did. This view is supported by some recent judgments,
which we now discuss.

2.15   In *Re H (Leave to Remove)*, Wilson LJ cautioned about the need to look
at what *Payne v Payne* actually says, rather than at a parody of the decision.[37]
In other words, his Lordship is reminding those who use the guidance that they
need to read what it actually says, and to resist the temptation to paraphrase it
inaccurately, or to give it a gloss which is not there on its face.

2.16   In practical terms, these comments aim to ensure that judges and
advisers do not read into *Payne* any assumptions in favour of the applicant. In
particular, para 40(c), combined with para 41, of Thorpe LJ's discipline was
sometimes read as if the effect on the applicant parent of refusing permission
to relocate, and the consequent effect on the child, were being
pre-determined.[38] A good explanation of how to read the *Payne* guidance
without any gloss came from the High Court in the case of *J v S (Leave to
Remove)*.[39]

---

34   *Re G (Leave to Remove)* [2007] EWCA Civ 1497, [2008] 1 FLR 1587; *Re H (Leave to Remove)*
       [2010] EWCA Civ 915, [2010] 2 FLR 1875; *Re W (Relocation: Removal Outside Jurisdiction)*
       [2011] EWCA Civ 345, [2011] 2 FLR 409.
35   See, eg, *Re B (Removal from Jurisdiction); Re S (Removal from Jurisdiction)* [2003] EWCA Civ
       1149, [2003] 2 FLR 1043 (leave refused 1 April 2004); *Re W (A Child) (Removal from
       Jurisdiction)* [2005] EWCA Civ 1614, [2006] 1 FCR 346 (leave refused 21 June 2006); *Re W
       (Leave to Remove)* [2008] EWCA Civ 538, [2008] 2 FLR 1170 (leave refused 9 June 2008); *Re F
       (Permission to Relocate)* [2012] EWCA Civ 1364, [2012] 3 FCR 443 (leave refused 4 February
       2013).
36   See, eg, P Pressdee, 'Relocation, Relocation, Relocation: Rigorous Scrutiny Revisited' [2008]
       Family Law 220. See also the views of practitioners and judges interviewed about relocation
       law in R George, *Relocation Disputes: Law and Practice in England and New Zealand* (Oxford,
       Hart Publishing, 2013), Ch 4. One trial judge is quoted from that research as saying that 'at
       one stage, *Payne v Payne* appeared to say, "A + B + C always equals relocation" ... [but] there's
       been just a bit of a change in the wind'.
37   *Re H (Leave to Remove)* [2010] EWCA Civ 915, [2010] 2 FLR 1875 at [21]; see also *K v K*
       at [86].
38   This impression was created in part by cases like *Re B (Removal from Jurisdiction); Re S*

Case Example: *J v S (Leave to Remove)* **[2010] EWHC 2098 (Fam), [2011] 1 FLR 1694**

The Japanese mother and Swedish father had lived in London for twenty years. The children, who were bilingual in English and Japanese, and who spent considerable time in both Sweden and Japan, were now 10 and 8. Following a change in the father's work patterns, he sought increased time with the children; but the maternal grandmother, who had previously spent prolonged periods in England, was now unwell, and the mother sought to relocate to Japan. She complained of being lonely and isolated in England (and medical evidence supported serious depression), and thought that she had better prospects of obtaining suitable employment in Japan.

In the High Court, Eleanor King J granted the mother leave to relocate, subject to various security precautions. Her Ladyship explained that, while the *Payne* guidance was binding on trial courts, it needed to be read carefully and in its entirety; in particular, it needed to be remembered that the effect of refusal on the applicant was only one of many factors to take into account.

> '[81] [Counsel for the father] properly and appropriately accepted in submissions that this court is bound by the Court of Appeal decision in *Payne*. I have, therefore, to decide this case on the basis of the *Payne* discipline regardless of whatever a growing tide of opinion may or may not say about that approach. What [counsel] says is that, at the end of the day, *Payne* says one thing namely that the welfare of these two children is paramount. I agree. This court, he submits, must be careful not to allow itself to become confined in a strait-jacket, with the series of questions presenting the only test. Care, he says, must be taken to ensure that the question of the impact of refusal of the mother is but one component of an assessment of the best interests of the boys and not the only feature. I unhesitatingly agree.
>
> [82] The welfare of these boys is paramount. In conducting the balancing exercise I am bound by the discipline of *Payne*, not limited to the questions set out by Thorpe LJ, but also with the judgment of Lady Butler-Sloss P (as she then was) at the forefront of my mind. I consider *Payne* only under the➡

(Removal from Jurisdiction) [2003] EWCA Civ 1149, [2003] 2 FLR 1043, *Re B (Leave to Remove: Impact of Refusal)* [2004] EWCA Civ 956, [2005] 2 FLR 239 and *Re G (Removal from Jurisdiction)* [2005] EWCA Civ 170, [2005] 2 FLR 166. These cases led Professor Mary Hayes to say in 'Relocation Cases: Is the Court of Appeal Applying the Correct Principles?' [2006] *Child and Family Law Quarterly* 351, pp 370–371: 'The weight to be given to the wishes and feelings of the [applicant] mother has been elevated to a matter of principle ... The Court of Appeal has ruled that a judge makes a serious error where he gives less weight to the impact on the mother of denial of leave than he does to other factors relevant to the welfare checklist'. More recent cases appear to have moved away from this position: see, eg, *Re AR (A Child: Relocation)* [2010] EWHC 1346 (Fam), [2010] 2 FLR 1577; *Re H (Leave to Remove)* [2010] EWCA Civ 915, [2010] 2 FLR 1875; *K v K.*

[39] *J v S (Leave to Remove)* [2010] EWHC 2098 (Fam), [2011] 1 FLR 1694; see **Appendix 3.2**.

> umbrella of the paramountcy rule and using the welfare checklist as a tool
> to assist me, whilst always bearing in mind the Art 8 rights of these
> children.'

2.17 In other words, the effect of refusal on the applicant parent, and the
further effect of that on the child's welfare, are matters of fact to be assessed
and weighed by the trial judge. *Payne* does not pre-empt that assessment, and
question (c) within Thorpe LJ's discipline is a genuine question, not a loaded
one. It asks what the impact of refusal will be on the applicant parent, and the
full range of answers, from 'none at all' to 'complete devastation', is available to
the trial judge, based on the evidence. In the event that the judge finds that
there will be a significant effect, *Payne* highlights that the emotional and
psychological well-being of a primary carer is an important factor when
assessing the child's welfare; but again, it is the judge who is tasked with
making the overall assessment in each case, and while this factor will be
important, it is not *all*-important.

2.18 Eleanor King J's remarks in *J v S (Leave to Remove)* were endorsed by
the Court of Appeal in *K v K*.[40] The Court of Appeal also reiterated that *Payne*
offers important guidance but does not represent any statement of legal
principle.[41] It follows that Eleanor King J's point about the effect of refusal on
the applicant parent can be applied equally to all other elements of the
guidance. The aim of *Payne* is to highlight factors which are usually relevant to
the decision, but its effect is to ask questions, not answer them.

Variations on the guidance

2.19 The principal guidance from *Payne* always has to be applied in a nuanced
way which starts with the facts of the case and adapts the guidance as required,
rather than trying to argue that the facts of the case can be squeezed into any
particular sub-category of case. In particular, we think there to be much force
in the view expressed by Black LJ in *K v K*,[42] and reiterated by Munby LJ in *Re
F*,[43] that arguments about 'categories of case', and therefore about different
'tests' to be applied, are unlikely to be helpful.

2.20 The fact-specific approach required is especially apparent in cases which
do not fit within the 'classic facts' of the cases which laid down the guidance. In
international relocation cases, those classic facts are, in short, that:

- the applicant parent is reasonably clearly identifiable as the main
  day-to-day care-giver of the child;

---

[40] *K v K* at [84]; see **Appendix 3.3**.
[41] See **2.3–2.6**.
[42] *K v K* at [145]; see **Appendix 3.3**.
[43] *Re F (Permission to Relocate)* [2012] EWCA Civ 1364, [2012] 3 FCR 443 at [58].

- the proposal is for a permanent relocation, rather than a short-term or fixed-term one;

- the plan for relocation has a genuine motivation (ie it is not designed to exclude the respondent parent from the child's life);

- the respondent parent's opposition is based on the effect on the child of damage to the existing relationship with that parent;

- the main alternative which is proposed by the respondent parent is for the applicant parent to continue providing the child's main day-to-day care in the current location.

2.21 When these characteristics are not present, or where there are additional characteristics which complicate matters in some way, the guidance has to be interpreted with special care. One of the significant variations – applications for temporary relocation – we address in a separate chapter of this book, because those cases are often quite different in character from other relocation cases.[44] Three other variations we deal with here, though others may arise.

Shared care cases

2.22 As a preliminary point, when we talk about 'shared care cases', it is the child's day-to-day care arrangements that matter, and not the name attached to any court order already in place. Thorpe LJ emphasised this point in his judgment in *K v K*:[45]

> 'What is significant is not the label 'shared residence' because we see cases in which for a particular reason the label is attached to what is no more than a conventional contact order. What is significant is the practical arrangements for sharing the burden of care between two equally committed carers. Where each is providing a more or less equal proportion and one seeks to relocate externally then I am clear that the approach which I suggested in paragraph 40 in *Payne v Payne* should not be utilised. The judge should rather exercise his discretion to grant or refuse by applying the statutory checklist in section 1(3) of the Children Act 1989.'

2.23 In his Lordship's view, shared care applications are likely to represent a small minority of relocation cases,[46] so caution should be exercised in determining that the child's care arrangements call for significant modification of the guidance. That said, the right approach is always to fit the guidance to the case, and not to try to fit the case into rigid categories of guidance.

2.24 There is some debate about how the guidance in relocation cases involving a substantially shared care arrangement should be modified. One view is that the *Payne* guidance is of minimal relevance and that the welfare

---

44   See **Chapter 7**.
45   *K v K* at [57]; see **Appendix 3.3**.
46   *K v K* at [59]; see **Appendix 3.3**.

checklist provides the principal structure for the decision; this view was taken by Thorpe LJ in *K v K*,[47] and has the support from earlier Court of Appeal authority.[48] The alternative approach suggests that *Payne*'s guidance is still helpful, but that the different elements in it will be weighed differently in a shared care case; this approach was favoured by Black LJ in *K v K* and Munby LJ in *Re F (Permission to Relocate)*.[49]

2.25 While the lack of clarity over the correct approach to take may be thought somewhat unhelpful, in practice it is unlikely to matter. If the *Payne* guidance does not apply to a shared care case, nonetheless many of its questions will be relevant to any international relocation application. Conversely, if the *Payne* guidance does apply, then it is applied with the express recognition that it should be modified to the extent called for by the facts of the case being decided.

2.26 It may be helpful to explain that point with examples. In terms of the things which should be a central focus, whether taken directly from the *Payne* guidance or not, we would include:

- the motivation for the application, in particular whether the applicant parent is trying to exclude the respondent parent from the child's life;

- the level of planning and preparation that supports the application;

- the basis for the respondent parent's opposition to the proposals, in particular whether the respondent parent is focused on the child's welfare rather than having some ulterior motivation;

- the extent of the detriment to the child's relationship with the respondent parent if the relocation went ahead, including a focus on the proposals being put forward for on-going contact or sharing of care.

2.27 Other factors from the *Payne* guidance are often given less weight in shared care cases (though we emphasise that the weight that any factor should be given in any case, shared care or not, is fact-dependent and should not be approached in a mechanistic manner). In particular, because the alternative options which are available to the court in a shared care case are often different from a sole care case, it is often the case that the effect on the applicant parent of a refusal of the plan is a factor which receives less focus in shared care cases.

---

[47] See **Appendix 3.3**.
[48] See *Re C and M (Children)* [1999] EWCA Civ 2039, unreported; the case is discussed in detail in R George, 'Reviewing Relocation?' [2012] *Child and Family Law Quarterly* 110, pp 120–125.
[49] *Re F (Permission to Relocate)* [2012] EWCA Civ 1364, [2012] 3 FCR 443. For discussion and criticism of *Re F*, see R George, 'International Relocation, Care Arrangements and Case Taxonomy' [2012] *Family Law* 1478.

2.28 Finally, there are aspects which are not usually at the forefront of a relocation application brought by a primary carer, but which are important in a shared care case. These include:

- the existing care arrangements in place for the child;

- whether the applicant parent intends to relocate even if the child cannot go with her;

- depending on the answer to the previous questions, what the alternative options being presented to the court are for the child's main care if the relocation is either allowed or refused, and how each of those options would affect the child (the answers to these questions are often quite different in a shared care case from in a sole care case);

- from the welfare checklist, a factor which can be important here which is usually of less central relevant in a sole care case is 'the range of powers available to the court', since creative solutions are often needed.

Other possible variations

2.29 We deal here with two further variations as illustrations of the courts' approach to international relocation cases in different factual circumstances, with a particular focus on how the relocation guidance should be used in such cases.

2.30 One example might be a case where the care arrangements for the child are not yet settled following the parents' separation. Both parents propose to be the child's main carer, and one proposes to live abroad. That such a case calls for modification of the guidance was recognised in *Payne* itself, since the President observed that her summary was:[50]

> 'made on the premise that the question of residence is not a live issue. If, however, there is a real dispute as to which parent should be granted a residence order, and the decision as to which parent is the more suitable is finely balanced, the future plans of each parent for the child are clearly relevant. If one parent intends to set up home in another country and remove the child from school, surroundings and the other parent and his family, it may in some cases be an important factor to weigh in the balance.'

2.31 In such cases, as seen in the case example below, the courts are clear that the relocation proposal is but one aspect of what is really best seen as a residence dispute.

---

[50] *Payne* at [86]; see **Appendix 3.1**.

Case Example: *Re H (A Child)* **[2010] EWCA Civ 789, (2010) 154(21) SJLB 29**

The parents separated when the child was 2. Care arrangements were reasonably settled, with the mother being the primary care-giver and the father being strongly involved in the child's care. The father had, on a number of occasions, sought to increase his involvement with the child, including seeking a residence order in 2008. When the mother's plan to relocate to Australia developed, the father renewed his application for the residence of the child, either as a shared residence arrangement if the mother remained in the UK or as the main care-giver if the mother chose to relocate.

The trial judge granted the mother permission to relocate with the child, and the father appealed. The appeal was dismissed, but Thorpe LJ explained that the approach taken to the judicial guidance in a case like this should differ from the classic approach to international relocation cases set out in *Payne*:

> '[13] ... [F]or reasons which I will explain, I do not think that the decision in *Payne* was of direct application [to the facts of this case]. The decision in *Payne* is directed to the paradigm relocation application where the judge has to choose between permitting the mother to go, with detrimental effect on the father's contact regime, or refusing the mother, confining her in this jurisdiction in order to succour the contact arrangement. Here the judge had a very different choice. He had to choose between the mother's residence order application, which was for her responsibility as primary carer discharged in an Australian community with her new partner, and the father's competing residence order application, which proposed an English future and the continuation of an English childhood in the family created by his new relationship ...
>
> [15] So where there are cross residence order applications, the judge has to apply the ordinary principles that apply in any competition by parents for the responsibility to provide primary care. It is of course an unusual case in which one parent will be proposing care on one continent and the other on some other, but it does not change the essential character of the issue raised by the trial or the essential task that the judge has to undertake.'

2.32 A similar analysis was seen in *Re J (Children) (Residence Order: Removal from Jurisdiction)*.[51] Two children lived with their mother and had contact with the father, and three lived with the father, two of whom refused even to speak to the mother. The father was unemployed in the UK, but had a good job offer in Bulgaria where his parents had also moved. He decided that he would relocate with the children in his care, and the mother applied for residence. The trial judge granted leave based on the practical reality that

---

[51] *Re J (Children) (Residence Order: Removal from Jurisdiction)* [2006] EWCA Civ 1897, [2007] 1 FLR 2033.

residence with the mother was not a realistic option for the children. In upholding the decision, Thorpe LJ said:[52]

> 'The judge ultimately had to decide between a mother's proposal for a residence order to be implemented in this jurisdiction and a father's residence order application to be implemented in another state. In those circumstances the discipline suggested in paragraphs 40 and 41 of my judgment in *Payne v Payne* hardly applies.'

2.33 The focus of the decision was on which parent was better able to care for the children, with the other elements of the relocation guidance taking a subsidiary role in the assessment. In *Re J*, for example, the children currently had no direct contact with the respondent mother, so the damage to their relationship with her from relocating to Bulgaria was of less central relevance than in most relocation cases. Conversely, the fact that the father could not find employment in the United Kingdom but had a job offer in Bulgaria was thought to be very significant in the overall welfare analysis, whereas that factor might play less of a role in other cases.

2.34 A different variation arises if the respondent parent's basis for opposition is not (or not only) the effect on the child of the change in the relationship with the respondent parent, but is in fact that the applicant parent is motivated by a desire to exclude the respondent from the child's life. Again, we illustrate this point with a case example. The relocation being litigated here was in fact a proposed internal move, but as the facts of the case show, the family had earlier been involved in an international relocation dispute with much the same basis.

Case Example: *Re L (Internal Relocation: Shared Residence Order)* **[2009] EWCA Civ 20, [2009] 1 FLR 1157**

After the parents' separation, the mother was initially the main care-giver with the father strongly involved in the child's life. Two years later, the mother applied to the court for permission to take the child to live with her in Israel. The judge refused permission and made a number of findings adverse to the mother, including that she had not been honest with the court, and that her proposed relocation was motivated by a desire to exclude the father from the child's life. A shared residence order was made. The mother then, with no warning to the father, moved from their original location in south London to north London; the father then followed so as to continue the shared care arrangement. Shortly after the father's move, the mother applied for permission to move from London to Somerset, where she had been offered a job. ➡

---

52   Ibid at [27].

> The same trial judge refused permission for the internal relocation, on essentially the same basis that the mother was motivated by a desire to exclude the father from the child's life. The trial judge said this:[53]
>
> > 'The mother's search for work out of London intensified after the father's move to [north London]. The juxtaposition of this is in my judgment no coincidence and in my judgment the mother is driven by an objective of undermining [the] shared residence order, possibly with the intention of renewing an application to relocate abroad. Part of that motivation may stem from the fact that the mother finds the father a difficult man to deal with and I am sure that from her perspective he is. I consider it likely that he has at times been inflexible and unreasonable. In part it may stem from his temperament, although I note that he is a respected longstanding employee of [a named company], but also from acute anxiety and concern at what he perceives as an attempt to take L from him.'
>
> The mother's appeal to the Court of Appeal was dismissed. Giving the main judgment, Wall LJ said:[54]
>
> > '[The trial judge] knew the case well, and found as a fact that the mother's motivation in seeking an internal relocation was 'driven by an objective of undermining shared residence'. Given his findings in the previous [international relocation] proceedings and his findings about the mother in the current proceedings, this was plainly a conclusion which he was entitled to reach: furthermore, it was plainly a factor which militated strongly against L's best interests and thus against relocation.'

2.35 Again, the approach required varies depending on the individual facts. In most cases, there will not be evidence to support a claim that the applicant parent is motivated by a desire to exclude the respondent from the child's life – but where there is, that aspect can be of such importance that it dominates the analysis.

Issues that apply if international relocation is to occur

2.36 If relocation is allowed, thought will need to be given to any consequent legal issues which may arise. While there may be other issues arising in a particular case, the main question is usually about the enforcement of contact arrangements. The amount of consideration which needs to be given to this issue depends on a number of factors, not least of which is the destination country.[55]

---

[53] Quoted in *Re L (Internal Relocation: Shared Residence Order)* [2009] EWCA Civ 20, [2009] 1 FLR 1157 at [47].

[54] Ibid at [61]; see further extracts from *Re L* in **Appendix 4.2**.

[55] See also **5.79–5.81** or **6.68–6.70**. As we discuss there, post-relocation contact orders are standard practice and, we think, very advisable in most cases; but cf *Re R (Leave to Remove: Contact)* [2010] EWCA Civ 1137, [2011] 1 FLR 1336 at [22] for a contrary view.

2.37 For moves within the EU, apart from Denmark, any orders made by the English court will be automatically enforceable in the destination country, subject to any application there to vary the order.[56] The English courts retain jurisdiction for three months after the relocation in most cases. There is no need to obtain mirror orders for these countries. Similarly, if the destination is a signatory to the 1996 Hague Convention then orders from the English courts may be recognised and enforced in the destination country without the need for mirror orders, depending on the detail of national laws implementing the Convention in the relevant country.[57]

2.38 However (and this point applies regardless of whether the proposed destination is within the EU or not), it is possible for the English courts to retain jurisdiction if 'the jurisdiction of the courts has been accepted expressly or otherwise in an unequivocal manner by all the parties to the proceedings at the time the court is seised and is in the best interests of the child'.[58] This provision probably includes both a binding acceptance before proceedings begin, and an unequivocal acceptance after the proceedings have begun (such as by instructing lawyers to appear in the proceedings and partaking in those proceedings).[59]

2.39 If the relocation is not to an EU country or another country where the legal system is well understood by practitioners in England and Wales (we are thinking of countries such as New Zealand, Australia and Canada), then it may be advisable to get specialist advice as to things like:

- the availability of mirror orders;

---

[56] See the Brussels II Revised Regulation, Council Regulation (EC) No 2201/2003 of 27 November 2003. We address this Regulation here only briefly, but it has considerable complexity as well as a great deal of scope for affecting international moves within the EU; for more detail, see N Lowe, M Everall QC and M Nicholls, *The New Brussels II Regulation: A Supplement to International Movement of Children* (Bristol, Jordan Publishing, 2005); K Boele-Woelki and C González Beilfuss (eds), *Brussels II Bis: Its Impact and Application in the Member States* (Cambridge, Intersentia, 2007).

[57] Hague Convention on Jurisdiction, Applicable Law, Recognition, Enforcement and Co-operation in Respect of Parental Responsibility and Measures for the Protection of Children 1996, Arts 23–28. We address this Convention here only briefly; for more detail, see N Lowe and M Nicholls QC, *The 1996 Hague Convention on the Protection of Children* (Bristol, Jordan Publishing, 2012). A list of signatory countries is found in **Appendix 6.2**, or online at www.hcch.net/index_en.php?act=conventions.status&cid=70.

[58] Brussels II Revised Regulations, Art 12(3). This provision is sometimes used as a bargaining tool in relocation cases: the respondent might agree to the relocation going ahead on condition that all parties expressly accept that the English courts will retain jurisdiction. However, note that there are reasons why jurisdiction may be declined by the English courts even when the parties have purported to accept that jurisdiction, including simply that the court does not consider that it will be in the child's best interests for decisions to be made in England rather than in the country of habitual residence: Brussels II Revised Regulations, Art 15; see, eg, *B v B (Brussels II Revised: Jurisdiction)* [2010] EWHC 1989 (Fam), [2011] 1 FLR 54.

[59] This was Lady Hale's preferred interpretation in *Re I (Contact Application: Jurisdiction)* [2009] UKSC 10, [2010] 1 FLR 361 at [35]; see also *VC v GC (Jurisdiction: Brussels II Revised Art 12)* [2012] EWHC 1246 (Fam), [2013] 1 FLR 244.

- the enforceability of contact orders;

- the approach that the courts in the destination country would have towards issues of residence and contact if the case ended up being litigated there in the future.

2.40   While it is worth investigating whether a mirror order can be obtained, it is fair to say that many non-Hague Convention countries will also not recognise the idea of a mirror order. Consequently, more creative ideas may need to be explored. Many of the measures which are commonly adopted with temporary international relocations can be considered.[60] If the applicant parent has family members or other close connections with the UK, there may in particular be scope for finding a form of security which is likely to be reasonably effective. Possible courses of action include:

- notarised agreements by family members that specify what contact arrangements will be put in place;

- monetary bonds, where the applicant (or a family member who is remaining in the UK) is required to deposit a sum of money in a bank account; the money is then not released for a specified period, and can be made available to the respondent (usually after a court application) to fund his efforts to enforce contact;

- undertakings given by the applicant parent to comply with the contact arrangements;

- solemn, witnessed declarations by the applicant and by family members to ensure that contact arrangements are complied with.

2.41   Indeed, regardless of the proposed destination country, it is relatively common for the applicant parent, and/or other family members, to give undertakings to the court, the detail of which will vary depending on the facts of the case. It remains surprisingly common for an undertaking to be given that the applicant will return the child to this jurisdiction if so ordered by the court of England and Wales, though there must be some doubt about the effectiveness of such undertakings in many cases.[61]

2.42   It is common, though not inevitable, that if the relocation is allowed then no further child maintenance will be paid, with that money being used by the respondent parent instead to fund ongoing contact. In the relatively unusual case that the applicant parent is in receipt of ongoing periodic payments as part of a financial settlement after divorce, these may also be subject to negotiation.

---

[60]   See **7.11** *et seq.*

[61]   This point was noted in *Re S (Residence Order: Forum Conveniens)* [1995] 1 FLR 314 (FD), but seems to have had little effect in practice. Such an undertaking could be one factor supporting a claim that the English court retains jurisdiction, though by itself it would not be sufficient in most cases.

However, if there are to be ongoing payments then, again, specialist advice may be required as to how these orders can be made enforceable in the new international situation.

2.43 If there is enough money, a specific fund is sometimes set up to fund ongoing contact. Either in addition to that, or in the alternative, the applicant parent will sometimes be required to place money in a bond to be used by the respondent as a litigation fund in the event of difficulties over contact.

Key Summary: International Relocation Law

- The welfare of the child is the paramount consideration, and all other factors feed into this question.

- In assessing which outcome will best meet the child's welfare, regard should be given to the guidance set out in the welfare checklist and in *Payne*.

- However, that guidance needs to be read carefully and without making any assumptions about the answers that will be given to the questions asked; the guidance should also be adapted as required to make it applicable to the particular facts of the case.

- In all cases, it will be important to be sure that the application is being made in good faith (ie it is not a ruse intended to damage or end the child's relationship with the non-moving parent).

- It is also vital that the practical planning is adequate in the circumstances of the case (a return to a location where the applicant parent lived for many years may require less investigation than a proposed move somewhere new, for example).

- If the application is being brought by a parent who is clearly the primary carer of the child, and on whom the child relies heavily for his or her welfare, then an assessment of the effect on the parent of refusal of her plans for relocation will be an important part of the case – but this factor may be important in any case.

- The potential effect on the child of any diminution in his or her relationship with the respondent parent will also be very important in every case.

- It will be crucial to assess the practical feasibility of proposed contact arrangements, and to compare the likely circumstances of such contact with the child's present relationship with the parent. ➡

> • The views, wishes and feelings of the child, particularly if he or she is older, are very important.

INTERNAL RELOCATION LAW

2.44 Whereas international relocation is prima facie not allowed because of s 13 of the Children Act 1989, there is no such restriction on relocation within the United Kingdom. The onus therefore lies on the parent seeking to prevent the relocation, who must obtain a court order to that effect if he wishes to use legal means to stop the move. (Despite that, for consistency, we refer to the parent seeking to relocate as 'the applicant' and the parent seeking to stop the relocation as 'the respondent' throughout this book.)

The legal basis

2.45 There are four main legal mechanisms that can be used to try to stop an internal relocation, all under s 8 of the Children Act 1989. First, the respondent can seek a transfer of residence. If the child is mainly living with the applicant parent then the court's general hostility to transferring children's main residence needs to be borne in mind;[62] on the other hand, where there is a shared care arrangement in place already, this approach can be more viable. Second, if there is an existing residence order in favour of the applicant, the respondent might seek to have conditions imposed on that order as envisaged by s 11(7).[63]

2.46 The third approach is to seek a 'prohibited steps order' under s 8, specifically preventing the applicant from changing the child's place of residence.[64] Finally, but less directly, a s 8 'specific issue order' might be sought about, for example, the school that the child is to attend, which has the effect of requiring the resident parent to live within a reasonable distance of that school.[65]

2.47 Whichever legal approach is adopted, the welfare of the child concerned is the paramount consideration, informed by the welfare checklist.[66] That said, the law in England and Wales approaches internal relocation very differently from international relocation. In general, the courts consider that a parent who has a residence order in their favour (or, if there is no such order in force,[67] a

---

[62] See, eg, *Re G (Residence: Same-Sex Parents)* [2006] UKHL 43, [2006] 2 FLR 629; *Re B (A Child)* [2009] UKSC 5, [2010] 1 FLR 551.

[63] See, eg, *B v B (Residence: Condition Limiting Geographic Area)* [2004] 2 FLR 979 (FD); see **Appendix 4.1**; for Children Act 1989, s 11(7), see **Appendix 1.1**. Note that the conditions are imposed under s 8, not under s 11(7), since the latter says 'a section 8 order may ... impose conditions'.

[64] See, eg, *Re B (Prohibited Steps Order)* [2007] EWCA Civ 1055, [2008] 1 FLR 613.

[65] See, eg, *Re G (Contact)* [2006] EWCA Civ 1507, [2007] 1 FLR 1663.

[66] Children Act 1989, s 1; see **Appendix 1.1**.

[67] *Re S (Residence Order: Internal Relocation)* [2012] EWCA Civ 1031, [2012] 3 FCR 153 at [59]

parent providing the child's main care) should not normally be restricted in terms of where he or she should live with the child within the United Kingdom.[68]

Case Example: *Re E (Residence: Imposition of Conditions)* [1997] 2 FLR 638 (CA)

The mother was given a residence order but, in order to facilitate contact between the children and the father, the trial judge imposed conditions on that residence order requiring the mother to remain in London, her current location, when she had planned to move to Blackpool where she had previously lived and where her family was. The mother successfully appealed against the conditions. Giving the leading judgment, Butler-Sloss LJ commented on both the legal powers available to the court, as specified under s 11(7) of the Children Act 1989, and on the policy which guided the use of those powers:[69]

> 'There is no statutory requirement of consent or leave of the court in respect of moving the child anywhere within the UK. Section 11(7) applies to all four s 8 orders, including prohibited steps orders and specific issue orders. The wording of the subsection is wide enough to give the court the power to make an order restricting the right of residence to a specified place within the UK. But in my view a restriction upon the right of the carer of the child to choose where to live sits uneasily with the general understanding of what is meant by a residence order ...
>
> A general imposition of conditions on residence orders was clearly not contemplated by Parliament and where the parent is entirely suitable and the court intends to make a residence order in favour of that parent, a condition of residence is in my view an unwarranted imposition upon the right of the parent to choose where he/she will live within the UK or with whom.'

The development of the current guidance

2.48 Until the last few years, the judicial guidance on internal relocation disputes was clear, namely that although internal relocation cases were decided based on the welfare of the child concerned, geographic restrictions would be imposed only in 'truly exceptional' circumstances.[70] The logic was that placing a restriction on the place of residence of the primary carer involved an undue restriction on that person's freedom, which would impact adversely on the

---

makes clear that the same approach applies whether the parties have a particular order or whether 'the parties have operated what is effectively [the equivalent] arrangement without the interposition of a previous order'.

[68] *Re E (Residence: Imposition of Conditions)* [1997] 2 FLR 638 (CA).

[69] *Re E (Residence: Imposition of Conditions)* [1997] 2 FLR 638 (CA) at 641–642.

[70] *Re B (Prohibited Steps Order)* [2007] EWCA Civ 1055, [2008] 1 FLR 613 at [7].

child's welfare.[71] At the same time, since contact orders would still be enforceable after an internal relocation, the court could be confident of preserving the child's relationship with the respondent after such a move.

2.49 In practical terms, although there were few reported cases, the kinds of facts which seemed to count as 'exceptional' mostly related to there being particular reasons why the child would not cope well with a move, or with a change in the pattern of contact with the respondent parent. In *Re S (A Child) (Residence Order: Condition) (No 2)*,[72] for example, the eight year old child had Down's Syndrome and would have struggled to understand why she was no longer able to see her father several times per week after a move from London to Cornwall. Similarly, in *Re H (Children) (Residence Order: Condition)*,[73] the applicant was prevented from moving to Northern Ireland because the respondent parent's role in the children's lives was thought to be important and, on the facts, unlikely to be maintained after a relocation.

2.50 Other facts can make a case 'exceptional'. In *Re E (Residence: Imposition of Conditions)*, Butler-Sloss LJ gave an example of a private law case 'where the court ... has concerns about the ability of the parent to be granted a residence order to be a satisfactory carer but there is no better solution than to place the child with that parent'.[74] In the more recent case of *Re F (Internal Relocation)*,[75] the trial judge's view that the distance involved, and the arduous nature of the proposed contact arrangements, in a move from England to the Orkney Islands made the case 'exceptional' was upheld by the Court of Appeal.

2.51 However, following three Court of Appeal decisions on internal relocation, it is now less clear that this 'exceptionality' test remains dominant,[76] though it has never been over-ruled.[77] The position now seems to be best expressed as being a pure welfare decision, albeit with an acknowledgement that restrictions on a parent's movement within the United Kingdom will probably, as a matter of fact, be unusual because more often the welfare

---

71   *Re E (Residence: Imposition of Conditions)* [1997] 2 FLR 638 (CA).
72   *Re S (A Child) (Residence Order: Condition) (No 2)* [2002] EWCA Civ 1795, [2003] 1 FCR 138.
73   *Re H (Children) (Residence Order: Condition)* [2001] EWCA Civ 1338, [2001] 2 FLR 1277.
74   *Re E (Residence: Imposition of Conditions)* [1997] 2 FLR 638 (CA) at 642.
75   *Re F (Internal Relocation)* [2010] EWCA Civ 1428, [2011] 1 FLR 1382; see **Appendix 4.3**; for commentary, see R George, 'Re F (Internal Relocation) [2010] EWCA Civ 1428' (casenote) [2011] *Journal of Social Welfare and Family Law* 169.
76   Two earlier judgments of Ward LJ also cast some doubt on this approach. His Lordship once said that the exceptionality approach taken in *Re E (Residence: Imposition of Conditions)* [1997] 2 FLR 638 (CA) is one 'with which many may disagree' (*Re W (Children)* [2005] EWCA Civ 717 at [12]), and later reiterated of *Re E* that 'many may think it a little unsatisfactory' (*Re G (Contact)* [2006] EWCA Civ 1507, [2007] 1 FLR 1663 at [26]). On the other hand, *Re E* was quoted by the House of Lords (seemingly with approval though no explicit comment was made, and the point was obiter) in *Re G (Residence: Same-Sex Parents)* [2006] UKHL 43, [2006] 2 FLR 629 at [15].
77   See *Re F (Internal Relocation)* [2010] EWCA Civ 1428, [2011] 1 FLR 1382 at [26]; see **Appendix 4.3**.

analysis will suggest that relocation, particularly over short or medium distances within the UK, should be allowed.[78]

2.52 The first case to start marking a shift away from any exceptionality test was *Re L (Internal Relocation: Shared Residence Order)* in 2009.[79] Wall LJ's leading judgment makes a number of important points. The first is that there is no difference of law or practice between sole care and shared care cases in terms of the guidance offered on internal relocation.[80]

2.53 Most significantly for the development of the law in general, while Wall LJ cited at length from the previous authorities, his Lordship's summary of the correct approach to take was couched in this way:[81]

'In each case what the court has to do is to examine the underlying factual matrix, and to decide in all the circumstances of the case whether or not it is in the child's interest to relocate with the parent who wishes to move ...

For the reasons which I have given ... the correct approach, in my view, is ... to look at the underlying factual substratum in welfare terms, bearing in mind the tension which may well exist between the freedom to relocate which any parent must enjoy against the welfare of the child which may militate against relocation. In my judgment, it is this balance which is critical, and ... the court [must not] lose sight of, or give insufficient weight to the former consideration.'

2.54 In other words, while Wall LJ made clear that a parent's freedom to relocate within the United Kingdom is an important factor, the core of the analysis is to be based on the child's welfare and not on any generalisations.

2.55 In the second of the three cases, *Re F (Internal Relocation)*,[82] the leading judgment came from Wilson LJ. His Lordship analysed internal relocation law at some length, expressing that he was 'puzzled by three features of the authorities'.[83] The first feature was the multitude of orders which might be sought in an internal relocation case.[84] The second was the link between

---

[78] Cf Lady Hale's point in *Re W (Children) (Abuse: Oral Evidence)* [2010] UKSC 12, [2010] 1 FLR 1485 at [22], that a careful balance of all relevant factors 'may well mean that [a particular outcome is reached] in the great majority of cases, but that is a result and not a presumption or even a starting point'.

[79] *Re L (Internal Relocation: Shared Residence Order)* [2009] EWCA Civ 20, [2009] 1 FLR 1157; see **Appendix 4.2**.

[80] Ibid at [36] and [51]; see **Appendix 4.2**.

[81] Ibid; for discussion of the way that Wall LJ expressed this point, see R George, 'Re L (Internal Relocation: Shared Residence Order) [2009] EWCA Civ 20, [2009] 1 FLR 1157' (casenote) [2010] *Journal of Social Welfare and Family Law* 71.

[82] *Re F (Internal Relocation)* [2010] EWCA Civ 1428, [2011] 1 FLR 1382; see **Appendix 4.3**; for commentary, see R George, 'Re F (Internal Relocation) [2010] EWCA Civ 1428' (casenote) [2011] *Journal of Social Welfare and Family Law* 169.

[83] Ibid at [22]; see **Appendix 4.3**.

[84] See **2.45–2.46**.

internal relocation and international relocation, questioning why the two lines of authority should have developed differently.[85]

2.56 The third feature for Wilson LJ, and most important for this discussion, was the development of the 'exceptionality' test. While considering himself to be bound by the previous authorities on this point,[86] Wilson LJ thought that an exceptionality criterion was both unhelpful and 'an impermissible gloss on the [welfare] inquiry mandated by s 1(1) and (3) of the [Children] Act'.[87]

2.57 The final Court of Appeal case to consider here is *Re S (Residence Order: Internal Relocation)*.[88] Giving the leading judgment, Sir Mark Potter referred to Wall LJ's earlier decision and, in similar vein, summarised the correct approach to an internal relocation case as being 'to look at the factual matrix and determine what was in the child's best interests'.[89]

2.58 The drift of these authorities is away from an exceptionality test and towards a general welfare analysis, albeit one in which the court considers that '[n]o one could quarrel with a proposition that it would rarely be in the interests of a child for the residential parent to be prevented from moving home with the child within the UK'.[90] We consider this to be the best way for any internal relocation case to be approached,[91] though it may still be appropriate to note that restrictions on internal relocation are unlikely to be imposed frequently.

Factors to consider in internal relocation cases

2.59 It is to be noted that, whereas the guidance on international relocation is extensive and covers many aspects of the practicalities which inform the welfare assessment, the guidance on internal relocation law is minimal. There is no case setting out the kind of guidance which *Payne* gives in the international context.

---

[85]   The authors take the view that the two lines of authority ought to be brought together. For fuller analysis of this point, see R George, *Relocation Disputes: Law and Practice in England and New Zealand* (Oxford, Hart Publishing, 2013), ch 6.

[86]   For a different view on whether the Court of Appeal is bound in this way, see R George, 'Re F (Internal Relocation) [2010] EWCA Civ 1428' (casenote) [2011] *Journal of Social Welfare and Family Law* 169.

[87]   *Re F (Internal Relocation)* [2010] EWCA Civ 1428, [2011] 1 FLR 1382 at [26]; see **Appendix 4.3**.

[88]   *Re S (Residence Order: Internal Relocation)* [2012] EWCA Civ 1031, [2012] 3 FCR 153.

[89]   Ibid at [37].

[90]   *Re F (Internal Relocation)* [2010] EWCA Civ 1428, [2011] 1 FLR 1382 at [25]; see **Appendix 4.3**.

[91]   There is some equivocation in *Re S (Residence Order: Internal Relocation)* [2012] EWCA Civ 1031, [2012] 3 FCR 153 at [56]–[65] (Sir Mark Potter) and at [79]–[82] (Black LJ), about whether the exceptionality test continues to apply if the applicant is clearly the child's main carer, rather than the case involving truly shared care. As a matter of principle, Wall LJ thought that there should be no difference in *Re L (Internal Relocation: Shared Residence Order)* [2009] EWCA Civ 20, [2009] 1 FLR 1157, and the Court of Appeal made no criticism of the trial judge's decision to adopt a broad welfare analysis in *Re S*, despite that being a case where the applicant was clearly the primary carer.

2.60 Nonetheless, it may be valuable to draw together some of the threads which can be seen in the various authorities. In doing so, we emphasise two points. First, this list is not to be found in any one authority; it is our summary of factors which we think emerge. Second, as with the international relocation guidance, our view is that the facts of the case should be the starting point around which any guidance is to be fitted, rather than trying to force the case into the straitjacket of the guidance.[92] With those caveats in mind, we offer the following suggestions.

2.61 First, as is evident, the decision must be based on the welfare of the child concerned. If there is more than one child, each child's welfare must be taken separately.

2.62 Second, since the legal mechanism for allowing or refusing an internal relocation case is always a s 8 order, the welfare checklist in s 1(3) is a mandatory part of the analysis.[93] While any of the elements of the checklist might be important (and all should be considered), the ones which are most likely to be important in an internal relocation case are:

(a)   the ascertainable wishes and feelings of the child concerned (considered in the light of his age and understanding);

(c)   the likely effect on him of any change in his circumstances;

(f)   how capable each of his parents, and any other person in relation to whom the court considers the question to be relevant, is of meeting his needs.

2.63 Next, the court should ask whether the motivation for moving is a legitimate one, or whether her motivation is to cut the respondent parent out of the child's life. If the judge concludes that the motivation is illegitimate, that is likely to be a powerful argument against the move going ahead.[94] Similarly, the court should assess the respondent parent's motivations for opposing the move, essentially to ensure that they are based on a legitimate concern for the child's welfare rather than an ulterior motivation to control the applicant's life.

2.64 The court should ask about the practical plans associated with the proposed move, though bearing in mind that the level of planning required is likely to be less significant than for an international move since the change involved compared with the present living arrangements will, in some ways, be less significant. Within this question, factors which may be important to consider include:

---

[92]   Cf **2.19**.

[93]   Children Act 1989, s 1(3) and (4); see **Appendix 1.1**.

[94]   For examples where this has happened, see, eg, *B v B (Residence: Condition Limiting Geographic Area)* [2004] 2 FLR 979 (FD) especially at [16] (see **Appendix 4.1**) and *Re L (Internal Relocation: Shared Residence Order)* [2009] EWCA Civ 20, [2009] 1 FLR 1157 (see **Appendix 4.2**).

- housing in the new location;

- schooling for the children in the new location;

- what employment, if any, the applicant parent will have in the new location;

- what family or other support network will be available in the new location;

- what plans there are regarding contact arrangements or shared care between the children and the respondent parent, including details about the frequency and location of the contact, and the mode and cost of transport.

2.65 The court should assess the likely effect (if any) on the applicant parent of refusing the internal relocation, together with the likely impact (if any) of that on the child. In this regard, the court may bear in mind that adults are not normally restricted in their decisions about where to live, but also that there are many practical reasons why people do and do not move.

2.66 Another important factor will be the effect of the move, if it goes ahead, on the child's relationship with the respondent parent. The distance involved, the nature of the existing relationship, the age of the child, and the financial resources of the parties are all likely to be relevant factors in making this assessment.

2.67 If the respondent parent is proposing that the child should have his or her main residence with him, as an alternative to relocating with the applicant parent, then the viability of that proposal will need careful consideration. An important aspect of that assessment will be the nature of the existing care arrangements, and therefore the extent of the change that would be involved from the child's point of view. If this option is being considered, the applicant parent will need to indicate whether she intends to relocate without the child if the court refuses leave: if she does, detailed contact proposals will need to be drawn up.

Issues that apply if internal relocation is to occur

2.68 If relocation is to be allowed, there are potentially different legal issues which may arise depending on whether the move is within the legal jurisdiction of England and Wales or, conversely, is to Scotland or Northern Ireland.

Moves within England and Wales

2.69 No legal issues arise following a move within England and Wales which did not apply before the relocation. The jurisdiction of the court is unchanged, and there will be no additional hurdles involved in enforcing or varying a court order compared with the pre-relocation position.

Moves to Scotland or Northern Ireland

2.70 The change of legal jurisdiction involved in a move to Scotland or Northern Ireland has potential consequences which do not arise for a move within England and Wales. For example, while a shared residence or contact order made in England and Wales would be automatically *recognised* by the courts of Scotland and Northern Ireland, such an order would need to be registered in the new jurisdiction before it could be *enforced*.[95]

2.71 There can also be issues to consider regarding jurisdiction itself, as discussed in the following case example:

Case Example: *Re W-B (Family Proceedings: Appropriate Jurisdiction Within the UK)* **[2012] EWCA Civ 592, [2013] 1 FLR 394**

The parents separated in 2005 when the child was just over a year old. The child lived with the mother and had contact with the father for about a year, whereupon the mother made an unannounced move from Southend to Scotland. The father immediately initiated proceedings in the Southend County Court, seeking a residence order and orders tracing the child's location. The mother was traced some months later, and proceedings continued in the Southend County Court.

Some two years after the mother's move to Scotland, in 2008, a residence order was made in her favour by the Southend Court. The child had resided in Scotland all this time, and the order merely formalised the position. In 2009, contact proceedings were initiated in the Southend Court, and contact was indeed ordered; the s 9(5) guardian who had been appointed was discharged, and the case appeared to have ended. Matters then rested for 15 months, before the father initiated fresh proceedings to vary the terms of the contact order in mid 2010. A consent order was made, but in June 2011 the father re-initiated proceedings, this time seeking residence of the child.

It was at the hearing of this application in September 2011 that the mother's counsel first raised the question of jurisdiction. That issue went on appeal, and McFarlane LJ, giving the lead judgment, considered the details of the Family Law Act 1986.[96] The normal rule is that, as between the three United Kingdom jurisdictions, a court does not have jurisdiction unless the child is habitually resident in that jurisdiction.[97] ➤

---

[95]   Family Law Act 1986, ss 25 and 27.

[96]   For the avoidance of doubt, the Brussels II Revised Regulation has no applicability as between the three legal jurisdictions of the United Kingdom: see *Re W-B (Family Proceedings: Appropriate Jurisdiction Within the UK)* [2012] EWCA Civ 592, [2013] 1 FLR 394 at [10].

[97]   Family Law Act 1986, s 3(1)(a). Under s 3(1)(b), if the child is not habitually resident in any of the United Kingdom jurisdictions, then jurisdiction is granted by the physical presence of the child.

However, as an exception to that normal rule, since the child had been removed without consent, the English court retained jurisdiction for a year from the date of her removal.[98]

The father's initial application following the mother's move was made well within the one-year time limitation. However, the Court of Appeal was clear that, contrary to the trial judge's view, the remaining proceedings could not all then be tied to that initial application.[99] The case which began in 2006 had run its course by mid-2009 when the court made a final order and discharged any ongoing proceedings. Consequently, despite the mother's participation in the subsequent hearings – including agreeing to consent orders, giving undertakings, and even making her own applications – the English courts had no jurisdiction after 2009.

2.72 In general, though, moves within the United Kingdom do not raise the potential legal complications which are seen in the international cases.

Key Summary: Internal Relocation Law

- In each case, the welfare of the child will be the court's paramount consideration, taking into account all the matters set out in the welfare checklist.

- If a child is in the primary care of the applicant parent and cannot reasonably be expected to live with the other parent, the court will be reluctant to impose a restriction upon the applicant parent's freedom to choose where to live.

- Although the court will be reluctant to restrict a primary carer in the circumstances set out above, if the proposed move is motivated by a wish to diminish the relationship between the child and the remaining parent the application is likely to be refused.

- Equally, if the circumstances are such that it will be against the best interests of the child to move, then the court will act to prevent it.

- If, however, the child could reasonably live with the respondent parent, the case is likely to be determined on a purely welfare basis of whether or not, in all the circumstances, it is in the best interests of the child to live with the applicant or the respondent.

- The views, wishes and feelings of the child, particularly if he or she is older, are very important.

---

[98]   Family Law Act 1986, s 41.
[99]   *Re W-B (Family Proceedings: Appropriate Jurisdiction Within the UK)* [2012] EWCA Civ 592, [2013] 1 FLR 394 at [21].

Chapter 3

BRINGING A RELOCATION APPLICATION: THINGS TO THINK ABOUT BEFORE YOU START

3.1   This chapter sets out in detail the kinds of matters which a parent who is thinking about relocating (and their legal adviser) should think about before a relocation case gets to court. In the next chapter, we consider the position of the parent who is opposing a relocation application, though of course there is some overlap between the factors for the two parents to consider. The issues discussed are relevant to both international and internal relocation cases except where otherwise indicated.

3.2   Our aim here is to help applicant parents plan their moves carefully and in such a way as will minimise the chances of the proposals themselves being criticised. But we also think that careful consideration of the proposals at an early stage can help to avoid the need for litigation in some cases, because it is more likely that the other parent will agree to proposals if they are well thought through and if he has been consulted at an early stage.

THINGS TO THINK ABOUT AT THE OUTSET

3.3   Deciding to try to relocate is a serious decision. Most of this chapter, and indeed most of this book, is focused on the practicalities of how to proceed once that decision has already been taken, but it is always worth making sure that the decision itself has been taken carefully and after all the options have been weighed. There are no guarantees that a relocation application will succeed, no matter how well thought through it is, so before starting the process a parent should think about why they want to go, what the pros and cons of doing that will be, and what the alternatives are.

3.4   In any intact family where a move is contemplated, the parents will consider all the circumstances. Are the reasons for moving good ones? What will the new home and area be like? What about schools, friendships and other opportunities? What will be the effect upon the child of the disruption involved?

3.5   For a separated family, the question to be asked in addition to all this is obviously the effect upon the relationship that the child has with the respondent parent. If current arrangements for seeing that parent would no longer be practicable, what arrangements would be? Is it possible to re-jig things so that the relationships do not suffer? Can time lost during term time be made up in the holidays, for example? What about the use of Skype, text messages and emails?

3.6   As we discuss in the next chapter,[1] the respondent parent will have a number of possible options to consider. The most obvious courses of action are seeking to take on the child's main care and seeking to stop the relocation entirely; but we also suggest that the respondent parent should be thinking about agreeing to the move and then moving himself.

3.7   The equivalent thought process for the parent thinking about relocation is to ask whether staying put is a realistic option. To what extent can the benefits of the proposed move be achieved in other ways? For example, if the reason for wanting to move is to return to the parent's original home in order to get support from family, could that support be obtained in other ways? How often could family members visit the current location, and how many holidays (and of what length) could the parent have back home?

3.8   Bringing a relocation application is likely to involve significant financial cost, unless the other parent can be persuaded to agree to the plan.[2] If the case ends up at a final hearing in court, there will be legal costs, usually running into the tens of thousands of pounds. Some families can afford that without particularly noticing, but most people find the financial aspects of legal action a significant consideration. Money spent on litigation is money that is not available later to pay for flights, accommodation and holidays if the relocation ends up being allowed by the court.

3.9   Perhaps more important than that, though, is the potential damage to the relationship between the parents, and between each parent and the child. As we set out in Chapter 1,[3] some relocation cases are the culmination of years of ongoing disputes between the parents, but in many cases the parents have either always been amicable with one another or have now settled into an amicable pattern after previous difficulties. While the applicant parent will no doubt see good reasons for wanting to move, and will not want to think that her former partner gets to determine what she now does with her life, it is worth being aware that many respondents see relocation applications as likely to sever their relationship with their child. Much will depend on the personality of the parents, on the reasons for seeking relocation, and on each parent's attitude and behaviour during the course of discussions – but it is worth asking what effect the relocation application is going to have before doing anything else.

---

[1]   See **4.7** *et seq.*
[2]   See **3.48** *et seq.*
[3]   See **1.12**.

CONSIDERING THE BASICS: WHERE, WHEN AND WHY

3.10   A relocation case could, of course, involve a proposed move anywhere in the world. Historically, proposed international moves tended to involve Commonwealth and other English-speaking countries, especially Canada, the USA, Australia and New Zealand. That pattern has become less pronounced in the last couple of decades, and in particular there has been a noticeable rise in cases involving EU countries as EU citizens increasingly take advantage of their rights to free movement within the Union.

3.11   As we set out in Chapter 1,[4] there are many reasons why a parent might seek to relocate – and, indeed, many applicants have a number of reasons. While there are no hard-and-fast rules, cases involving a *return home* tend to arise fairly soon after the parents' relationship has broken down, whereas cases involving *specific opportunities* in a new location, a *new partner*, or a move for a *better lifestyle* tend to arise a little later.

3.12   A surprisingly large number of parents appear to believe that if their children live with them or spend most of their time with them, then they are free to move with them to live wherever they like. For the avoidance of any doubt, that is not the case. As we set out in detail in Chapter 2,[5] there is an automatic prohibition on removing a child from the United Kingdom for more than one calendar month.[6] Technically, that rule applies only where there is a residence order in force with respect to the child, but even in cases where there is no residence order the unilateral removal of a child may constitute child abduction,[7] and therefore it is highly advisable to proceed in the same way regardless of the legal arrangements for residence.

3.13   For international moves, if the applicant parent who seeks to relocate permanently with their child or children outside of the United Kingdom is unable to obtain the written consent of every person with parental responsibility for each child, that parent will be required to make a freestanding application to the court for permission to remove the child or children permanently from the jurisdiction. This application must be made in accordance with Part 12 of the Family Procedure Rules 2010, and the application should be made in Form C100.[8] If the proposed move is for a fixed period of longer than one calendar month, but is not intended to be permanent, then an application for temporary removal must be made in the same way.[9] However, the one-month minimum threshold for requiring

---

[4]   See **1.13–1.18**.

[5]   See **2.7–2.9**.

[6]   Children Act 1989, s 13(1)(b); see **Appendix 1.1**.

[7]   Child Abduction Act 1984, s 1; Hague Convention on the Civil Aspects of International Child Abduction 1980.

[8]   We deal with the process of making an application more fully in **Chapter 5**.

[9]   On temporary relocation, see **Chapter 7**. Temporary moves for less than one month may be opposed by the respondent, but the onus will be on him to make an application to court.

permission means that a parent wanting to go on a family holiday with their child for two weeks need not seek permission.[10]

3.14 For moves within the United Kingdom, a parent with a residence order has more freedom to determine where he or she will live.[11] However, even though written consent from the other parent is not technically required before a move within the United Kingdom can take place, it is inadvisable to proceed unilaterally if the move is likely to have any significant effect on the child's relationship with the other parent. Although technically it would fall to the respondent to seek a court order preventing the move, any disruption to shared residence or contact arrangements could put the moving parent in danger of breaching an existing court order.

3.15 Although an application for permission to remove a child or children permanently from the jurisdiction can be made in any court, it should normally be issued in the local county court or the Principal Registry of the Family Division. Onward transfer to the High Court or arrangements for the case to be determined by a specialist family law circuit judge authorised as a deputy High Court judge will depend on the complexity and difficulty of the decision.[12] If the proposed destination is international and the country in question is *not* a signatory of the Hague Convention on the Civil Aspects of International Child Abduction 1980,[13] then the case ought normally to be commenced in (or immediately transferred to) the High Court.[14] Otherwise, the application will normally be determined by a circuit judge, a district judge of the Principal Registry or a part-time judge with similar powers (eg a recorder).

3.16 District judges in county courts do not normally deal with the final hearings of international relocation cases unless they have particular expertise,[15] though they will often be involved in giving directions. By contrast, internal relocation cases which are litigated are almost always heard in the county courts, either by circuit judges or district judges depending on their complexity (and, in practice, on the availability of the various judges for hearings).

DETAILED PLANS FOR A RELOCATION APPLICATION

3.17 In this section, we talk about the kinds of issues that a parent thinking about relocation needs to consider. These matters are important for a number

---

[10]   If the other parent is concerned about a move of less than a month, he may still seek to prevent the move or to have conditions imposed before it happens, but such a course is likely only where there is a serious risk of the child not being returned: see **Chapter 7**.

[11]   *Re E (Residence: Imposition of Conditions)* [1997] 2 FLR 638 (CA).

[12]   *MH v GP (Child: Immigration)* [1995] 2 FLR 106 (FD). See also *Practice Direction: Allocation and Transfer of Proceedings* [2009] 1 FLR 365.

[13]   A list of countries that have acceded to the Convention can be found in **Appendix 6.1**, or online at www.hcch.net/index_en.php?act=conventions.status&cid=24.

[14]   See *Practice Direction: Allocation and Transfer of Proceedings* [2009] 1 FLR 365, para [5.2].

[15]   *Re D (Children)* [2009] EWCA Civ 957 at [3].

of reasons. One is simply that they all form part of a smooth move and careful planning will help to minimise any difficulties if the move goes ahead. Another is that the best way to proceed with a relocation case is to agree the outcome with the other parent, and that is most likely to happen if the plans are drawn up carefully and so can be discussed in an informed way. Finally, in the event that agreement cannot be reached, the court will demand to see highly detailed plans and cases can easily fail if the plans put forward by the applicant are not 'founded on practical proposals both well researched and investigated'.[16] The court will also be keen to see that the applicant parent has a genuine motivation for seeking to relocate, and in particular that the proposal is 'not motivated by some selfish desire to exclude the father from the child's life'.[17]

3.18 When it comes to considering the details of the proposals, there will be some elements that are common to all applications, which we address below.[18] Other elements vary somewhat depending on the case, and we have therefore broken this section down into sub-sections based around the main reasons for seeking to relocate. As we said in Chapter 1, these are not legal categories and there is no legal difference based on these reasons for seeking relocation,[19] but in purely practical terms there are differences.

Going home cases

3.19 Many parents feel isolated and unhappy following a relationship or marriage breakdown. If a parent originally comes from another country, or another part of the United Kingdom from where they are presently living, they may miss the support of their family and friends and wish to return to the place they think of as home.

3.20 In these *going home* cases, it is important for the parent to explain (to the other parent, and later to the court if the case gets that far) how they feel at the moment living in the present location, and how going home will benefit the parent and, importantly, how the move would benefit the child. The benefit to the child might be direct benefit, but is also likely to include indirect benefit from the improvement caused to the parent.

3.21 The applicant parent should be able to provide details of their support network in their home country and identify members of their family and friends living there, especially if they have been or are currently providing support to the applicant (whether financial, emotional or other support). The applicant parent should be prepared to produce statements from a few family members or friends explaining how they will be able to support her and the children.

---

[16] *Payne v Payne* [2001] EWCA Civ 166, [2001] 1 FLR 1052 at [40(a)]; see **Appendix 3.1**.
[17] Ibid.
[18] See **3.38–3.43**.
[19] See **1.19–1.21**.

3.22 It is important not to over-generalise because every case is unique, but experienced practitioners tend to think that the *going home* cases are the most likely to succeed. The applicant parent has experience of living in the proposed destination, an existing (often extensive) family network and other connections there, and the court can usually be reasonably confident that the planned life in the new location will run at least as smoothly as life runs anywhere else. However, the fact that the parent is proposing to go 'home' is not in itself a trump card, and other factors in a case can lead to refusal of permission.

Case Example: *Re Y (Leave to Remove From Jurisdiction)* [2004] 2 FLR 330 (FD)

The 5 year old child was subject to an informal shared care arrangement between his divorced parents (American mother and English father who had settled in Wales as a young man). The mother felt increasingly isolated in Wales and wanted to return to family and friends in Texas and, she believed, better employment prospects. The High Court judge, Hedley J, held that it was in the child's best interests to continue the shared care arrangements and not move.[20]

3.23 It is important that a parent wishing to return home does not give the impression that she is running away from the other parent, nor seeking to punish the other parent for the relationship or marriage breakdown or undermine the other parent's relationship with the child. A parent seeking to return home may need to be more careful about this than a applicant parent for another reason, because *going home* cases more often arise in the immediate aftermath of the breakdown of the relationship.

Specific opportunity cases

3.24 If the reason for the proposed relocation is to enable the applicant parent to move to pursue a new employment or other opportunity, then she will need to explain how she will benefit from taking up the opportunity, and how the children will benefit. The parent will also need to explain the impact on her and the children of being unable to take the opportunity. There will need to be clear documentary evidence about the nature of the opportunity, how it arose and when it must be taken, if it is to be taken.

3.25 The court does not specifically say this, but there is an impression that the court asks about the extent to which the proposed move is necessary, rather than merely desirable. For example, if the parent's company is closing its existing office and the parent has been offered a transfer to an office elsewhere, that opportunity may be more compelling than cases where there is a new job, but the parent currently has an acceptable job in their present location.

---

[20] Because *Re Y* involved an equal shared care arrangement, many of the factors identified in *Payne v Payne* [2001] EWCA Civ 166, [2001] 1 FLR 1052 carried less weight than they do in many cases; see **2.22–2.28**.

> **Case Example:** *Re F (Internal Relocation)* **[2010] EWCA Civ 1428, [2011] 1 FLR 1382**
>
> The mother wished to move to the Orkney Islands, and she and her new husband had accepted a job share as the GP on one of the islands. The court found that the move would cause the children (aged 14, 12, 11 and 9) emotional harm and huge emotional strain. All four children had been brought up in the town in the North East of England where they currently lived, and they were firmly rooted there. Their contact with their father (on Wednesday evenings, alternate weekends and for longer holiday periods) was important to them and the tortuous nature of the proposed contact journeys raised doubt over the sustainability of the proposed contact arrangements. Three of the children opposed the move and the judge found that the application had become almost unarguable once the children's views were known. Importantly, the mother and her new partner could continue with their careers in the North East even though they would have preferred to move their practice to the Orkneys.[21]

New partner cases

3.26   Cases where the proposed move involves a new partner come in many varieties. Sometimes the new partner is fairly unconnected to the reasons for seeking relocation, such as in a case where the applicant has a new partner and they both seek to move to the partner's original home, or where the applicant has a new partner but the proposed move is really a lifestyle decision. Those cases are best considered under the respective headings. Our discussion here is focused on the case where the applicant has a new partner who is already in the new location.

3.27   The applicant will need to explain the nature and duration of her relationship with the new partner, setting out (for example) how they met, how long they have known each other, how long the relationship has been going on, and so on. The applicant will need to set out the benefit of moving and the effect of not being allowed to relocate, both on her and on the children. The applicant will also need to be prepared to produce a statement from her new partner, explaining why the new partner cannot relocate to her present location.

3.28   Cases involving new partners who are already in the proposed relocation destination are complex. On the one hand, the court will not be keen to force a couple to remain apart; but on the other hand, if the relationship is relatively new or the couple has not previously lived together, there may be significant risks involved and the court may think that the proposed move involves too many uncertainties to be in the child's best interests.

---

[21]   See extracts from this judgment in **Appendix 4.3**. For an example of a proposed international move which was refused for similar reasons, see *Re W (Relocation: Contact)* [2009] EWCA Civ 160, [2009] All ER (D) 120 (May).

> **Case Example: *Re D (Leave to Remove: Shared Residence)* [2006] EWHC
> 1794 (Fam), [2006] Family Law 1006**
>
> The mother of three children (aged 16, 11 and 10) wanted to marry her
> new partner who was American and live with him in America where he
> already lived and worked. The mother and the father had shared the care
> of their children exactly equally since their divorce, and the High Court
> Judge, Hedley J, referred to his own decision in *Re Y (Leave to Remove
> from Jurisdiction)*[22] and approached this case as a factor-specific case to
> be determined in accordance with s 1 of the Children Act 1989.[23] The
> Judge considered the welfare checklist and made a shared residence order
> on the basis that the children would spend significant amounts of time in
> the United Kingdom and the United States. The Judge considered that
> the mother was better able to meet the pressing emotional needs of the
> children and granted her application for leave to remove the children to
> the United States.

Lifestyle cases

3.29 It is easy to understand a client's motivation when they seek to move to
live close to the beach on a Caribbean island, to put their children in a local
school within walking distance of the new home and beach, and to work less
and spend more time with the children. However, caution needs to be exercised
if the reason for relocation is a better lifestyle, as there is a significant risk that
the applicant parent will not be successful.

3.30 As we explained in Chapter 1,[24] we define *lifestyle* cases in way: the
applicant parent is seeking to move somewhere new because she thinks that, in
general, that location will offer a better quality of life, or better life chances, for
her and/or her child than staying where she is at the moment. These cases are
distinguished from *going home* cases because the applicant usually has only
limited (or even no) previous connection with the proposed destination – and if
the applicant has a new partner, he too has no particular connection with the
proposed destination. Similarly, *lifestyle* cases are distinguished from *specific
opportunity* cases because, although the applicant may in fact have obtained an
offer of employment or something like that before bringing a *lifestyle* case, the
decision to move came first, and the job offer followed; in a *specific opportunity*
case, the applicant was not thinking about moving until the opportunity
presented itself.

3.31 The Court of Appeal has made clear that *lifestyle* cases do not face any
additional *legal* hurdles not faced by all relocation cases.[25] However, as a matter

---

[22] *Re Y (Leave to Remove from Jurisdiction)* [2004] 2 FLR 330 (FD); see **3.22**.
[23] For discussion of this legal approach, see **2.22** *et seq*.
[24] See **1.17**.
[25] See, eg, *Re B (Leave to Remove: Impact of Refusal)* [2004] EWCA Civ 956, [2005] 2 FLR 239
at [16]–[17].

of practice, it is harder for an applicant to show that refusal of the plan will have significant detrimental effects if the reason for seeking to move is based primarily on the lifestyle that would be enjoyed in the new location.

Get away cases

3.32   It is most unusual for an applicant to propose a relocation based on an explicit desire to get away from the other parent, and the vast majority of parents would face certain refusal if they brought their case on this basis because their motivation would be seen as illegitimate.[26] However, in wholly exceptional cases, a relocation application can be brought on this basis if the respondent parent poses a serious, objective risk to the child or the applicant parent. The danger would need to be of the gravest seriousness in order to form the basis of an application, such as an ongoing risk of serious violence towards the applicant parent,[27] or criminal convictions for child pornography and paedophilia offences.[28]

PLANNING FOR A RELOCATION

3.33   When a parent first starts to think about relocation, whether their plan is to move in the near future or not for some time, they should do their best to promote contact between the children and the other parent before they seek to relocate. This is because the respondent parent and, in due course, the court will need to be able to have confidence that the applicant parent will continue to facilitate contact arrangements following relocation. If the court is not sure that the relationship between the respondent parent and the children can be maintained in spite of the distance between them, relocation is unlikely to be sanctioned.

3.34   Parents seeking to relocate sometimes think that the less contact between the other parent and the children leading up to the proposed relocation, the greater the chances of being able to relocate. However, except in the rare case where the other parent both does not have and does not seek a significant relationship with the child, or where that parent is an objective danger to the child, we think that to be incorrect. It is more important for the applicant parent to have shown herself to have understood the importance of the child having a strong relationship with the other parent, and to be reliable and committed in promoting that relationship.

3.35   Moreover, a proven record on the part of the applicant of being positive about the other parent's relationship with the child is likely to make the other parent more open to the idea of allowing the relocation. It will also alleviate

---

[26]   *Payne v Payne* [2001] EWCA Civ 166, [2001] 1 FLR 1052 at [40(a)]; see **Appendix 3.1**.

[27]   Although not litigated as a relocation case, see for example the facts of *Re A (Contact: Witness Protection Scheme)* [2005] EWHC 2189 (Fam), [2006] 2 FLR 551.

[28]   One such case is discussed briefly in R George, 'Relocation Research: Early Ideas from Ten County Court Cases' [2012] *Family Law* 700.

concerns on the part of the court that relocation is being used as an opportunity by the applicant to minimise the other parent's involvement in the child's life. Of course, the applicant parent may need to bear in mind that if the child's care arrangements are such that there is no clear primary carer, that can make it more difficult to succeed in a relocation case.

3.36 Any applicant parent should think carefully about the ages at which it would be better for their children to move overseas. There are no hard-and-fast rules, but we have the impression that the courts are more reluctant to grant permission to remove when the children are very young. This is because replacing the existing contact with more infrequent but longer blocks of time may not be possible or developmentally appropriate for a baby or very young child. At the same time, there is likely to be concern that it will be difficult for the relationship between a young child and the other parent to be sustained from a distance, since young children are less able to use Skype, phone or text messaging to maintain meaningful contact between face-to-face visits.

3.37 In addition to being concerned about granting leave to remove in situations where the children are very young, the courts will be concerned about granting permission to remove when the children are at crucial stages of their education, particularly secondary education. An applicant parent will need to show that they have a child-focused approach to their planning, including adjusting the timing of their plans to suit their children's needs if necessary. So, for example, a plan that involves moving at the end of a school year (or moving to enter the new school at the start of the new school year in the destination) is more child-focused than a plan that involves moving mid-term.

INFORMATION AND PRACTICALITIES

3.38 It is difficult to overstate the importance of careful and detailed planning during the initial stages of any intended relocation. Although the courts often make only a cursory assessment of the details of the planning, the fact that there has been careful research into the realities of the proposed move is a crucial aspect of bringing a relocation application. That said, the level of detail required will vary somewhat depending on the case. Where a parent is proposing to return to a location where she lived herself for many years until the comparatively recent past, less planning is required than for a case where the parent proposes to move to a new location where she has no prior experience of living.[29]

3.39 In every case, though, the applicant parent will need to provide full details of their plans for the proposed relocation and should consider the following matters at an early stage:

---

[29] See, eg, *Re F and H (Children: Relocation)* [2007] EWCA Civ 692, [2008] 2 FLR 1667 at [9].

- where would the applicant parent and the children live in the chosen country?

- where would the children go to school?

- what work would the applicant parent do (if relevant)?

- what support would the applicant parent and the children have from family and friends?

- would the relocating parent and the children have access to healthcare provided by the state in the chosen country? If not, what arrangements will be made for private healthcare?

- would there be any immigration issues and, if so, how would they be addressed?

- how would the children maintain their relationships with the other parent, including what proposals would the applicant parent make for direct and indirect contact?

- how would the costs of contact be met?

- would the other parent be able to relocate to the chosen country with the relocating parent and the children? If not, would the other parent be able to travel to and spend time in the chosen country?

3.40 For all of these matters, the applicant parent will need to provide documentary evidence, such as school prospectuses, information on a range of possible housing options (unless, for example, the plan is to move to live with a family member for the first year), and so on.

3.41 In respect of proposals for direct and indirect contact, the applicant parent should make proposals that would give the other parent and the children the best chance of maintaining their relationships in spite of the distance. If the other country is within Northern Europe, the applicant parent may be able to make contact proposals which will not reduce the frequency of contact significantly – for example, contact every third weekend, or one weekend each month during term-time as well as up to half of the holidays, depending on the distance involved and the resources available. If the proposed destination is further away (especially if it is as far away as Australia or New Zealand) the applicant parent is unlikely to be able to do this, and may need to consider proposing that the children spend a larger proportion of their holidays with the other parent. Proposals for indirect contact, including by Skype or other webcam program, will be very important.

3.42 The applicant parent is likely to need to bring the children to this country on a regular basis (unless she agrees to the children flying unaccompanied) and she should also welcome the other parent visiting the children in the other country to reduce the time which the children will need to spend travelling. While it is important that these proposed plans involve the maximum amount of contact that is feasible, the proposals also need to be realistic. The court will look in detail at the applicant parent's budget and the proposals will be scrutinised with care.

3.43 In terms of direct contact, this scrutiny will involve questions not only about finances, but also about timing. For example, if the respondent parent has a job which allows him only 20 days of holiday per year, it may not be realistic for the applicant parent to propose four weeks of staying contact in the summer holidays and a week each at Christmas and Easter (though if there are grandparents or other family members who can help with child care, then the position may be different). Similarly, plans for indirect contact need to take into account both the developmental stage of the child concerned (how long will the child realistically spend interacting on Skype each time?), but also practical issues like time zones.

THE CHILD'S WISHES AND FEELINGS

3.44 The wishes and feelings of the child involved in any family court case are an important factor for the judge. The older the child gets, and therefore the greater the child's maturity and understanding, the more weight will be given to his or her views. It is not uncommon for the views of older children to be virtually determinative of the application.[30] It is important, however, to make clear to a child of whatever age that the burden of the decision making does not rest on his shoulders: either the parents will make the decision together or, if they cannot agree, it will be the judge who determines the outcome and the child's views will be but one factor.

3.45 There is a fine line to be walked in this regard. On the one hand, the child should be introduced to the possibility of a move fairly early in the process so that his or her views can be incorporated into the process. On the other hand, it is important that the applicant parent does not present the move as being inevitable (because it is not), and that neither parent places pressure on the child to support their position. Such actions can seriously backfire. The parents need to demonstrate that they are listening to their child, and not trying to put words into his or her mouth.

3.46 The older the child is, the more likely it is that their views will be influential with the court. But more than that, both parents should listen carefully to what their child is saying, because it may influence how they themselves feel about the decision. If the child is adamantly opposed to the move, the applicant parent might ask herself whether the move is really in the child's interests. Conversely, if the child is strongly in favour of the proposed

---

[30] See, eg, *Re F (Internal Relocation)* [2010] EWCA Civ 1428, [2011] 1 FLR 1382, discussed briefly above, **3.25**, and with fuller extracts in **Appendix 4.3**.

move, the respondent parent might ask whether opposing the move is likely to be best, overall, for his relationship with the child.

3.47 If there is more than one child, it is important to remember that the court will consider them separately,[31] and therefore thought must be given to *each* child's wishes and feelings. It is not inevitable that the children will have the same views about a possible relocation and, while in general the courts think that siblings should be kept together if possible, it is not impossible that one child might relocate and the sibling remain.

TALKING TO THE OTHER PARENT AND TRYING TO REACH AN AGREEMENT WITHOUT LITIGATION

3.48 Parents should be aware that if they end up applying to court and require a multi-day hearing to determine an application for relocation, there may be a delay of anything up to nine or ten months between filing the application and the case being heard. If there is an appeal, that can easily add another three to five months.

3.49 An applicant parent should also be aware that if her application for relocation is fully contested by the other parent, she may have to meet tens of thousands of pounds of legal costs. This may have an impact on her plans for relocation, including potentially affecting her ability to purchase or rent suitable housing in the proposed destination and potentially reducing the amount of contact which can be facilitated by the relocating parent between the children and the other parent.

3.50 The court process must therefore be understood to be slow and expensive, and a much better solution in every way will be to try to agree the result without litigating. A parent wishing to relocate should attempt to talk to the other parent at an early stage, after having given careful thought to their plans. Ideally, this would be at a time when there are settled contact arrangements between the children and the other parent. A parent wishing to relocate should invite the other parent to discuss their plans in mediation with a mediator who has experience of mediating in this area of law. There is a Pre-Application Protocol for Mediation Information and Assessment that applies to applications to relocate.[32] Parties are expected to have attended an information meeting about family mediation and other forms of alternative dispute resolution, unless either:

(a)   there have been allegations of domestic violence resulting in a police investigation, or

---

[31]   *Re S (Relocation: Interests of Siblings)* [2011] EWCA Civ 454, [2011] 2 FLR 678.
[32]   Practice Direction 3A; see **Appendix 2.1**.

(b)   a mediator has determined that the case is not suitable for a mediation and assessment meeting.[33]

3.51   The court will expect all applicants for orders to have complied with the Protocol,[34] and will wish to know whether mediation has been tried or considered. In considering the conduct of any relevant family proceedings, the court will take into account any failure to comply with the Protocol and may refer the parties to a meeting with a mediator before the proceedings are permitted to continue.[35]

3.52   As an alternative to mediation, the applicant parent may wish to consider suggesting that each parent instructs a collaborative lawyer and that they try to reach an agreement by engaging in the collaborative law process.[36] The parents may be assisted by this process to agree a more 'creative' solution than would be likely to be imposed upon them by the court process.

3.53   An applicant parent should not be surprised if the other parent does not feel able to consent to the proposed relocation. It understandably can be very difficult for a parent to wave their children off willingly to live in another location and thereby agree a reduction in the amount of time the children will be able to spend with the parent in the future.

WHEN TO GET HELP

3.54   It is vital that an applicant parent consults a solicitor or barrister who specialises in family law and has experience of representing parents in relocation cases (either international or internal, as the case may be) at an early stage. Furthermore, because of the slowness of the litigation process, an applicant parent should not delay in making an application to the court if the other parent is unlikely to agree to the proposed relocation. This is particularly the case if the plan of the applicant parent is time-sensitive (such as because of a need to fit with the child's school year, or because of the start-date of a job offer).

3.55   The reason why it is important to get a specialist family lawyer to work on the case is that relocation litigation is complicated. The law involves pitfalls

---

[33]   Practice Direction 3A, Annexes A and C; see **Appendix 2.1**.
[34]   In December 2012, Holman J, then Acting President of the Family Division, wrote to all Family judges reminding them of Practice Direction 3A and inviting them to apply the requirements more rigorously.
[35]   Practice Direction 3A, para [4.1]; see **Appendix 2.1**.
[36]   In the collaborative law process, each parent appoints their own trained collaborative lawyer and the parents and their lawyers meet together (in four-way meetings) to work things out face-to-face. The parents and the lawyers commit to try to resolve the issues without the involvement of the courts, and they sign an Agreement which disqualifies the lawyers from representing the parents in court if the collaborative process breaks down. More information can be obtained at www.resolution.org.uk/collaborative_family_law.

that are not common to other areas of family law, and the preparation that is required before bringing a case is both greater and more specific than most cases require.

3.56 In the case of a proposed international move, it may also be necessary to get advice from a lawyer in the proposed new country. In particular, the court in this country will need to be sure that any contact arrangements that are proposed for after the move will be enforceable. While some specialist family lawyers will have enough experience to advise about this issue with regard to some international destinations, it may be necessary to get specific advice in an individual case.

3.57 The main issues, other than possibly immigration questions, will usually relate to finding out about how contact would be enforced in the new location, and whether any order made by the English court can be registered in the new country, or whether a 'mirror order' can be obtained. A mirror order is where the local court in the new location is asked to make an order there in identical terms to the order made in the English court. Many jurisdictions will happily do this, though often not until the child is physically present in the new country, but it is worth being aware that in some countries the idea of a mirror order is not recognised and therefore such an order cannot be obtained.

3.58 If advice from a lawyer in another jurisdiction is required, the following questions are likely to be important:

- Would an English court order, expressed in terms of a residence order in favour of the applicant parent and a contact order in favour of the respondent parent, be capable of being mirrored in the other jurisdiction?

- Would an English court order expressed as being a shared residence order in favour of both parents be capable of being mirrored in the other jurisdiction?

- If the answer to question 1 or 2 above is 'yes', what is the procedure for obtaining a mirror order? What is the likely timescale and cost?

- In the event that one of the parents breaches the terms of the English order, what enforcement options would be open to the other parent in the other jurisdiction?

- If, after the children become habitually resident in the other jurisdiction, one of the parents makes an application to the court in the other jurisdiction to change the arrangements for children:

  — what principles would the court in the other jurisdiction apply when determining the application?

— how much time would the court in the other jurisdiction be likely to order that the children should spend with the opposing parent in the circumstances of the case?

• Is there any particular form of words that can or should be incorporated in the English order in order to minimise the risk of the court in the other jurisdiction interfering with the decision of the English court?

CASE STUDY

3.59 To illustrate some of the issues that have arisen in this chapter, we have set out the following case study. Of course, the issues arising in any particular case will be unique, but we hope that this example gives a flavour of how cases can develop.[37]

Case Study

Nick and Jennifer met in Chicago, US whilst Nick was on secondment with his work as a lawyer in a commercial law firm in the City. Jennifer joined Nick in London six months after the end of his secondment, and they married six months later. They were married for 14 years and have two children, Brad aged 13 and Victoria aged 11. They divorced a year ago after Jennifer discovered that Nick had been having an affair with his secretary. Since the divorce, the children have had staying contact with Nick on alternate weekends from Friday at 6.00pm to Sunday at 6.00pm and they have had visiting contact with him every Wednesday from the end of their after-school activities until 7.30pm. The children have stayed with Nick for two weeks during the summer, a week at Christmas and at Easter and for half of their half-terms.

In an email to Nick, Jennifer explains that she is very upset about the breakdown of the marriage, she has never felt at home here and she wishes to return to live in Chicago where her parents and siblings (two sisters and a brother) still live. Nick responds angrily to Jennifer suggesting that she is trying to punish him for his affair by taking their children away from him.

Answer to Case Study

Jennifer should invite Nick to attend mediation with her. If he agrees, she should explain how she feels isolated and lonely here. She should explain fully her plans, including where she proposes to live with the children and where she proposes the children will go to school. She should explain that ➡

---

[37] See also **4.43**, where we include another case study raising different factual issues; in **Appendix 5** we include sample application and response materials relating to the case study set out in Chapter 4.

she intends initially to live with her parents in their large house. She should make it clear that she has thought carefully about the timing of the children moving to a new school or new schools and that she believes the children could transfer smoothly at their respective ages. She should explain that she hopes that she would be able to work part-time in her family's retail business.

Jennifer should explain how she and the children will benefit from living close to her family and support network and how they will benefit from Jennifer being able to return to the workplace (having not worked outside of the home since her move to the United Kingdom). She should remind Nick of the relationships Brad and Victoria have with members of her family, and explain what she believes the children's wishes and feelings will be about the proposed move.

Jennifer will need to make proposals for contact that will enable the children to continue to spend time with Nick and his family regularly.

Nick's law firm still have an office in Chicago and Jennifer hopes that Nick will be able to combine regular business trips with contact visits, particularly during school term-time. She agrees to facilitate arrangements for the children to spend extended periods of time in the United Kingdom with Nick during school holidays. She also agrees to facilitate indirect contact between the children and Nick by Skype, telephone, email etc. She should offer to take advice from a specialist family lawyer in Chicago with a view to providing reassurance to Nick about the enforcement of English contact orders by the Chicago courts and the approach of those courts to contact. She should try to avoid contested leave to remove proceedings and, if necessary, offer additional contact, as the family's resources will be better spent on travel costs for contact rather than legal costs.

Chapter 4

OPPOSING A RELOCATION APPLICATION: THINGS TO THINK ABOUT BEFORE YOU START

4.1   This chapter sets out in detail the kinds of matters which a parent who is thinking about opposing a relocation application (and his legal adviser) should think about before the case gets to court. Our aim here is to help respondent parents to understand what they should be looking for when they assess a relocation application, as well as matters separate from that which they should consider.

THINGS TO THINK ABOUT AT THE OUTSET

4.2   A few years ago, many family lawyers would have said to a parent who was considering opposing a relocation application that, although there was a chance of winning, they were likely to face difficulty. That would have been particularly true if the applicant was clearly the primary carer of the child. The general view was that a well-planned and genuinely motivated application was likely to succeed. However, the last few years have seen something of a shift in attitude, and it is now generally thought that the law is more evenly balanced.

4.3   Because of the way that the law has developed, if it seems likely that the other parent will seek to relocate at some point, the parent not wanting to relocate will be well advised to remain as involved as possible in the child's day-to-day care. If the parents are sharing the child's care in more or less equal proportions – or, at least, if both parents are providing enough of the daily care that the child could realistically live with either of them and do well – then the parent opposing the relocation is in a much stronger position.

4.4   If arrangements like these are formalised in a court order, they would no doubt be called 'shared residence' – but the name of the order is not important. What matters is the arrangements on the ground, as seen from the child's perspective.[1] As we explained in Chapter 2,[2] in these shared care cases the guidance given by the Court of Appeal needs to be modified, and may make it harder for an applicant parent to succeed in obtaining permission to relocate.

---

[1]   See *K v K (Relocation: Shared Care Arrangement)* [2011] EWCA Civ 793, [2012] 2 FLR 880 (hereafter, *K v K*) at [57]; see **Appendix 3.3**.

[2]   See **2.22** *et seq.*

4.5   If the parents are not able to agree on a shared care arrangement informally, a court application for a shared residence order can be made.[3] The order that the judge makes will depend on what arrangement is best for the child concerned in the circumstances of the case, and it is important to note that the parent seeking shared care does not necessarily need to aspire to achieving an equal division of the child's time under the shared care arrangement. However, they should aim to achieve a position where they are spending significant time with the child, for example at least alternate weekends from Friday to Monday, one night during the week and half of school holidays, and where they are making a significant contribution to their care. The aim is to make clear to the child (and therefore to anyone else, including the court if necessary) that the child has a home with both parents, and is happy living in both households.

4.6   A parent who believes that there is a possibility that the other parent may wish to relocate should be supportive of the other parent, including (if applicable) supporting visits to family and friends on a regular basis. The parent should endeavour to be positive about the other parent at all times, especially in front of the child. He should also be flexible and accommodating towards the other parent and not micromanage the other parent's care of the child.

CONSIDERING THE ALTERNATIVES

4.7   Furthermore, the applicant parent should not remove any of her children from the United Kingdom, even if there is no residence order in place, as any removal without the consent of every person with parental responsibility may amount to an offence of child abduction.[4]

4.8   If an applicant parent notifies the respondent parent that she wishes to relocate with the children and the respondent parent opposes, or is likely to oppose, the proposal to relocate, the respondent parent will have a number of options. It is important to think carefully about all the possible options and the pros and cons of each, including some options which the parents may not initially want to think about.

4.9   Before deciding what to do, it is worth thinking about how things are likely to play out both if the relocation goes ahead and if it does not. The respondent parent needs to decide whether the overall best course of action is to oppose the planned relocation or to endorse and agree to it. That requires careful thought, and it is best to avoid immediate responses when the idea is likely to be raw and upsetting.

---

[3]   Note, however, that applications made on a purely tactical basis solely as a means of opposing a relocation have been deprecated by the Court of Appeal, see *Re F (Permission to Relocate)* [2012] EWCA Civ 1364, [2012] 3 FCR 443 at [60].

[4]   Child Abduction Act 1984, s 1; Hague Convention on the Civil Aspects of International Child Abduction 1980.

4.10   In the end, the most common decision that the respondent parent reaches is that he wants to oppose the application, and we will consider in a moment various ways in which that can be done.[5] First, though, there are two other alternatives to which thought might be given, even if in the end the parent rejects both.

4.11   One alternative is to agree to the applicant parent's suggestion and give written consent to her taking the children permanently to live somewhere else. The downside to this option is obvious, but it is worth thinking about what the reality would be if the relocation went ahead. How often could contact take place? For how long could the child visit, and for how long could the parent visit them in their new home? How old are the children? If they are, say, in their early or mid teenage years, they may well choose to return to the United Kingdom for university or employment, so the time away may not be as long as it initially seems.

4.12   It is also worth considering the effects and financial cost of opposing the relocation. If the case ends up at a final hearing in court, there will be significant legal costs, usually running into the tens of thousands of pounds. Some families can afford that without particularly noticing, but most people find the financial aspects of legal action a significant consideration. Money spent on litigation is money that is not available later to pay for flights, accommodation and holidays if the relocation ends up happening.

4.13   Perhaps more important than that, though, is the potential damage to the relationship between the parents, and between each parent and the child. As we set out in Chapter 1,[6] some relocation cases are the culmination of years of ongoing disputes between the parents, but in many cases the parents have either always been amicable with one another or have now settled into an amicable pattern after previous difficulties. While the parent opposing the relocation may, justifiably, see any potential problems that arise from the relocation dispute as having been 'caused' by the applicant parent, it is worth asking what life will be like after the case is over if he has succeeded in his application to the court to stop her from moving. Much will depend on the personality of the parents, on the reasons for seeking relocation, and on each parent's attitude and behaviour during the course of discussions – but it is worth asking the question.

4.14   The other alternative that the respondent parent may wish to consider is whether he too might relocate to the proposed destination, so as to maintain his proximity to the children. In many cases, this will not be a realistic option – for example, the applicant may be proposing to move to a location where the respondent would struggle to get permission to immigrate, the respondent may

---

[5]   See **4.16** *et seq.*
[6]   See **1.12**.

have a job which could not readily be moved to another location, or the respondent may have other family responsibilities in the present location which could not be discharged if he moved.

4.15 In some cases, though, it may in fact be an option for both parents to move, and careful and open-minded thought may lead the respondent parent at least to consider this approach. In a case where, for example, both parents originally moved together to the United Kingdom from another country and, their relationship having broken down, one now seeks to go back, it would be possible – if perhaps not desirable for whatever reason – for both parents to return. Increasingly, the courts expect to see evidence that the respondent to a relocation application has at least considered this option.[7]

4.16 In the event that the respondent parent decides to oppose the relocation, there are a number of ways of doing that. The two main options are to seek to become the child's sole main carer in the original location, or to prevent the applicant parent from relocating so that she remains in the original location with the child.

4.17 On the assumption that this outcome cannot be achieved by negotiation, the respondent parent will need to apply for one or more of the following court orders:

(a) a residence order transferring the main residence of the children from the applicant parent's home to the respondent parent's home;

(b) a shared residence order providing that the children spend increased time with him;

(c) a prohibited steps order preventing the applicant parent from removing the children from the jurisdiction of England and Wales (in the case of a proposed international move) or from their present town or city (in the case of a proposed domestic move);

(d) a specific issue order enabling the court, for example, to determine where the children should go to school.

4.18 The court's paramount consideration when deciding whether to exercise these powers is the welfare of each child concerned,[8] having regard in particular to the factors set out in the welfare checklist.[9]

4.19 Every case is different, and a parent thinking about opposing a relocation should take advice from a solicitor or barrister who specialises in

---

[7]   *K v K* at [47].
[8]   Children Act 1989, s 1; see **Appendix 1.1**.
[9]   Children Act 1989, s 1(3); see **Appendix 1.1**.

family law and is experienced in relocation cases as to when and if it would be appropriate to make an application for any of these orders, and which would be most appropriate.

4.20 In some cases, it may be important for the respondent parent to make an application for a residence order or a shared residence order before the other parent makes an application for leave to remove the children. In other cases, it may be best to avoid raising the temperature by making an application to the court before all efforts to reach an agreement in respect of any relocation proposal have been exhausted. If the respondent parent has reason to believe that the applicant parent may attempt to remove the children from the jurisdiction of England and Wales without the respondent parent's consent or permission from the court, he should not delay in making an application to the court for a prohibited steps order, together with other standard anti-abduction measures which an experienced solicitor or barrister will know well.[10]

ASSESSING THE APPLICANT PARENT'S PROPOSALS – WHAT TO LOOK FOR

4.21 A parent who is presented by the applicant parent with a proposal to relocate with the children from this jurisdiction, should consider carefully the applicant parent's reason for the proposed relocation and whether she has made any previous proposal(s) to relocate. As discussed earlier,[11] her reason may be that she wishes to return home to live close to her family and/or friends, to move to live with a new partner, or to take up a new employment opportunity. Alternatively, she may simply hope to enjoy an improved lifestyle.

4.22 While there are no 'categories' of relocation cases based on the applicant's reasons for wanting to move,[12] the reason is still very relevant because the likely effect on the applicant parent of refusing the application is one factor in the court's assessment, and the reason why the parent wants to move is usually relevant to that assessment. In general, applicants find it easiest to establish that there will be a significant detrimental effect on them from refusal in *going home* cases, while respondents find it easiest to suggest that there will be no major long-term effect of refusal in *lifestyle* cases.

4.23 A parent who is presented with a relocation proposal should consider carefully the applicant parent's plans, including her proposals for the children's

---

[10]   Abduction is not a matter that we address in this book, but measures like ordering the surrender of the child's passport, ordering that no new passports be issued in the child's name, and ordering that the child's name be put on the 'port stop' or 'port alert' list are all standard anti-abduction precautions. It is also possible for the child to be made a ward of court (see Practice Direction 12D: Inherent Jurisdiction (Including Wardship) Proceedings). For further information about anti-abduction measures, see Part 4 of Practice Direction 12F: International Child Abduction.

[11]   See **1.13–1.18** and **3.19–3.32**.

[12]   See, eg, *Re B (Leave to Remove: Impact of Refusal)* [2004] EWCA Civ 956, [2005] 2 FLR 239 at [16]–[17].

contact with the respondent parent. In the current judicial climate,[13] the effect of the children's removal on the relationship between the respondent parent and the children is likely to be the factor which provides the respondent parent with the greatest scope for challenging the applicant parent's plans.

Helpful Hint

Ten points for a respondent parent to think about when thinking about a relocation application for the first time:

(1) What would be the difference in the frequency of the children's direct contact with the respondent parent following the relocation?

(2) How are the children likely to cope with less frequent contact? How are the children likely to be affected? The respondent parent should bear in mind that young children are considered to need more frequent contact with the parent with whom they do not spend the majority of their time, whereas older children can more readily adjust to long blocks of time such as extensive holiday contact.

(3) How will the children maintain contact with the respondent parent's extended family?

(4) What will be the difference in the quality of the children's direct contact with the respondent parent following relocation? Is it proposed that the contact or a significant proportion of it should take place in the location in which the children will be living or in another location between the two parents' homes? If so, where will the children and the respondent parent stay during their time together? Is it proposed that they should stay in a hotel or hotels? (The respondent parent should consider that 'hotel contact' is likely to be less natural and relaxed, and thus of a lesser quality, than contact within the parent's home.)

(5) Do the working arrangements and commitments of the respondent parent allow him to travel/spend extended periods with the children at the level which will be required for the relationship(s) to be maintained?

(6) How is it proposed that the children will travel for contact at the respondent parent's home? Will the applicant parent be accompanying them? Are the children too young to travel as 'unaccompanied minors'? Can the costs of contact be afforded? How is it proposed that these costs are to be met? (In many cases, a compromise is➡

---

[13]   This is thought to be so in particular since *K v K* in mid-2011; see **Appendix 3.3**.

reached whereby the respondent parent ceases to pay child support
if the relocation goes ahead, with that money being put towards
travel costs for contact instead.)

(7)   What will be the effects on the children of the proposed travel
arrangements?

(8)   What proposals are made for indirect contact (including by email,
Skype, etc)? Is it likely that the proposed indirect contact can
compensate for the reduced frequency of direct contact? What is the
quality of indirect contact likely to be? Indirect contact may be
beneficial and successful for older children and their parents but is
likely to be less beneficial and successful for younger children and
their parents (though of course each child is unique, so the parent
should think about this with regard to his own child).

(9)   Can the applicant parent be trusted to facilitate contact and
promote the position and role of the respondent parent in the
children's lives? What is the background in this respect? Has the
applicant parent facilitated contact and promoted the children's
relationship with the respondent parent to date?

(10) Is it possible for any order granting leave to remove and specifying
the contact arrangements to be registered and/mirrored in the other
jurisdiction? How will contact be enforced in the other jurisdiction
in the event of difficulties? It is very important that advice is taken
from a family law specialist in the other jurisdiction on these issues.

4.24   In addition to the applicant parent's contact proposals, the respondent
parent should consider the applicant parent's practical plans, in particular for
housing in the new location and for the education of the children. Although
there is often limited scope for challenging the applicant parent's practical
plans (particularly when the applicant parent is represented by a lawyer who is
experienced in international relocation cases and is likely to help the applicant
parent to present a satisfactory 'business case'), the plans should still be
scrutinised.

4.25   The respondent parent should consider whether the proposed housing in
the other country will be of a similar standard to the children's housing in this
country and whether it will be in a safe, pleasant and child-friendly
environment. If the proposed housing does not meet these criteria, the
respondent parent can think about challenging the detail of the relocation
plans. That said, it is worth bearing in mind that in many cases the plans can be
fleshed out and improved as the case goes on, and so if this is the only basis for
challenging the plan then it may be worth asking whether it is likely to lead to
the outcome that the respondent is seeking.

4.26 Depending on the location to which the applicant parent seeks to relocate, the respondent parent may raise concerns about the safety of the country/home environment. Whilst, on the face of it, a proposal to move to a country/city that is regarded as having safety issues may seem open to challenge, such a proposal may still be authorised by the court.

Case Example: *Re K (Application to Remove from Jurisdiction)* **[1998] 2 FLR 1006 (FD)**

The Nigerian mother applied for leave to remove the children from this jurisdiction to Nigeria, where her family lived and she would be able to further her teaching career. The Nigerian father who opposed the mother's application contended that living conditions, especially in relation to crime, health and general amenities were lower than in England.

Charles J held that adverse or significantly different living conditions in the country to which the custodial parent sought leave to take the children was a factor to be taken into account as part of the general consideration of the welfare of the children. In this case, the central and crucial point was whether the differences in the living conditions, environment and culture in England and Nigeria were such that, accepting that adverse conditions existed in Nigeria, the medium to long term welfare of the children could best be promoted by them remaining in England. Matters such as both parents having families in Nigeria would make it easier for the children to adjust to the environment and would ameliorate the adverse conditions in Nigeria so far as they affected or might affect them.

4.27 While there may be exceptions to this general perception, in most cases the courts take the view that one location is unlikely to be inherently so much more unsafe than another that this factor will be decisive in a relocation case. If the case gets to trial, the judge will need to assess the relative risks and the parent's ability to protect the child from those risks, but it would be a most unusual case when the judge thought that a parent was planning to move to a location which was dangerous but where the applicant parent did not have plans in place to keep her child safe.

4.28 The respondent parent should consider the ages of the children and their stages of education. If a child is at the end of their primary education and has secured a place at a good school for their secondary education, the respondent parent might want to look carefully at the proposed education in the new location. If the proposed schools there look less advantageous than those available in the original location, the parent may want to challenge the relocation proposal on the basis that the child would be losing this opportunity. If the case involves a child aged 13 or above, the respondent parent may want to argue that the child is at an important stage of his/her secondary education and that a relocation would be unsettling and potentially damaging as far as his/her education is concerned.

4.29 There are three other issues which a parent opposing a relocation application may want to think about at this early stage of the process:

(a) Will the applicant parent have a support network in the new location? Is what the applicant parent says about the support network they will have in the new location genuine? If the applicant parent seeks permission to relocate because she feels unhappy or isolated in the present location and she does not have a support network in the new location, the respondent parent may argue that she is unlikely to feel happier or less isolated in the new location.

(b) If the proposed move is an international one, what will the applicant parent's immigration status be? The respondent parent may need to take advice from an immigration law specialist in the other country to establish whether the applicant parent and the children will be able to live permanently in the other country without any issues. There may also be issues with the respondent parent's immigration status in the new country for the purposes of contact visits; in most cases holiday visas are reasonably straightforward to obtain, but it is worth checking with the relevant Embassy or High Commission in London.

(c) Does the applicant parent have any lifestyle issues that may undermine her reliability or trustworthiness, or impact upon her ability to care for the children? These issues would need to be reasonably serious to be worth raising, because in general the respondent should endeavour to remain positive about the other parent – the case must be focused on the child's welfare, and not come across as the parents fighting over the past.

THE CHILD'S WISHES AND FEELINGS

4.30 The wishes and feelings of the child involved in any family court case is an important factor for the judge. The older the child gets, and therefore the greater the child's maturity and understanding, the more weight will be given to his or her views. It is not uncommon for the views of older children to be virtually determinative of the application.[14] It is important, however, to make clear to a child of whatever age that the burden of the decision making does not rest on his shoulders: either the parents will make the decision together or, if they cannot agree, it will be the judge who determines the outcome and the child's views will be but one factor.

---

[14]   *Re F (Internal Relocation)* [2010] EWCA Civ 1428, [2011] 1 FLR 1382; see **3.25** and **Appendix 4.3**.

4.31   There is a fine line to be walked in this regard. On the one hand, the child should be introduced to the possibility of a move fairly early in the process so that his or her views can be incorporated into the process. On the other hand, it is important that the applicant parent does not present the move as being inevitable (because it is not), and that neither parent places pressure on the child to support their position. Such actions can seriously backfire. The parents need to demonstrate that they are listening to their child, and not trying to put words into his or her mouth.

4.32   The older the child is, the more likely it is that their views will be influential with the court. But more than that, both parents should listen carefully to what their child is saying, because it may influence how they themselves feel about the decision. If the child is adamantly opposed to the move, the applicant parent might ask herself whether the move is really in the child's interests. Conversely, if the child is strongly in favour of the proposed move, the respondent parent might ask whether opposing the move is likely to be best, overall, for his relationship with the child.

4.33   If there is more than one child, it is important to remember that the court will consider each separately,[15] and therefore thought must be given to *each* child's wishes and feelings. It is not inevitable that the children will have the same views about a possible relocation and, while in general the courts think that siblings should be kept together if possible, it is not impossible that one child might relocate and another remain.

TALKING TO THE OTHER PARENT AND TRYING TO REACH AN AGREEMENT WITHOUT LITIGATION

4.34   Parents should be aware that if they end up applying to court and require a multi-day hearing to determine a relocation dispute, there may be a delay of anything up to nine or ten months between filing the application and the case being heard. If there is an appeal, that can easily add another three to five months.

4.35   A parent wishing to oppose a relocation application should also be aware that if the relocation case is fully contested, he may have to meet tens of thousands of pounds of legal costs. Depending on the available resources, this expenditure may have a significant effect on his financial position regardless of the outcome of the case, as well as reducing the money available to pay for ongoing contact if the relocation does go ahead.

4.36   The court process must therefore be understood to be slow and expensive, and a much better solution in every way will be to try to agree the result without litigating. A respondent parent should attempt to talk to the applicant parent at an early stage, after having given careful thought to the

---

[15]   *Re S (Relocation: Interests of Siblings)* [2011] EWCA Civ 454, [2011] 2 FLR 678.

plans that have been put forward. The parents may find it helpful to talk about the decision in mediation with a mediator who has experience of working in this area of law. Before commencing any legal proceedings relating to children, an applicant will, save in certain specified circumstances,[16] be expected by the court to have attended a mediation information assessment meeting.[17]

4.37 As an alternative to mediation, the respondent parent may wish to consider suggesting that each parent instructs a collaborative lawyer and that they try to reach an agreement by engaging in the collaborative law process.[18] The parents may be assisted by this process to agree a more 'creative' solution than would be likely to be imposed upon them by the court process.

4.38 Relocation cases are particularly fraught, and both parents should try to keep in mind how the other parent is feeling. It is not at all unusual for the parents to be unable to agree about the right outcome to a relocation dispute, but keeping an open mind can help to smooth the process.

WHEN TO GET HELP

4.39 It is vital that a parent opposing a relocation proposal consults a solicitor or barrister who specialises in family law and has experience of acting for parents in relocation cases (either international or internal as the case may be) at an early stage. Depending on the facts of the case, there may be a need to act quickly. For example, if the respondent does not have parental responsibility for the child concerned,[19] it may be necessary for him to start legal proceedings to ensure that the relocation does not take place without his agreement. Similarly, for moves within the United Kingdom, there is no legal onus on the applicant to obtain court sanction before moving,[20] so it will be down to the respondent to commence legal proceedings, and that will be done much more effectively before the move takes place.

4.40 The reason why it is important to get a specialist family lawyer to work on the case is that relocation litigation is complicated. The law involves pitfalls

---

[16] The relevant circumstances are set out on Mediation and Information Assessment Form (Form FM1).

[17] Practice Direction 3A: Pre-Application Protocol for Mediation Information and Assessment; see **Appendix 2.1**.

[18] In the collaborative law process, each parent appoints their own trained collaborative lawyer and the parents and their lawyers meet together (in four-way meetings) to work things out face-to-face. The parents and the lawyers commit to try to resolve the issues without the involvement of the courts, and they sign an Agreement which disqualifies the lawyers from representing the parents in court if the collaborative process breaks down. More information can be obtained at www.resolution.org.uk/collaborative_family_law.

[19] There will be increasingly few such cases as legal changes in the early 2000s mean that most parents have parental responsibility for their children.

[20] See **2.44** *et seq.*

that are not common to other areas of family law, and the preparation that is required before bringing a case is both greater and more specific than most other cases involve.

4.41 For international moves, there may be cause to seek expert legal advice from a lawyer in the proposed destination country. The main issues, other than possibly immigration questions, will usually relate to finding out about how contact would be enforced in the new location, and whether any order made by the English court can be registered in the new country, or whether a 'mirror order' can be obtained. A mirror order is where the local court in the new location is asked to make an order there in identical terms to the order made in the English court. Many jurisdictions will happily do this, though often not until the child is physically present in the new country, but it is worth being aware that in some countries the idea of a mirror order is not recognised and therefore such an order cannot be obtained.

4.42 If advice from a lawyer in another jurisdiction is required, the following questions are likely to be important:

- Would an English court order, expressed in terms of a residence order in favour of the applicant parent and a contact order in favour of the respondent parent, be capable of being mirrored in the other jurisdiction?

- Would an English court order expressed as being a shared residence order in favour of both parents be capable of being mirrored in the other jurisdiction?

- If the answer to question 1 or 2 above is 'yes', what is the procedure for obtaining a mirror order? What is the likely timescale and cost?

- In the event that one of the parents breaches the terms of the English order, what enforcement options would be open to the other parent in the other jurisdiction?

- If, after the children become habitually resident in the other jurisdiction, one of the parents makes an application to the court in the other jurisdiction to change the arrangements for children:

    - what principles would the court in the other jurisdiction apply when determining the application?
    - how much time would the court in the other jurisdiction be likely to order that the children should spend with the opposing parent in the circumstances of the case?

- Is there any particular form of words that can or should be incorporated in the English order in order to minimise the risk of the court in the other jurisdiction interfering with the decision of the English court?

CASE STUDY

4.43   To illustrate some of the issues that have arisen in this chapter, we have set out the following case study. Of course, the issues arising in any particular case will be unique, but we hope that this example gives a flavour of how cases can develop.[21] We have also included sample C100 (application) and C2 (cross-application response) forms relating to this case study in Appendix 5.

Case Study

Pete and Sue were married for 12 years and they have three children, Charlie aged ten, Millie aged seven and Freddie aged three. Pete is a property developer and Sue is a photographer. Both of them have flexibility in their working hours. During their marriage, Pete was generally able to look after Charlie and Millie whilst Sue worked. When Pete and Sue divorced two years ago, the children continued to live for the majority of their time with Sue in the former family home in a pleasant area of Surrey. Charlie and Millie began immediately to stay with Pete on alternate weekends from Friday after school to Monday morning and on Wednesday nights each week. Pete and Sue agreed that Charlie and Millie would stay with Pete for two weeks in the summer holidays, one week at Christmas, one week at Easter and for half of half terms. He would also take or collect Charlie and Millie to and from school occasionally when Sue was working. At the age of one, Freddie was very attached to Sue at the time of the divorce. Pete and Sue agreed that Freddie would visit Pete for three hours each Saturday morning initially and that Freddie's time with Pete would gradually increase so that, by the age of three, Freddie would be ready to stay with Pete on alternate weekends and Wednesday nights.

A year after their divorce, Sue has formed a relationship via an internet dating site with an English banker who is based in Cape Town, South Africa. Although Freddie is now visiting Pete for the day on alternate Saturdays, Sue says that he is unsettled after his visits and she has not yet agreed to him making the transition to staying overnight with Pete. Charlie is promising to be a very good sportsman and has been offered a place on a sports scholarship at a local grammar school.

During a meeting over lunch with Pete, Sue tells him that she wishes to move with the children to Cape Town to live with her new partner. She tells him that she intends to sell the former family home and move into the partner's large apartment with the children. She will continue to work and arrange for the children to attend international schools in Cape Town.   ➡

---

[21]   See also **3.59**, where we include another case study raising different factual issues.

Answer to Case Study

Pete should talk to the older two children about their wishes and feelings in relation to Sue's proposed relocation, without placing any undue pressure on them. Charlie, in particular, may be reluctant to move as he is especially close to Pete and if he moves, he will lose the opportunity of moving to the grammar school on a scholarship with some of his closest friends.

In relation to the children's contact with Pete, he should discuss with Sue her proposals for the children to spend time with him. He should explain to her that he is concerned that the effect of any proposals she makes will inevitably be a reduction in the amount of time the children spend with him and significantly longer gaps between the children's periods of time with him. He should question how he and the children would be able to maintain their relationship. He should ask Sue how she proposes Freddie is going to make the transition to staying overnight with Pete for long periods, given that he has not yet stayed overnight with Pete, and question how Freddie is going to cope with the gaps between the periods of time they spend together. Pete may, understandably, be concerned that there will be difficulties and he should take advice from a specialist family lawyer in Cape Town about how any contact arrangements agreed by Pete or Sue or ordered by the court would be enforced by the South African courts and what their general approach is to the issues of residence, contact, and shared residence/contact.

Pete should question whether it will be in the children's best interests to move from a relatively spacious house with a garden to an apartment which is likely to be situated in a gated block with high security fencing and is likely to have no private garden/outdoor space. Pete should raise concerns about the safety/security of Cape Town and may consider it appropriate to suggest it will not be in the children's best interests to live in those conditions. Pete should also question whether the international schools in Cape Town would provide the children with as good a standard of education and as good opportunities as the schools they will have the benefit of attending here.

Pete should consider whether he could do anything to persuade Sue to stay. Sometimes, it may be possible in cases where a mother wishes to return home for the father to offer the mother assistance to help her to feel happier and less isolated living in this jurisdiction, for instance, arrangements which will enable the mother to travel regularly with the children to visit her family in the home country. In the above scenario, it is likely to be more difficult to offer Sue assistance that will persuade her against the proposed relocation. Pete could suggest that Sue spends regular periods of time with her partner in Cape Town while he looks after the children. He should also question whether Sue's partner could return to live in this country (he is English) to avoid the children having to ➡

relocate. If Sue cannot be persuaded to stay in this country and her partner cannot return to live here, Pete will need to consider carefully the advice of his legal representatives about his prospects of being successful in opposing Sue's proposed relocation. If he is advised that he does not have good prospects, he may wish to consider moving to Cape Town/South Africa himself so that he can continue to make a significant contribution to the children's day-to-day care. His work as a property developer may be sufficiently portable to enable him to relocate and he and the children are likely to benefit from the costs that he will save by not becoming embroiled with Sue in a fully contested leave to remove case.

Chapter 5

BRINGING A RELOCATION APPLICATION

5.1   This chapter sets out everything that needs to happen from an applicant parent's point of view between the completion of the initial stages of the case (which we addressed in Chapter 3) and the completion of a final hearing in a relocation case. For this purpose, relocation means an application to remove a child permanently from the United Kingdom or to move permanently within the United Kingdom.[1]

DECIDING WHETHER TO MAKE A FORMAL APPLICATION

5.2   Any thought of relocating a significant distance is a serious decision and should not be undertaken lightly. Even internal relocations and many comparatively short international moves (to Ireland or France, say) would be likely to have significant effects on the child's relationship with the parent who did not move, as well as involving other changes to the child's life relating to matters like schooling or, for some international moves, language and culture.

5.3   These are all things which the other parent is entitled to know about, discuss and, if he thinks best, oppose, and the parent proposing the relocation needs to take that into consideration. The courts frown on parents who act unilaterally,[2] often regarding such conduct as evidence of that parent lacking respect for the role of the other, or worse still as evidence of a deliberate attempt to undermine the relationship the other parent has with the children. Only in cases of real need, for example if there is fear of domestic violence, may such conduct be excused.

5.4   If parents are able to discuss proposed arrangements face-to-face, this is obviously the first and best step to take. If this is not possible, the best course of action is to inform the other parent in writing of the proposals. Many people by this stage will have consulted a solicitor, who will write the letter on their behalf. The letter should contain details of the proposal, including precisely where it is intended to move, why the move is being contemplated, the possibilities for schooling, and proposals for contact (and the costs of travel if substantial).

---

[1]   For temporary international relocation, this chapter should be read along with **Chapter 7**.
[2]   A unilateral move to another country will usually amount to international child abduction: see **2.7–2.9**.

5.5   If the parents cannot agree to the move and the consequences that will ensue, either parent can apply to the court. Litigation, however, should never be undertaken lightly. It is expensive, distressing and time-consuming. That is just for the parents. For the children it can cause real anguish. Nonetheless, in some cases it cannot be avoided.

5.6   Once it is known that the respondent parent does not intend to agree to the applicant's proposed relocation, the best way to proceed is to seek a residence order (if the applicant does not already have one), together with a specific issue order sanctioning the move and a defined contact order (or defined shared residence arrangement) for the respondent parent.[3]

PREPARING AN APPLICATION

5.7   Once it has become apparent that there is unlikely to be an early agreement to relocation, and a letter has been written to the other parent formally setting out the proposals (and giving time for a response), the next step is to apply to the court. This can be done before or after going to mediation.[4] If time is of the essence it may be sensible to apply to the court before mediation has been started or concluded, because the few weeks that it will take to list the case for a first hearing can be used to see whether agreement can be reached notwithstanding the court application.

5.8   In an ideal world, by the time a case gets to the stage where an application is being prepared, the applicant's decision to seek relocation will have been given the fullest consideration. Detailed plans will have been drawn up for the future, having regard to the housing, education and individual needs of the children, any job prospects that the applicant parent has, proposals for post-relocation contact arrangements with the respondent parent, and so on. Detailed discussions will have taken place with the respondent parent, and the level and nature of his opposition will be clear. Serious attempts to negotiate the outcome will have been made, and the case will have proceeded to the point where the only remaining option is to issue an application to the court.

5.9   However, this ideal world is not a reflection of how many relocation cases actually proceed. Many applications are made late in the day. Perhaps the applicant parent did not initially realise that permission was needed to relocate. Perhaps the respondent parent had initially acquiesced in the wish to relocate, but changed his mind late in the day for whatever reason. In some cases, these factors mean that timing is starting to become crucial – the new term, when the

---

3   See, eg, *Re F (Internal Relocation)* [2010] EWCA Civ 1428, [2011] 1 FLR 1382 at [23]; see **Appendix 4.3**. Whether the applicant is first to file or not, the order which she seeks is a specific issue order. If the respondent is first to file, whether seeking a residence order for himself or a prohibited steps order preventing the child from relocating, the applicant parent should issue a cross-application for a specific issue order using Form C2, as well as defending the applications brought by the respondent. In practical terms, seeking one order and defending the other will amount to the same thing.

4   See **3.50** and **4.36**.

child was meant to start in the new school, is starting to approach, or the job which the applicant parent hopes to take is due to start. The fact that the case is starting to become urgent is not in itself a reason to worry: much of the detailed preparation can be done in the period after the application is issued but before the first court appointment.

5.10 The application to move a child within the United Kingdom or to remove a child from the United Kingdom is an application for a *specific issue order* pursuant to s 8 of the Children Act 1989.[5] If there is not already a residence order in force, it should be included within the application that must be made on Form C100 and accompanied by Form FM1.[6] The C100 must be served on the other parent, and on anyone else who has parental responsibility for the child.

5.11 The application may be filed in either the county court or in the High Court, depending on its factual complexity. If the case involves a proposed relocation to a country which is not a signatory of the Hague Convention on the Civil Aspects of International Child Abduction 1980,[7] then the application must be made in or immediately transferred to the High Court.[8]

5.12 Form C100 requires essentially only basic information about the children and the parents, and there is provision at Part 7 of the form to make only a short statement of about 200 words setting out the reasons for making the application. Although this is short, it is important to set the tone of the application in this section from the very outset. Careless words at this stage may well come back to haunt the applicant parent in cross-examination months later. It is essential to have well in mind that the decision that will eventually be made will be guided by the welfare checklist and the other applicable legal principles.[9] It is therefore good practice to refer to those of the principles that support the application at this early stage.

---

[5] See **Appendix 1.1**. It is sometimes said that the order in international relocation cases is made pursuant to s 13 of the Children Act 1989. However, a careful reading of that section shows that its effect is to require consent to be obtained, but no separate power is provided there to grant such consent. The appropriate application, as with all private law applications about the child's upbringing, is therefore for one of the section 8 orders.

[6] See also **Appendix 5.1**, where we include a sample C100 relating to the case study set out at **4.43**. In the case where the parent opposing the relocation is first to file (most common in an internal relocation case, where the applicant parent does not always need to seek a court order: see **2.44**), Form C2 should be used to issue a cross-application. A sample C2 is included in **Appendix 5.2**, though there relating to the respondent parent's case.

[7] A list of countries that have acceded to the Convention can be found in **Appendix 6.1**, or online at www.hcch.net/index_en.php?act=conventions.status&cid=24.

[8] See *Practice Direction: Allocation and Transfer of Proceedings* [2009] 1 FLR 365, para [5.2].

[9] See **Chapter 2**.

Helpful Hint

Part 7 of Form C100 includes provision for a short statement setting out the applicant's reasons for making this application. As an example,[10] that paragraph might say something like this:

'I am making this application because I believe that it is in the best interests of the children to relocate to [country/new part of UK] with me. I have been their primary carer throughout their lives. They have predominantly lived with me since my separation from their father on [date]. The reason that I am seeking to relocate to [country/new part of UK] at this time is [reason]. It would not meet the children's welfare if I was no longer to care for them and therefore they need to move with me to [country/new part of UK]. I have made enquiries about education and housing, and good arrangements that meet their needs are available as of [date]. Although the pattern of contact with their father will have to change, I remain anxious to continue to facilitate the children's relationship with their father and am confident that appropriate arrangements can be made. I have tried to agree these future plans with the children's father but to no avail. Further delay in resolving the children's future is not in their best interests and I have therefore been left with no alternative other than to issue this application.'

5.13 Part 8 of Form C100 asks about what efforts have been made to resolve the disputed issue by agreement, including by way of mediation. Form FM1 should be completed setting out whether a mediation information and assessment meeting has been attended and if not, why not.[11] If mediation was not attempted or a mediation information and assessment meeting was not attended, there is a box in Part 8 requiring a short explanation.

5.14 Part 9 of the C100 asks about whether the children have experienced or are at risk of experiencing harm in one of the following categories: domestic abuse/violence; child abduction; child abuse; drug, alcohol or substance abuse; other safety or welfare concerns. If one or more of these categories are alleged, full details are required by completion of Form C1A.[12]

5.15 As with Part 7, it is important to get this right from the start. Any issues which the applicant seeks to rely on later in proceedings should be raised at this point, and the applicant may be open to criticism later if they are not set out here. The truth of what is later said may be undermined if the facts were known at the time of the issuing the application but the form is silent about them.

5.16 On the other hand, an extravagant list of allegations in the application form that cannot subsequently be substantiated by reliable evidence will be equally damaging to the applicant. It will be suggested that by raising

---

[10]   See also **Appendix 5.1**, where we include a sample C100 relating to the case study set out at **4.43**.
[11]   See **3.50**.
[12]   Form C1A, Section 3.

unsustainable allegations, the applicant's motive is to denigrate the respondent parent and undermine his relationship with the children.

5.17 Service is generally effected by the court sending the documents to the respondent parent's address as supplied by the applicant parent.[13] Once the application has been issued, the court will set a date for a first hearing dispute resolution appointment ('FHDRA').[14]

5.18 All disputes between parents about the upbringing of their children are covered by the Private Law Programme.[15] According to Practice Direction 12B, the Private Law Programme works on the following main principle:[16]

> 'Where an application is made to a court under Part II of the Children Act 1989, the child's welfare is the court's paramount concern. The court will apply the principle of the 'Overriding Objective' to enable it to deal with a case justly, having regard to the welfare principles involved. So far as practicable the Court will –
>
> (a) deal expeditiously and fairly with every case;
> (b) deal with a case in ways which are proportionate to the nature, importance and complexity of the issues;
> (c) ensure that the parties are on an equal footing;
> (d) save unnecessary expense;
> (e) allot to each case an appropriate share of the court's resources, while taking account of the need to allot resources to other cases.'

DOMESTIC VIOLENCE

5.19 If either party makes allegations of domestic violence by the other party, or there is reason to suppose that a child or party has experienced domestic violence perpetrated by the other party, or that there is a risk of violence, then Practice Direction 12J applies. Domestic violence includes physical violence, threatening or intimidating behaviour and any other form of abuse which, directly or indirectly, may have caused harm to the other party or to the child or which may give rise to the risk of harm.[17]

5.20 If that is the case, the judge at the FHDRA will identify the factual and welfare issues involved, and consider whether the nature of any allegation or admission of domestic violence would be relevant in deciding whether to make an order about residence or contact. If the parties to such a case come to an agreement, the court will not endorse the order without the parties in court unless it is satisfied there is no risk to the child in so doing.[18] The court will scrutinise all the evidence available and may order a welfare report (from

---

[13] Family Procedure Rules (FPR) 2010, r 6.4.
[14] FPR 2010, r 12.5(a) and see **5.20**.
[15] Practice Direction 12B; see **Appendix 2.2**.
[16] Practice Direction 12B, para [2.1]; see **Appendix 2.2**.
[17] Practice Direction 12J, para [2].
[18] Practice Direction 12J, para [4].

Cafcass, or, if appropriate, from the local authority), either as a separate report on this issue alone or as part of the main report.

5.21 In cases where there are allegations of domestic violence, the court may order a preliminary fact finding hearing to determine the allegations, although in relocation cases it is more common to have all issues determined at the same hearing. The court will order statements to give particulars of the allegations made and responses given in such a way as to identify the disputed facts with clarity.

5.22 The parties and the court will also be required to consider whether any third party evidence should be obtained – for example, evidence from the police or health services which may support or refute the allegations. When the court finds domestic violence has occurred or that there is a risk that it may occur, then these matters will be taken into account when considering what outcome is in the best interests of the child.

5.23 It is beyond the scope of this book to look at issues of domestic violence in detail. For those cases where the issues do arise, careful note should be taken of all matters set out in Practice Direction 12J and the relevant case law.[19]

FROM ISSUE TO THE FIRST HEARING DISPUTE RESOLUTION APPOINTMENT

5.24 Upon issue of the application, the court will list an FHDRA where practicable within 4 weeks and in any event no later than 6 weeks.

5.25 If full preparation was not possible in advance of issuing the application, this is now the window in which enquiries and plans can be made regarding housing, schools, travel etc. No further evidence will be filed in advance of the FHDRA but if there is to be any possibility of negotiating an agreement at the FHDRA, these details need to be resolved to the satisfaction of both parents. Even if an agreement proves not possible at the FHDRA, the information will be vital to the next stage of proceedings.

5.26 Also in this interim period, the court will send a copy of the application to Cafcass who will allocate an officer to make enquiries in advance of the FHDRA confined to matters of safety. No other matters should be discussed by or with Cafcass in advance of the FHDRA other than relates to safety.[20] Neither parent should be invited to talk about any other issues including in relation to the substantive application, or more general welfare issues regarding the child.

---

[19]   See in particular *Re L, Re V, Re M and Re H (Contact: Domestic Violence)* [2000] 2 FLR 334 (CA).

[20]   Practice Direction 12B, para [3.9]; see **Appendix 2.2**.

5.27 In reality, this is a somewhat artificial restriction. The allocated officer will telephone both parents for a brief discussion and it is impossible to control so strictly what is said at that stage. The officer will also make checks with the local authority and police regarding any records they may hold of the parents or children. If any risks of harm are identified, Cafcass may invite the parents to meet separately with an officer before the FHDRA. However, the officer will not meet with the children at this stage.

5.28 The Cafcass officer will then report on the outcome of the enquiries to the court in what is known as a Schedule 2 Letter. Unless Cafcass considers that disclosure of the letter would in itself create a risk of harm to a parent or child, the letter would ordinarily be disclosed to the parents in advance of the FHDRA. If it is not, the court itself will inform the parents of its content subject to any consideration of risk.

5.29 In preparation for the FHDRA it is good practice[21] to produce a succinct written position statement that summarises the order sought by the applicant parent, the reasons for the application, the points in favour of the application, the proposed arrangements for contact with the staying-behind parent and any important deadlines for a decision perhaps regarding education or employment. The position statement may include a brief chronology of significant events in children's lives in advance of this application.

5.30 The position statement has to be comprehensive enough to set out a convincing case on behalf of the applicant parent, but also brief enough to be read quickly by the judge who may be dealing with a dozen such cases in a morning. As with all documents to be placed before the court, its focus should be on the issues that will influence the court's decision. It will be helpfully structured if it sets out the relevant facts organised in accordance with the welfare checklist and, for international relocations, the guidance/discipline set out in *Payne v Payne*.[22]

5.31 While we have addressed most of the planning issues before,[23] because the applicant ought ideally to start addressing them at the very start of the process, in some cases there will be new issues to deal with at this stage. For example, if there is a need to obtain expert evidence about the legal position in another jurisdiction, this should be done now. The position about the enforceability of orders in the new location may also need to be investigated.

---

[21] It is a requirement if the FHDRA is (unusually) listed to be heard by a High Court judge or in the Royal Courts of Justice: see Practice Direction 27A.

[22] *Payne v Payne* [2001] EWCA Civ 166, [2001] 1 FLR 1052; see **Appendix 3.1**. See further **Chapter 2**.

[23] See **3.17** *et seq*.

THE FIRST HEARING DISPUTE RESOLUTION APPOINTMENT

5.32   The parties and Cafcass officer are expected to attend the FHDRA.[24] At the FHDRA, the court will consider whether the parents can safely resolve some or all of the issues in dispute with the assistance of a Cafcass officer and any available mediator. The court will also:

- seek to identify and manage any risks to the children;

- consider further dispute resolution;

- consider the avoidance of delay by the early identification of issues and timetabling future hearings.[25]

5.33   Where possible, the Cafcass officer will speak separately with each parent at court but before the hearing. The Cafcass officer will explore the reasons for the application and attempt to resolve any issues between the parents that will enable the application to be agreed. For example, if the Cafcass officer identifies that the respondent parent would agree to the application provided the future contact arrangements are satisfactory, then the applicant parent may be encouraged to adopt those proposals. The Cafcass officer, by direct informal communication with each parent, is trying to get to the core of the issues and concerns of each of them, and suggest ways in which those disputed issues may be resolved.

5.34   It may be that the Cafcass officer identifies even at this stage that there is scope for a mediated settlement. In some courts, a mediator will be present or available to conduct mediation on the day of the hearing and detailed arrangements are in place at each court to facilitate this. Alternatively, consideration may be given to adjourning the application to permit mediation to be attended away from court.

5.35   A hearing will then be conducted by a district judge in private in the presence of the Cafcass officer who will further advise the court and the parents. If an agreement has been reached, the court will scrutinise it and almost certainly approve it. In the absence of agreement, the judge can be expected to adopt an interventionist approach and challenge each party or their legal representatives about their respective cases.

5.36   The judge may well make suggestions as to the terms of a settlement that he would consider appropriate and invite the parties to continue negotiations to this end. It is not possible for the judge to impose a final order on the parties and resolve the application against their will at this stage. However, a strong

---

[24]   In some courts, children above a certain age are expected to attend court as well to be seen by the Cafcass officer. If the court to which you apply operates this system, full details will be provided when the application is issued/served.

[25]   Practice Direction 12B, para [2.2]; see **Appendix 2.2**.

indication from the judge creates considerable pressure to settle the case on his terms or, if they can be negotiated, on more favourable terms.

5.37 In general Children Act proceedings, these hearings have a high degree of success in resolving disputes between parents about children at this early stage. However, the stakes in relocation cases (particularly in international cases) are so high that it is more likely for such cases to proceed beyond this stage to a contested hearing. The court will consider (with the assistance of the parties and the Cafcass officer) what evidence is necessary to be filed for the court to be able to resolve the application at a final hearing on some future date.

5.38 As a minimum each party will need to prepare, exchange and file a written statement of evidence setting out the facts that they each rely upon in support of their respective cases. Each party may have other witnesses who can speak to relevant facts in dispute between the parties but serious consideration should be given to whether such witnesses are really necessary. The more witnesses who give evidence, the longer the final hearing will become and the longer the wait before a hearing can be listed.

5.39 It is normal practice, though not essential,[26] for a full Cafcass report to be ordered at this point.[27] To prepare that report, the Cafcass officer will, of course, need to make his or her own enquiries so as to report to the court on the welfare checklist, particularly the wishes and feelings of the children and the effect of relocation on their education and relationship with the respondent parent. Depending on local arrangements, such a report may take as long as 16 weeks to complete, thereby delaying any final hearing for up to 5 months from the date of the FHDRA or approximately 6 months after the application was issued.

5.40 As an alternative, if resources allow, the parties may agree to instruct and pay for an independent social worker ('ISW') to undertake the same enquires that Cafcass would perform. An ISW often has considerable previous experience in working for Cafcass and presenting reports and giving evidence in the family courts. Typically such a report could be available in a much shorter timescale than Cafcass, thereby facilitating an earlier final hearing date where time is of the essence. If it is intended that an ISW should be used, then the proposed expert's curriculum vitae, estimate of cost and timescale to report should be made available to the opposing party in advance of the FHDRA,[28]

---

[26] *Re R (Leave to Remove: Contact)* [2010] EWCA Civ 1137, [2011] 1 FLR 1336 at [18].

[27] It is sometimes thought that Cafcass enquiries are of limited use in international relocation cases because of the difficulty that the officer has in assessing the applicant's proposals. For this reason, some judges prefer to order a report limited to the child's wishes and feelings or, in a case of a young child where the parents are not in dispute about the importance that each has in the child's life, to forego a report entirely.

[28] Practice Directions 25A (Experts – Emergencies and Pre-Proceedings Instructions), 25B (The Duties of an Expert, the Expert's Report and Arrangements for an Expert to Attend Court) and 25C (Children Proceedings – the Use of Single Joint Experts and the Process of Leading to an Expert Being Instructed or Expert Evidence Being Put Before the Court); see **Appendices 2.4, 2.5 and 2.6**, and also **5.42**.

together with a draft letter of instruction setting out a neutral background to the case and the questions for the ISW to answer. Invariably the ISW will be instructed jointly by the parties although the costs need not be shared equally depending on the respective financial circumstances of the parties.

5.41 It is expected that the children's views will be communicated to the court through the parents and the Cafcass officer (or ISW).[29] It is therefore highly unusual for the children to be parties themselves to the litigation with separate legal representation.[30]

5.42 The court will also consider what other evidence may be needed for the resolution of the dispute. If necessary, reports from experts may be ordered, although this must be justified by the particular facts of a case and it will be necessary to convince the court about the necessity of having an expert at all and about the extent of the expert's role. This is something that the parties should have given thought to before the FHDRA. Expert evidence is by no means the norm,[31] but there may be cases where the mental health of the applicant or respondent is fragile and may be affected by the refusal or allowing of the application and where expert evidence might assist. Alternatively, the child may have special needs or health problems that would be affected (for better or worse) by a move. If the parties wish to propose that an expert is instructed they should pay close attention to Practice Direction 25C, specifying details such as:

- the discipline, qualifications and expertise of the proposed expert;

- the matters which the party wishes the expert to assess;

- the likely cost of the report;

- the availability of the proposed expert to file the report and attend any hearing;

- why the proposed assessment cannot be carried out by Cafcass.[32]

5.43 Assuming that no agreement is reached at the FHDRA, and that delay will not assist resolution, the court will seek to identify the disputed issues and make directions for a final hearing to decide the matter.

---

[29] See also **3.44** *et seq.*

[30] The rare circumstances in which children will be made parties to the proceedings are set out in Practice Direction 16A, para [7.2]; see **Appendix 2.3**.

[31] See *Re TG (Care Proceedings: Case Management: Expert Evidence)* [2013] EWCA Civ 5, [2013] 1 FLR forthcoming at [29]–[34]. An exception to this general rule may apply in the case of expert evidence regarding the legal system in a destination country which is outside the standard international agreements; we discuss this further at **7.12–7.13** with regard to temporary relocation cases.

[32] Practice Direction 25C, para [3.10]; see **Appendix 2.6**. The requirement which existed under the previous Practice Direction, that the proposal to instruct an expert be filed and served by 11am the day before the hearing, has been removed in the new version.

> **Helpful Hint**
>
> It really is important to get the case listed in front of the right tribunal.[33] All international relocation cases are complicated, and if the case is listed for a final hearing before a district judge in the county court then the advocates need to think carefully about whether they are happy to proceed on that basis. There are two reasons to be cautious. One is that the case may warrant a higher level of tribunal where there is greater experience of complex legal provisions and long-term consequences, as well as the kinds of orders required in the event the relocation is allowed.[34] The other is that the route of appeal from a district judge in a county court is to a circuit judge, and both parties to a relocation case may prefer to start their case before a tribunal whose decision is appealed to a more senior court.[35]

5.44 The court will then provide a date at which the final hearing can take place on the basis of a time estimate agreed with the parties having regard to the amount of evidence that is to be called. Typically at least two court days will be required given the need for: both parents to give evidence, perhaps also the Cafcass officer or ISW; legal submissions to be made on both sides; judicial reading time at the outset of the hearing; and time for judgment at the conclusion.

BETWEEN THE FIRST HEARING DISPUTE RESOLUTION APPOINTMENT AND THE FINAL HEARING

5.45 The potential for reaching a negotiated settlement does not end at the FHDRA. Negotiations that stalled at or before the FHDRA may be capable of being re-started in correspondence, at a round-table meeting or in mediation. Sometimes it takes a few days for the advice of Cafcass, or the district judge's steer, to be fully appreciated by the parties. Alternatively, the full enormity of a contested hearing and all that it entails may only have been brought to life as the directions were being made at the FHDRA. It is never too late to attempt to reach a compromise.

5.46 At the same time, it is never too soon to start preparing the evidence ready for compliance with the court's direction for a final hearing. Typically the court will require statements to be filed within 28 days of the FHDRA.

5.47 The importance of getting the contents of the applicant's statement correct cannot be over-emphasised. This is the one opportunity to place the

---

[33] On listing, see also **3.15–3.16**.
[34] See **5.79–5.81**; on means of enforcing orders, see **7.7** *et seq*.
[35] On appeals, see **Chapter 8**.

applicant's case before the court in its entirety and in the best possible light. This is the opportunity to demonstrate that the application is well researched and the plans for relocation watertight. By this stage, all the core information should be available, ready to collate in one document. It is no time for errors and half-baked assertions that will be brutally exposed in cross-examination at the final hearing. Where possible, documentary evidence should be exhibited to support the contents of the statement.

5.48 The statement therefore needs to address the following points (which are in no particular order):

- the current situation regarding the care, education and housing arrangements for the children, together with consideration of any particular needs that the child may have (eg particular medical or educational needs);

- the reasons and motivation for the proposal to relocate;

- the timescale for the relocation;

- any immigration issues which need to be addressed, and the likely timing for resolving them;

- the practical arrangements for housing, employment, education etc in the relocation country including, in particular, details of possible schools that the child may attend with information about their academic credentials, class sizes, extra-curricular programme, etc. If a particular school is preferred, it should be identified as such and reasons given. If the child has particular needs (eg medical or educational), the proposal should set out how they will be met in the new location;

- general information about the new location, such as leisure activities, local amenities, social opportunities, etc;

- the child's wishes and feelings;

- the proposals for contact with the respondent parent, together with detailed information about how this can be facilitated in practical terms eg how the financial costs will be met, when the contact will take place (for both direct and indirect contact), the proposed location(s) of direct contact, etc. In international cases, the applicant should also specify whether a mirror order or other legal enforcement mechanism will be available in the new location, and if so when and how it will be obtained;[36]

---

[36] If the destination is a signatory to the Hague Convention on Jurisdiction, Applicable Law, Recognition, Enforcement and Co-operation in Respect of Parental Responsibility and Measures for the Protection of Children 1996, then Arts 23–28 of that Convention may enable orders from the English courts to be recognised and enforced in the destination country without the need for mirror orders, depending on the detail of national laws implementing the

- the effect on the applicant and/or the child of a refusal of permission to relocate;

- the proposed working arrangements of the adults involved in the move, and/or general information about the family's finances showing that the move is economically viable.

5.49 It is equally important that the statement should avoid excessive and unnecessary criticism of the respondent or exaggerated minimisation of his role in the children's lives. It is potentially fatal to the success of the application for the court to be left with the impression from the contents of the statement that the applicant is motivated by a desire to separate father and child, or even that the applicant does not value the relationship between the child and the respondent.

5.50 Any opportunity given by the court to reply in a further statement to the evidence filed by the respondent should be limited to correcting any factual inaccuracies in his evidence and supplying any further information about the application that he has suggested is missing. It is inevitably therefore a short focused statement rather than an opportunity to rehash the evidence already filed.

5.51 Actions as well as words are important in this interim period. The applicant may well be faced with requests from the respondent for increasing levels of contact as he tactically attempts to strength his opposition to relocation by attempting to establish a shared care arrangement. This can be a double-edged sword. On the one hand, if the applicant parent agrees to the increased levels of contact in order to demonstrate a commitment to the respondent's relationship with the child, she can then run the risk that, by the time of the final hearing, the level of contact is such that it weighs against a relocation. On the other, a conflict over contact arrangements at this stage may leave the applicant open to being accused of being motivated by a desire to restrict the child's relationship with the respondent parent.

5.52 It is critically important, therefore, that the right tone is used in correspondence dealing with this issue. The focus as always should be on the best interests of the children and minimising any disruption brought about by these proceedings on their lives pending a final decision. A blatant attempt to disturb the status quo in an attempt to gain an advantage for the respondent is likely to speak for itself.

5.53 If the court has ordered an expert report, the terms upon which the expert is advising should have been set out clearly in the order. Any expert should be provided with a copy of the Practice Directions relating to Experts and Assessors in Family Proceedings, which contain information about details

---

Convention in the relevant country. A list of signatory countries is found in **Appendix 6.2**, or online at www.hcch.net/index_en.php?act=conventions.status&cid=70.

the expert should include in the report in addition to answering the questions that are asked of them.[37] The parties' solicitors are required to agree a letter of instruction to the expert within five days of the hearing at which the expert was appointed. If the parties are not legally advised they will have to do this themselves. Practice Direction 25C gives advice as to the content of the letter.[38]

5.54 In preparation for any hearing before a High Court judge, or any hearing lasting more than one hour in the Principal Registry of the Family Division or a county court, it is the responsibility of the applicant to prepare a bundle for the use of the court and the parties.[39] At the commencement of the bundle, in Section A, should be:

- an up-to-date case summary, confined to those matters which are relevant to the hearing or the management of the case, and if possible limited to one A4 page;

- a statement of issues to be determined at the final hearing;

- a position statement of each party including a summary of the order sought;

- an up-to-date chronology;

- skeleton arguments, with copies of authorities relied upon;

- a list of essential reading for the final hearing.

5.55 The key documents here are the position statement and the skeleton argument (commonly combined into one document). This is the advocates' opportunity to frame the way in which the court will approach its task at the final hearing. It will set out the key factual contentions and the way in which they meet the legal requirements for relocation. It is the opportunity to argue for a particular interpretation of the legal framework to be applied to the particular application. For a busy judge without time to read the whole bundle in advance of the hearing, the position statement is key to setting the background against which the oral evidence will be heard.

5.56 In addition to these preliminary documents and all the witness statements, documentary evidence and reports, it is also important that the key authorities which are to be relied upon are included, in full, in the bundle with the skeleton argument. For any international relocation case, *Payne v Payne* should be included, but the choice of supplementary authorities will vary from case to case. It depends, of course, on the points which are most pertinent to the applicant's case.[40]

---

[37] Practice Directions 25A, 25B and 25C; see **Appendices 2.4, 2.5 and 2.6**.
[38] Practice Direction 25C, para [4.1] and Annex A; see **Appendix 2.6**.
[39] Practice Direction 27A.
[40] See **Chapter 2** for a full exposition of the law and also **3.19–3.32**.

5.57 The other parties should be sent the bundle index not less than four working days before the hearing; counsel must have a paginated bundle delivered to them by not less than three days before the hearing and the bundle must be lodged with the court not less than two working days before the hearing.[41] If the hearing is at the Principal Registry of the Family Division or at the Royal Courts of Justice in London, the party lodging the bundle should obtain a receipt from the clerk accepting it if it is delivered personally, or if it is posted or sent by DX, obtain proof of posting/dispatch.[42] Otherwise, the bundle should be lodged at the appropriate court office. There are costs penalties for failing to lodge the bundle properly, or in proper form. Anybody preparing a case should take care to look at and comply with Practice Direction 27A.

CAFCASS/INDEPENDENT SOCIAL WORKER

5.58 At some point after the FHDRA, a Cafcass Officer (or ISW) will conduct full interviews with the parties and the child or children. Children will usually be seen separately from parents, sometimes in sibling groups, and sometimes individually. They will often be seen with parents as well.

5.59 The enquiries of the Cafcass officer or ISW and the resulting report will be key to framing the outcome of the application. The reporter is the 'eyes and ears' of the court, and the judge will follow the recommendations of the reporter unless there is good reasons for not doing so.[43] Consequently, although it is not impossible to relocate in the teeth of opposition from the Cafcass officer, a negative recommendation makes succeeding in the application considerably more difficult.

5.60 Because of the importance of the report, parents are often nervous about the interviews with Cafcass. There is little that can be done to prepare for the interviews, and the best advice is simply to be yourself and leave the child to be him- or herself.

5.61 The applicant's potential to influence the Cafcass officer begins from the moment that the officer is served with a copy of the applicant's initial statement. The influence to be brought to bear on the Cafcass officer will start when she is served with a copy of the statement. The well-prepared application with a positive focus on maintaining the children's relationship with the respondent parent will impress. A recognition of the needs of the children

---

[41] Practice Direction 27A, para [6].

[42] Practice Direction 27A, para [8].

[43] If the judge is departing from a clear recommendation of a welfare officer, the judge must explain why he has reached a different conclusion. That said, the overall question is only whether the judge's reasoning in an adequate explanation for his decision, and he need not recite, in a formulaic manner, 'I disagree with the welfare officer because...': see *Re V (Residence: Review)* [1995] 2 FLR 1010 (CA) at 1019.

rather than an emphasis on the wishes of the applicant and/or undue criticisms of the respondent will also carry favour.

5.62 This positive approach should be carried through in the meetings between the Cafcass officer and the applicant. Everyone responds well to a friendly and co-operative approach and Cafcass officers are no different in this regard. The more that can be done to help them undertake their task, the better. It should go without saying that basics such as flexibility over meeting times and sticking to appointments in an otherwise busy schedule are important.

5.63 The Cafcass officer is looking for some insight into the effect of relocation on the children and their relationship with the respondent parent, so a realistic approach to these potential difficulties will be rewarded. Do not gloss over the significance of the proposed change but accept that there may be problems and set out in practical terms how it is proposed that they will be addressed. Avoid lecturing or 'talking at' the reporter and give her the opportunity to ask the questions that she considers important. Nor is this an opportunity to denigrate the respondent or focus on criticisms of his response to the application. It is worth remembering to remain focused on the positives.

5.64 The Cafcass officer will want to meet the children and discuss the application with them in the absence of the parents. Obviously the children will need to be prepared for this meeting but it is counterproductive to actively groom a child in what should be said to the officer. A child's use of adult phrases and concepts soon becomes apparent to the Cafcass officer and not only are the child's expressed views discounted as a result, but it has a negative effect on the perception of the applicant's motivation. Cafcass officers are skilled in dealing with children and eliciting their wishes and feelings in a variety of ways.

5.65 The resulting report will contain a summary of the factual matters uncovered by the reporter's enquiries coupled with an analysis of the welfare checklist and (usually) some analysis of the main issues raised by the relevant case law.[44] The report may or may not reach a clear recommendation as to which outcome the Cafcass officer thinks would be best. The officer cannot be criticised either way for making or not making a recommendation, though in some cases she may depart from whatever conclusion she reached when giving evidence (either to give a recommendation on the witness stand when none was contained in the report, or to retract a recommendation given in the report).

5.66 If there are any errors of fact that are central to the report then they should be brought to the reporter's attention as soon as possible upon receipt of the report. Otherwise, any disagreement with the analysis or interpretation

---

[44]   In an international relocation case, *Payne v Payne* [2001] EWCA Civ 166, [2001] 1 FLR 1052, for example, may usefully be drawn to a Cafcass officer's attention, since it contains various considerations relevant to most international relocation applications; see **Appendix 3.1**.

of facts, and the resulting recommendation if relevant, is appropriately dealt with in cross-examination at the final hearing.

5.67 It may be that the Cafcass officer's attendance at the final hearing was directed at the FHDRA in any event. If the officer's presence has not already been requested, and there are significant matters contained in the report which are disputed and therefore require the officer's attendance at the final hearing for cross-examination, the Cafcass officer should be notified at the earliest opportunity.

5.68 Upon receipt of the Cafcass report and any expert reports, and in advance of the final hearing, it is advantageous for there to be a conference between the applicant parent and her advocate. This is a vital opportunity to consider the state of the evidence as it now stands in its entirety, and to agree the approach to be taken at the final hearing and the precise terms of the order sought. It is also a further opportunity to consider whether one more attempt may be made to negotiate an agreement by putting a further written offer to the respondent parent in the light of the recommendation of the Cafcass officer.

5.69 If the court has listed a pre-hearing review at this stage, this is also an opportunity to put pressure on the respondent parent if the Cafcass recommendation supports relocation. On the other hand, if the recommendation is against relocation, then careful consideration will have to be given about the way in which the application will be pursued (or even if it will be pursued).

5.70 If there are witnesses from overseas that need to be cross-examined at the final hearing, it may be possible to avoid their attendance at court by arranging video-link facilities. Every court has such facilities but they must be booked well in advance and arrangements made with the court office. If this is left to the last minute and an adjournment is then necessary, there may be adverse costs consequences.

THE FINAL HEARING

5.71 At the final hearing, the judge may have had time to read all the relevant documents by the morning of the first day, but more likely he or she will require two hours or more of reading time. Given proper advance preparation there should be no further need to describe the case orally to the judge at the outset of the hearing.

5.72 Typically, if the Cafcass officer or ISW is required to give oral evidence, that will happen at the outset of the hearing (though it can be later if there is a reason to delay it until after some other aspect of the case). Given the central importance of the Cafcass report, it is useful to have resolved any challenge to her evidence before the parties give their evidence to the court. It gives the parties the opportunity to address the recommendation that survives cross-examination.

5.73 If there is an expert, he or she will usually give evidence at the beginning, either before or after Cafcass/ISW, having regard to his/her convenience and the cost of attendance.

5.74 The applicant and any witnesses that she is calling will give evidence next and be cross-examined by the respondent's advocate. The best preparation for a witness giving evidence is to be fully familiar with the content of her statement, as that will form the basis for the questioning that will come from the respondent's advocate. Just as with the drafting of the statement and the interaction with the Cafcass officer, the tone of the evidence given is as important as its content. The judge will be forming a view not just of the content of the answers but the way in which they were given.

5.75 The court will assess the applicant in the round on the basis of the complete presentation in the witness box. Clear, succinct and straightforward answers are the order of the day. The ability to demonstrate a level of insight not only into the benefits of the proposed relocation but the potential problems too will be watched for. It is clearly important that there is no hint of malice towards the respondent and a willing acceptance of the importance of his role in the children's lives. Again this is not the opportunity to seek to undermine or criticise the respondent. It is important to remain positive. A repeated emphasis on the welfare of the children will be recognised.

5.76 The oral evidence of the respondent and any witnesses he is calling will follow. The technique used to challenge that evidence will differ between advocates and from case to case, depending on its facts and the strength of the application.

5.77 Closing submissions follow with the applicant's advocate speaking last. This is the opportunity to finally argue for the most appropriate legal framework and persuade the court how the facts of a particular application fit within it so as to allow the desired relocation.

5.78 The judge will then give a reasoned decision, either orally at the conclusion of argument, or at some future date in writing. Either way, the judge can be expected to review the evidence and decide which of any disputed facts he prefers, determine the legal framework within which he will make his decision, set out his analysis of the welfare checklist and reach a conclusion about the merits of the application and the final order to be made.

THE COURT ORDER

5.79 In general, court orders are drafted by counsel and approved or amended by the judge.[45] Every case will have its own details, but in general the order will:

---

45   If neither side has legal representation, the judge will draft the order.

- give an indication of how the decision was reached, noting for example that the court has read the bundle and heard oral evidence from the parties and the Cafcass officer;

- record any undertakings given in relation to the case by either parent or, in some cases, by someone else such as a grandparent,[46] generally making provision for requirements that the court cannot order or that the parties agree are appropriate. It is not possible to be prescriptive here: undertakings are an opportunity to be creative to suit the particular circumstances of your case;

  (i) if the relocation is being allowed, these may include things such as:

    — an agreement to keep the respondent informed about such details as are relevant (such as school progress, medical conditions, etc);
    — an agreement to promote a positive relationship between the child and the other parent;
    — an undertaking that the applicant parent will make a computer available so as to allow the child to use Skype and email to have indirect contact with the respondent parent;
    — details about any security being provided;
    — an agreement to return the child to the jurisdiction of the courts of England and Wales if so required by an order of the court;
    — an agreement about jurisdiction for future issues about the child's upbringing.

  (ii) if the relocation is being refused, there may still be undertakings, which may include things such as:

    — an agreement to promote a positive relationship between the child and the other parent;
    — an agreement to allow one parent to take the child on holidays abroad, as agreed, at particular intervals in the future.

- make the actual orders, which will include:

  — whether or not the relocation is allowed; if it is, then in an international relocation case the order should state specifically that the applicant parent is authorised to remove the child permanently from the jurisdiction;
  — if the relocation is allowed, the order should specify when it may take place, especially if the relocation is not to take place before a specified date or event (such as the end of the school term);

---

[46] See, for example, the undertakings given by the mother and maternal grandfather in *Re A (Security for Return to Jurisdiction) (Note)* [1999] 2 FLR 1 (FD), albeit there in the context of a temporary relocation; see **Appendix 3.4**.

— whether earlier orders made in relation to the child remain in force or not;

— what new orders are made in respect of residence and contact, or in relation to shared residence, which often include a very detailed contact schedule;

— any supplemental orders relating to moving or not moving (such as a specific issue order about which school the child should attend, or specific orders about future holiday arrangements).

5.80 To reiterate, these are just examples. Every case has its own particular issues, and it is not possible to set out an exhaustive list of the issues that may need to be addressed in the court order.

5.81 It is standard practice, and we think very advisable, for there to be a detailed contact order in the event of relocation being allowed.[47] The detail varies depending on the destination:

- **internal relocations within England and Wales**: orders are enforceable like any other Children Act order;

- **internal relocations to Scotland or Northern Ireland**: the order will be recognised automatically in the new location, but needs to be registered before it becomes enforceable;[48]

- **international relocation within the EU (except Denmark)**: contact orders and other matters relating to parental responsibility are automatically recognised and enforceable in the destination country, once that country becomes the child's place of habitual residence (usually after three months);[49]

- **international relocation outside the EU but to a 1996 Hague Convention country**: contact orders and other matters relating to parental

---

[47] But cf *Re R (Leave to Remove: Contact)* [2010] EWCA Civ 1137, [2011] 1 FLR 1336 at [22]: Wilson LJ indicated that, since a court order granting permission to remove a child from the jurisdiction amounted to 'surrendering [the court's] control over the child', it was 'contrary to principle' for a contact order to be attached to the grant of leave to remove. We note that it remains standard practice to make such orders and, with respect, we think that to be the better approach. Many international agreements (including the Brussels IIR Regulation, the 1996 Hague Convention, and the international understanding of mirror orders) work on the basis that the pre-relocation court will make orders about the child's upbringing which are then recognised and enforced, or mirrored, in the destination state. Indeed, Art 12(3) of Brussels IIR would enable the English court to retain jurisdiction after a relocation; see **2.38**. Even absent such considerations, it is hard to see any difficulty with the making of contact orders: the worst that could happen, so far as we can see, is that they might be ignored by the court in the destination country.

[48] Family Law Act 1986, ss 25 and 27.

[49] Brussels II Revised, Council Regulation (EC) No 2201/2003.

responsibility may be automatically recognised and enforceable, depending on the particular country's domestic laws implementing the Convention;[50]

- **international relocation to other countries**: mirror orders may be obtainable, but not all countries recognise this concept; either way, other measures to help safeguard contact may be required, depending on the facts of the case.[51]

AFTER THE FINAL HEARING

5.82 Whatever the outcome of the final hearing, the ideal thing is for the parents to tell the child what is going to happen together.[52] Even in the most amicable of cases, that will be difficult for the parent who has not achieved his/her desired outcome, and in many cases it will be simply too hard. If the parents cannot tell the child together, then each of them will need to speak with the child about it. If thought desirable, any ISW instructed in the case may be prevailed upon to assist, although Cafcass rarely have the resources to retain involvement after the final hearing.

5.83 So far as is possible, each parent should put the decision in the most positive light he or she can manage. Focus on what will be good about the decision, and about how things are going to be for the child in the coming weeks and months. Avoid talking about the parent's disappointment and upset, and if possible try to take ownership of the decision by saying things like 'we have decided that…'.

If the relocation is allowed

5.84 If the relocation is allowed, the order will usually have specified a date after which the applicant is allowed to move. While relocations sometimes happen in very short order after the completion of a final hearing, it is more common for there to be a delay of a few weeks or even months.

5.85 During this time, the applicant parent will be preparing for the move in all kinds of ways. That will include all the practicalities like finalising housing arrangements, arranging transportation to move to the new location, confirming a start date for a new job for the parent, or whatever is relevant. Sometimes there will be visa and other immigration matters to deal with, and that should be a priority.

---

[50] Hague Convention on Jurisdiction, Applicable Law, Recognition, Enforcement and Co-operation in Respect of Parental Responsibility and Measures for the Protection of Children 1996. We address this Convention here only briefly; for more detail, see N Lowe and M Nicholls QC, *The 1996 Hague Convention on the Protection of Children* (Bristol, Jordan Publishing, 2012). A list of signatory countries is found in **Appendix 6.2**, or online at www.hcch.net/index_en.php?act=conventions.status&cid=70.

[51] See also the measures that we discuss at **7.7** *et seq.*

[52] Obviously with babies and young infants, this aspect does not apply.

5.86 It is normal practice to facilitate as much contact between the child and the respondent parent, as well as any other family members in the current location (grandparents, cousins, etc), as possible between the final hearing and the move date. Sometimes the court will have ordered this, but usually the applicant parent is inclined to be pro-active in supporting increased contact in the run-up to the move.

If the relocation is refused

5.87 In many ways, there is less to do if the application is refused by the court. Very occasionally, the applicant parent has indicated that she herself will relocate whether or not the child goes. If such an indication has been given, this is crunch time – the applicant must now decide whether she is really going to go or not.

5.88 Most parents decide they will not, but if the parent does decide that she is going anyway then practical arrangements will have to be made for transferring the child's residence to the respondent parent. If there is time, the shift is best done gradually, slowly increasing the amount of time that the child spends at the respondent's house until that becomes the main base. Whatever the time period involved, though, both parents will need to be astute to the child's needs, wishes and feelings. It would be advisable to get assistance from a professional (perhaps from the Cafcass officer or ISW, if they are willing) about the practicalities of the change.

5.89 If, as is far more common, the applicant decides not to move, the issues arising are minimal. Arrangements will need to be made for future contact and residence arrangements, but there is no reason in principle why these should be any different after the relocation case than they were before. On the other hand, the case may be seen as an opportunity to make changes in one way or another. Those matters are tangential to the relocation case itself.

5.90 In many cases, arrangements for holidays (sometimes lengthy holidays) to the proposed destination will be sought by the applicant if the relocation is refused. Most of the time, so long as there are no concerns about non-return,[53] these are readily agreed, but it may be a matter that can be dealt with before the judge in the immediate aftermath of the relocation decision being taken if it is apparent that there is any difficulty.

Longer term issues

5.91 If a move to another jurisdiction has taken place (which includes, for this purpose, a move to Scotland or Northern Ireland[54]), that will have significant long-term consequences for the child. While it remains reasonably common for

---

[53] If there are concerns about non-return, the matters that we discuss at **7.7** *et seq* will be relevant.
[54] Family Law Act 1986; *Re W-B (Family Proceedings: Appropriate Jurisdiction Within the UK)* [2012] EWCA Civ 592, [2013] 1 FLR 394.

applicant parents to give undertakings to the English court that they will return the child to the jurisdiction of the English courts if ordered to do so, in reality the child will very quickly become habitually resident in the new country and therefore subject to the domestic family law of that country. This means that decisions about their future are likely to be determined in the new country.

5.92   So far as a country within the EU is concerned (except Denmark), the new country will acquire jurisdiction after a period of three months after the date of the move (unless the parties agree otherwise).[55] If the destination country is within the EU, a contact order will be directly enforceable there, subject to any application to vary it. If the country is not within the EU, subject to specialist legal advice that is likely to have been sought, and if it has been agreed that mirror orders be put in place before the move, now is the time to ensure that everything is in order before the departure.

5.93   If the relocation has not taken place, some unsuccessful applicants will think about applying again in the future. In principle, there is no reason why she should not, and the fact that she applied before will not normally be a major factor in any re-application (unless, for example, the judge made adverse findings about the applicant parent's motivation for seeking relocation the first time). In general, it is better not to think too much about this. The parent should focus as best she can on getting on with her life where she is.

5.94   Whatever the outcome, a court which has recently made orders – for residence, contact, preventing or allowing relocation – will expect them to be honoured unless there has been a change of circumstances or events have not turned out as would be expected. If there are difficulties with the orders that have been made, then the correct thing to do (assuming it is not possible to resolve matters by agreement) is to apply back to the judge who originally made the orders.

5.95   If matters proceed reasonably smoothly, and the need to vary arrangements arises only after a considerable amount of time, then the proper course (if matters cannot be agreed) is to apply to the court where the children are now living.

---

[55]   See further **2.36** *et seq*; Brussels II Revised, Council Regulation (EC) No 2201/2003, Art 9(1); *Re I (Contact Application: Jurisdiction)* [2009] UKSC 10, [2010] 1 FLR 361 at [35]; *VC v GC (Jurisdiction: Brussels II Revised Art 12)* [2012] EWHC 1246 (Fam), [2013] 1 FLR 244.

Chapter 6

OPPOSING A RELOCATION APPLICATION

6.1   Most practitioners would say that there has been a change in the way that the courts are considering relocation applications, such that opposing them is not the forlorn task that it once was. There are more reported cases where relocation was refused,[1] and more cases where the refusal was upheld on appeal.[2]

6.2   There may be many reasons for this shift in approach, but one important factor is probably the rise in shared care arrangements which means that there is a well-balanced case for each parent to have the care of the children. If the children can equally live with either parent, then the impact of the loss of day-to-day contact with one of them is much the same whether they leave or stay. A refusal of a relocation application does not prevent the applicant from moving without the children, who will suffer the loss of regular contact with a parent no more if they remain in the current location than if they go.

6.3   Respondents to an application for internal or international relocation should read Chapters 3, 4 and 5 carefully first. This chapter deals with the situation once it becomes clear that litigation is inevitable.

RESPONDING TO AN APPLICATION

6.4   A parent who wishes to relocate abroad with children will need to seek the permission of the court pursuant to s 13(1)(b) of the Children Act 1989. The respondent parent may answer with an application for a residence or shared residence order transferring residence, or may simply object to the relocation application. A respondent who is genuinely able to offer himself as a primary carer will be in a better position to oppose the application successfully, and therefore it is generally better to oppose an application by bringing an application for residence as well unless the prospects of success are very small.

---

[1]   See, eg, *Re AR (A Child: Relocation)* [2010] EWHC 1346 (Fam), [2010] 2 FLR 1577; *Re C (Children)* [2012] EWCA Civ 203 (permission to appeal refusal of leave refused).

[2]   See, eg, *Re B (Leave to Remove)* [2008] EWCA Civ 1034, [2008] 2 FLR 2059; *Re L (Internal Relocation: Shared Residence Order)* [2009] EWCA Civ 20, [2009] 1 FLR 1157; *Re W (Relocation: Contact)* [2009] EWCA Civ 160, [2009] All ER (D) 120 (May); *Re F (Internal Relocation)* [2010] EWCA Civ 1428, [2011] 1 FLR 1382.

6.5   Given that there is no statutory requirement for a parent wishing to relocate within the United Kingdom to apply to the court for leave to do so, a parent planning such a move may decide not to apply to the court at all. In those circumstances, assuming that it has not been possible to reach agreement via solicitors or through mediation, the opposing parent should apply to the court himself.[3] He should apply for a prohibited steps order preventing the move, and should also consider applying for a specific issue order to deal with issues such as schooling and also for residence and/or contact if appropriate. By doing this, the respondent parent will be bringing all the issues before the court to be resolved.

SITUATIONS WHICH ARE URGENT

6.6   There are cases where a parent acts unilaterally or is threatening to do so, when action needs to be taken urgently. If a parent believes that the other parent is about to abduct the children abroad, he should consult a solicitor immediately and go to court to get an order preventing a removal. Even if the proposed move is within the UK, it is still important to obtain orders preventing a removal if it is suspected that the other parent will act unilaterally (usually a prohibited steps order). It is important that the applicant parent does not establish a status quo in the proposed destination by the time of the hearing.

6.7   Short-term orders can usually be obtained very quickly at an *ex parte* hearing (where the other side does not attend), with the matter then listed to return to court within a short period to be heard 'on notice' (where the other side attends and makes her case against the orders).[4] In an urgent case which arises out of hours involving a likely international removal, the duty judge at the High Court should be contacted by telephone.[5] Measures taken in urgent cases can include:

- a prohibited steps order;

- an order to surrender passports;

- 'port alert' orders, which require customs officers at ports and airports to stop the child being taken over the UK border.

6.8   Indeed, if the case is very urgent then police assistance should be sought at once. The police have power to act to protect a child under the age of 16 and to act to prevent an unlawful removal from the jurisdiction without a court

---

[3]   Note that, for consistency of language, we continue to call the parent seeking to relocate the applicant and the parent opposing the relocation the respondent, regardless of whether that is technically the case or not.

[4]   See Practice Direction 12E: Urgent Business.

[5]   See President's Guidance (18 November 2010) [2011] 1 FLR 303.

order being obtained first.[6] This course is, however, exceptional, and should be reserved only for cases of the greatest urgency where there is an immediate and compelling risk of abduction.

6.9 If the applicant parent has already moved by the time of the application to court, in an international case it will be necessary to obtain orders for return in the court here, and to seek remedies for abduction in the destination country.[7] In the case of an abduction within the United Kingdom, the remaining parent should seek an urgent specific issue order requiring the children to be returned pending the hearing of the full relocation application and a prohibited steps order preventing a further attempt to move.[8]

6.10 A parent who brings an application to relocate before the court has clearly shown an intention to deal with things in a proper way, and therefore it is unlikely that there would be any grounds for an application for a prohibited steps order preventing a move pending the full hearing.[9] Nonetheless, there may be cases where the respondent parent has reason to believe that the applicant parent will take the law into her own hands, and if so, then an urgent application to the court should be made.

AFTER THE APPLICATION HAS BEEN ISSUED

6.11 As set out in Chapter 5, an application to the court, whether to remove a child from the jurisdiction or to prohibit a move, is made on Form C100. The person filing the C100 will be able to make a short statement in Part 7 of the form setting out the reasons for making the application.[10] The application will then be issued and served upon the respondent parent who will likewise be able to make a short statement giving reasons for opposing the application.

6.12 Assuming that the applicant parent filed Form C100, then if the respondent wishes to make his own application he will fill out a Form C2 (applying for an order within proceedings), which also contains a section in which reasons for making the application can be set out. This is not usually necessary if the parent is opposing the relocation but not seeking a residence order in his own favour. But where he is seeking such an order (or some other supplementary order), Form C2 will be needed.[11]

---

6   See Practice Direction 12F: International Child Abduction, para [4.3]. If there is a court order and police assistance is sought, a copy of the order should be provided to the police.

7   Abduction is not a matter that we address in this book, and if a child is abducted abroad the remaining parent must seek remedies not only in this country but also in the destination country. This will of course be easier if the destination country is a signatory to the Hague Convention 1980.

8   Children Act 1989, s 8; see **Appendix 1.1**.

9   Children Act 1989, s 8; see **Appendix 1.1**.

10 We give an example of the way such a statement will be made in **5.12**. See also **Appendix 5.1**, where we include sample Form C100 relating to the case study set out in **4.43**.

11 See also **Appendix 5.2**, where we include sample Form C2 relating to the case study set out in **4.43**.

Helpful Hint

If the respondent parent is seeking an order within the proceedings, such as a residence order in response to the relocation application, Form C2 includes provision for a short statement setting out the parent's reasons for making this application. As an example, that paragraph might say something like this:

'I am making this application because I believe that it is in the best interests of the children to live mainly with me, rather than relocating to [location]. I have been strongly involved in the upbringing of the children throughout their lives. This has included having them live with me for [whatever proportion] of their time since their mother and I separated, and they have an established home with me as well as one with her. I am focused on maintaining the present arrangements for the children's upbringing as much as possible, including their schooling and contact with their wider family in this area. Although the children's pattern of time with me and their mother would change, their interests are best met with a stable upbringing which I am providing for them. I am anxious to agree ongoing contact arrangements between the children and their mother if she decides to relocate to [location], and I am happy to have a shared residence arrangement whether she remains here or relocates.'

6.13   If the parties have not made efforts to resolve their dispute by mediation they will have to explain on the form why this has not happened. The dispute between the parents will be governed by the Private Law Programme.[12]

THE FIRST HEARING DISPUTE RESOLUTION APPOINTMENT

6.14   As set out in Chapter 5,[13] the court will list a first hearing dispute resolution appointment ('FHDRA') within four to six weeks of issuing the application. The Cafcass officer will make contact with the parents to make initial enquiries (which will be limited to safeguarding issues).[14] At the FHDRA, the parents and Cafcass will be expected to attend so that the court will be able to consider whether the parents can safely resolve some or all of the issues in dispute, or whether the matter will need to be set down for a full hearing. If the latter is the case, then the purpose of the hearing will be to identify the issues, and make directions as to the filing of evidence (including expert evidence) and the filing of the Cafcass report.[15]

6.15   In many private law cases parents are ordered to file their statements simultaneously, but in relocation cases it should be argued that statements

---

[12]   See **5.18**.
[13]   See **5.32** *et seq.*
[14]   Practice Direction 12B, para [3.9]; see **Appendix 2.2**.
[15]   Ibid.

should be filed sequentially so that each side has the opportunity to respond to the proposals of the other. Therefore, the parent who wishes to change the status quo and remove the children from their current home/situation should file a statement first setting out their proposals. The respondent parent should then file a statement in response. The applicant parent should then be able to file a short statement dealing with the objections.

6.16 As we explained in detail in Chapter 5,[16] it is normal for a report from Cafcass or an independent social worker ('ISW') to be ordered at this stage. If any party wishes the court to obtain expert evidence, then Practice Direction 25C applies.[17] Expert evidence is the exception not the rule and will need to be justified by the particular facts of a case. A party seeking to call expert evidence will need to convince the court about the necessity of having an expert at all and about the extent of the expert's role.[18] That party should file an application setting out various details, including:

- the name, qualifications and experience of the proposed expert or several possible experts, indicating a preference if there is one;

- the matters which the party wishes the expert to assess;

- the likely cost of the report;

- the availability of the expert to file the report and attend the hearing.[19]

6.17 If the court accedes to the application for expert evidence, the terms upon which the expert is advising will be set out clearly in the order and the parties' solicitors (or the parties themselves if they have no solicitors) will be required to agree a letter of instruction within five days. Practice Direction 25C gives advice as to the contents of the letter.[20]

6.18 If Cafcass is unable to provide a report within the timeframe that the parties are hoping for, it is common, where resources allow, for the parties to agree to instruct an independent social worker ('ISW') instead. This will cost money, but it is often worth it as the ISW may be able to make more detailed enquiries and to provide a report within a shorter timeframe. If an ISW is instructed, this is done in the same way as an expert is instructed: jointly, with an agreed letter of instruction.

---

[16] See **5.39–5.41**.
[17] Practice Direction 25C, paras [3.1]–[3.11]; see **Appendix 2.6**.
[18] See *Re TG (Care Proceedings: Case Management: Expert Evidence)* [2013] EWCA Civ 5, [2013] 1 FLR forthcoming at [29]–[34]. An exception to this general rule may apply in the case of expert evidence regarding the legal system in a destination country which outside the standard international agreements; we discuss this further at **7.12–7.13** with regard to temporary relocation cases.
[19] Practice Direction 25C, para [3.10]; see **Appendix 2.6**.
[20] Ibid, para [4.1] and Annex A; see **Appendix 2.6**.

6.19 It is always a good idea for a written position statement to be submitted by each party (or their legal representative if they have one) at the FHDRA. This should include a summary of the party's position on the application and the reasons for it, the points in favour of that position, and what evidence it is suggested the court will need to determine the matter at a final hearing. If it is suggested that expert evidence should be obtained then the reasons for this should be set out.

6.20 The position statement should be succinct – short enough to be absorbed quickly by a busy judge who is likely to have many cases in the list that day, but long enough to set out a convincing case.

6.21 Assuming that no agreement is reached at the FHDRA, and that delay will not assist resolution, the court will seek to identify the disputed issues and make Directions for a final hearing to decide the matter.

Helpful Hint

It really is important to get the case listed in front of the right tribunal.[21] All international relocation cases are complicated, and if the case is listed for a final hearing before a district judge in the county court then the advocates need to think carefully about whether they are happy to proceed on that basis. There are two reasons to be cautious. One is that the case may warrant a higher level of tribunal where there is greater experience of complex legal provisions and long-term consequences, as well as the kinds of orders required in the event the relocation is allowed.[22] The other is that the route of appeal from a district judge in a county court is to a circuit judge, and both parties to a relocation case may prefer to start their case before a tribunal whose decision is appealed to a more senior court.[23]

6.22 The court will then provide a date at which the final hearing can take place on the basis of a time estimate agreed with the parties having regard to the amount of evidence that is to be called. Typically at least two court days will be required given the need for: both parents to give evidence, perhaps also the Cafcass officer or ISW; legal submissions to be made on both sides; judicial reading time at the outset of the hearing; and time for judgment at the conclusion.

---

[21]   On listing, see also **3.15–3.16**.
[22]   See **6.68–6.70**; on means of enforcing orders, see **7.7** *et seq.*
[23]   On appeals, see **Chapter 8**.

SETTING OUT A CASE IN RESPONSE TO A RELOCATION APPLICATION

6.23 The opportunities that an opposing parent will have to set out his or her case will be:

- initially in correspondence with the other parent or other parent's solicitor;

- then, in short form on the response to the application form or in Form C2;

- in the position statement for the FHDRA and any other court hearing;

- in a witness statement for the court.

6.24 It is in the witness statement that most detail can be given. The matters that the respondent parent should be researching in detail, and advising the court about in the witness statement, are set out below.

General practicalities

6.25 The law in this field is undoubtedly in a state of flux,[24] but there are some principles that can be asserted with confidence. The first and most important is that the test is, and will remain, that the welfare of the child is the court's paramount consideration.[25] However, the welfare principle is then informed by judicial guidance, and judges are likely to continue to have regard to the guidelines in *Payne* in an international case,[26] because many of its points are of general application regardless of the details of the relocation application.[27]

6.26 Indeed, as we explained in Chapter 2,[28] many of the questions that the guidance in international relocation cases offers are also relevant to an internal relocation cases. For example, it will remain important for any applicant to demonstrate that the plans for a move are well thought through in terms of income, housing, schooling and contact, and that the purpose of the move is not to bring contact to an end.

6.27 In any case, therefore, the applicant's proposals as to accommodation, work and schooling should be carefully scrutinised. In the days of the internet, this is much easier than it once was. It is possible to get an idea of house prices or rental costs in most parts of the world. It is also usually possible to view the

---

[24] See further **Chapter 2**.
[25] Children Act 1989, s 1 (see **Appendix 1.1**); for case law affirming the centrality of welfare in relocation cases, see *K v K (Relocation: Shared Care Arrangement)* [2011] EWCA Civ 793, [2012] 2 FLR 880 at [39], [86] and [141] (see **Appendix 3.3**).
[26] *Payne v Payne* [2001] EWCA Civ 166, [2001] 1 FLR 1052; see **Appendix 3.1**.
[27] For detailed discussion of this issue, see **2.19** *et seq*.
[28] See **2.59** *et seq*.

types of housing or even the actual property that it is proposed the children live in. Of course, any properly prepared application will include these details, but research will demonstrate whether the proposed cost is a realistic one and whether, for example, the property is in a reasonable area.

6.28 Employment details are also important. If the applicant has not got a job yet, what are the prospects of obtaining one? Is a work permit needed? If so, what process needs to be gone through before it is obtained, and what is the likelihood that it will be refused? What are the timescales? These matters should have been dealt with in the application, but if they are not, questions should be asked, and information given should not be too difficult to check. These matters can then be raised in the respondent's statement if they are still causing concern.

6.29 What is the overall income of the family going to be? If there is a new spouse or partner, details of his income will need to be given unless there really can be no doubt that there is sufficient money available for the family. If the details given or the lack of detail is causing concern, this should be raised in the statement.

6.30 These matters then need to be placed in the balance with the overall cost of living in the chosen destination. This is not just the cost of rent or a mortgage, but also the cost of utilities, food, travel etc. If the respondent is not happy with the figures given by the applicant he should say so and explain why.

6.31 In an international case it is often asserted by the applicant that the cost of living will be lower in the country of destination. The United Kingdom is not a cheap place to live, so this could well be true. On the other hand, there is an understandable tendency of those seeking to relocate to be over-optimistic about the cost of living in the place that they wish to live, and a careful appraisal of the figures given will often reveal this. It is important, not only because it might undermine the strength of the application, but also because a poorer financial situation than had been anticipated will affect not only the standard of living, but also the ability to fund contact.

6.32 Schooling is a very important area for scrutiny. A parent has no less right to be involved in the choice of the schooling of his child if the child is living far away than if the child is close by. Therefore, the respondent should be prepared to investigate the proposed schools, and any other schools in the area, which might be suitable. Depending on the distances involved, and the cost, it would not be unreasonable to visit the school(s) and area where the children would be.

6.33 If one school is preferred to another this is a matter for negotiation (or if this does not work, for the court to decide). Many parents who oppose relocation are very reluctant to engage in issues about schooling for they feel that by doing so they are giving tacit approval to the move, and also that they might be assisting the applicant. This is not usually the best approach. A parent is more likely to be criticised for not becoming involved in the choice of schooling on the basis that this is not a child-focused response to the application. Moreover, engagement about possible schooling options does not signal an agreement to the move. It is simply a matter of being pragmatic in the event that the application succeeds and having the best interests of the children at heart. It also allows the respondent to comment properly upon the applicant's proposals.

6.34   As with everything else, if it is proposed that the children go to private schools, the cost of schooling should be considered. What do the quoted fees include? Are there any extras? How does the cost increase as the child gets older? If the child is young, what school is the child likely to be expected to go to later? What is the cost of that? How long are the holidays and when are they? When are exams taken? What is the curriculum? If the proposed move is abroad, how easy would it be for the child to return to the United Kingdom and fit into the school or university system here after a period away?

6.35   All these matters are of the greatest importance whether or not the applicant is a primary carer, or whether the applicant is an equal carer. In an international case in particular, if the court believes that the plans are badly thought through the application is likely to be dismissed. The bar may be set lower for an applicant who is going back somewhere they have been brought up and are very familiar with, and/or where there are wider family members.[29] The same of course is true of an internal relocation as the system of education/health care etc is well understood.

Motivation

6.36   The court will wish to consider the motivation behind the application to relocate. Is it because the applicant wishes to return home and feels isolated in this country/area? If this is what is given as a reason, is this really the case? Does the applicant have friends and support where she is now? If she is isolated, are there ways in which she could improve the situation for herself? Could her sense of isolation be relieved by visits to her home country/area rather than a wholesale move?

6.37   On the other side of the coin, is the applicant really likely to be happier if she returns to her roots? How long is it since she last lived there? What is her relationship with her family really like, and does she have friends and a social life there to return to? Is the wish to return soundly based, or is it really a wish to run away from current unhappiness in the false belief that everything will be better somewhere else? Could a current sense of isolation/unhappiness be due to something different, such as depression or as a result of the breakdown of the relationship, a situation which is likely to improve with treatment or time?

6.38   If the motivation to move is based upon a job or other opportunity which has presented itself, then this itself will need to be scrutinised. Is the

---

[29]   See *Re F and H (Children: Relocation)* [2007] EWCA Civ 692, [2008] 2 FLR 1667 at [9].

opportunity one that will not present itself at another time? Is it really such a wonderful opportunity or does it just seem like such to the applicant? Will the applicant not have other opportunities in time without needing to move?

6.39 Much the same considerations apply if the motivation to move is a result of a new relationship where the partner works away or has been offered a job far afield.

6.40 If the motivation is to follow (or join) a new partner, then there may be considerations as to the new relationship, for example how longstanding or secure the relationship is. If there are issues about this, they may be mentioned in the respondent's witness statement.

6.41 A respondent should always be aware of the potential of some matters, if raised, to cause distress and/or resentment. Therefore, allegations or queries about such things as the state of the applicant's new relationship, or as to whether the applicant really is distressed/depressed should only be raised if they really need to be, and then in as sensitive a manner as possible. At the end of the case, whoever wins or loses, the parents are going to have to try to get on.

Contact

Cases where there has been little or no previous conflict/acrimony over the children

6.42 Most relocation cases involve parents who have not really had any major disagreements about contact. Many of them will never have been to court before. In this type of case it will be very hard, if not impossible, to demonstrate that any part of the applicant's motivation is to bring contact between the children and respondent parent to an end. It makes an application harder to defeat but, on the other hand, if relocation is allowed then the respondent parent at least has the security of knowing that the other parent will not try to squeeze him or her out of the children's lives.

6.43 Assuming that it is not a 'high acrimony' case, then the important matters to focus upon so far as contact is concerned are the practical ones. Research suggests that some applicants, in their desire to succeed, are over-optimistic about the contact that can and will take place after any move.[30] The proposals may not take sufficient account of the distances involved, the extent to which older children will develop their own lives and wish to spend holiday times with their friends and in their main home, and also the cost. It is perfectly reasonable for a respondent to an application to query what appears to be a generous offer of contact on the basis that it is unlikely to be viable.

6.44 The cost of travel for contact, either that of the children or the respondent parent, as well as accommodation for the latter in the destination

---

[30]   See M Freeman, *Relocation: The Reunite Research* (London, Reunite, 2009).

country should all be considered very carefully. Is there really going to be sufficient money to sustain holiday (and, if the proposed relocation is not too far away, long weekend) contact? Who is to pay? The applicant parent will be aware that decent proposals for contact are a pre-requisite to a successful application so may be prepared to fund the travel and/or to forego child maintenance so that it can be put towards the cost. Another option is for a fund to be set up for the costs of travel in the future.

6.45   Indirect contact is also extremely important, and arrangements should be made for contact via emails and Skype or other webcam programme. At the time of writing, reception via Skype is still a bit unpredictable in certain places (and the places where high-speed broadband is unavailable are not necessarily the places that one would expect). It is likely that these issues, and call quality in general, will improve dramatically in time. The quality of the computer being used can also make a big difference.

6.46   The practicalities of contact are much more straightforward with older children than with very young ones, for obvious reasons. Young children cannot travel alone, and indirect contact is much more difficult. There is a much bigger risk of a loss of a meaningful relationship with the respondent parent by relocation where young children are concerned, and this is a point that should be made with force by a respondent, and should be given considerable weight by the court. With young children, the applicant parent should be expected to accompany them to this country for contact, and it is particularly important for provision to be made for the respondent parent to travel and stay in the destination country if relocation is allowed.

Cases where there has been previous conflict/acrimony over the children

6.47   These cases provide particular difficulty for the courts. Should the court decide that the purpose of the application is wholly or partially to bring the relationship between the child and respondent parent to an end, or to marginalise it as much as possible, it is very likely that an application to move far afield will be refused.

6.48   It can be difficult, however, to prove that this is the case. There are some cases where it is fairly easy to see that one parent is trying to marginalise the other, but there are many others where the history of acrimony does not reveal anything so clear cut.

6.49   Any parent who is concerned that the application is being made in an attempt to undermine the relationship between him and the children should undoubtedly set this out as soon as possible. Moderation in expression should be the order of the day, although it is important to set out clearly what the respondent fears will happen if the application is allowed and why.

6.50 The most important evidence in support of a claim that the applicant parent wishes to undermine contact or at the very least does not respect the value of contact is the history of what has happened to date. This should be set out clearly in the respondent's statement. What have been the contact arrangements since separation? Is there a history of litigation? What orders did the court make, and were they honoured by the applicant?

6.51 Additionally, examples of hostility by the applicant towards the respondent should be set out as well as examples of how the children may have been brought into the dispute, and/or influenced against him. It is important that such examples can be substantiated, as exaggerated claims or allegations are likely to damage the respondent's case and undermine all the evidence that he gives.

CAFCASS/INDEPENDENT SOCIAL WORKER

6.52 In Chapter 5, we dealt in detail with the kind of work that the Cafcass officer or ISW will undertake, all of which applies equally here. Rather than repeat ourselves, we refer readers to that section.[31]

6.53 The report which is produced at the end of these enquiries will contain a summary of the factual matters uncovered by the reporter's enquiries coupled with an analysis of the welfare checklist and (usually) some analysis of the main issues raised by the relevant case law.[32] The report may or may not reach a clear recommendation as to which outcome the Cafcass officer thinks would be best. The officer cannot be criticised either way for making or not making a recommendation, though in some cases she may depart from whatever conclusion she reached when giving evidence (either to give a recommendation on the witness stand when none was contained in the report, or to retract a recommendation given in the report).

6.54 If there are any errors of fact that are central to the report then they should be brought to the reporter's attention as soon as possible upon receipt of the report. Otherwise, any disagreement with the analysis or interpretation of facts, and the resulting recommendation if relevant, is appropriately dealt with in cross-examination at the final hearing.

6.55 It may be that the Cafcass officer's attendance at the final hearing was directed at the FHDRA in any event. If the officer's presence has not already been requested, and there are significant matters contained in the report which are disputed and therefore require the reporter's attendance at the final hearing for cross-examination, the Cafcass officer should be notified at the earliest opportunity.

---

[31] See **5.58–5.70**.
[32] *Payne v Payne* [2001] EWCA Civ 166, [2001] 1 FLR 1052, for example, may usefully be drawn to a Cafcass officer's attention, since it contains various considerations relevant to most international relocation applications; see **Appendix 3.1**.

6.56 Upon receipt of the Cafcass report and any expert reports, and in advance of the final hearing, it is advantageous for there to be a conference between the respondent and his advocate. This is a vital opportunity to consider the state of the evidence as it now stands in its entirety, and to agree the approach to be taken at the final hearing and the precise terms of the order sought. It is also a further opportunity to consider whether one more attempt may be made to negotiate an agreement by putting a further written offer to the applicant in the light of the recommendation of the Cafcass officer.

6.57 The court will normally list a pre-hearing review before the final hearing and once all the evidence has been filed, to ensure that all the evidence is available and that the case is ready. It is also an opportunity for a final attempt to see if the parties can agree as to what should happen to the children. In particular, if the Cafcass report was not favourable to the relocation proposal, this is a chance for the respondent to try to persuade the applicant to abandon the case. If that is not possible, it is also an opportunity for the parties and the court to decide which witnesses will need to be called, what issues will be relevant for the hearing, and which have fallen away.

6.58 If there are witnesses from overseas that need to be cross-examined at the final hearing, it may be possible to avoid their attendance at court by arranging video-link facilities. Every court has such facilities but they must be booked well in advance and arrangements made with the court office. If this is left to the last minute and an adjournment is then necessary, there may be adverse costs consequences.

6.59 The applicant will be responsible for the preparation and lodging of the bundle with the court not less than two days before the final hearing (and before any hearing in the High Court or lasting more than an hour in the county court). It should contain a case summary, schedule of issues and agreed chronology. It should also contain a skeleton argument on behalf of each party, together with copies of authorities relied upon, and a reading list for the judge.[33]

THE FINAL HEARING

6.60 At the final hearing, the judge may have had time to read all the relevant documents by the morning of the first day, but more likely he or she will require two hours or more of reading time. Given proper advance preparation there should be no further need to 'open' the case.

6.61 Typically, if the Cafcass officer is required to give oral evidence, that will happen at the outset of the hearing (though it can be later if there is a reason to delay it until after some other aspect of the case). Given the central importance of the Cafcass report, it is useful to have resolved any challenge to her evidence

---

[33]   Practice Direction 27A; see also **5.54–5.57**.

before the parties give their evidence to the court. It gives the parties the opportunity to address the recommendation that survives cross-examination.

6.62 If there is an expert, he or she will usually give evidence at the beginning, either before or after Cafcass. The applicant and any witnesses that she is calling will give evidence next and be cross-examined by the respondent's advocate (or by the respondent himself if he is acting without lawyers).

6.63 The respondent then gives evidence. The best preparation for a witness giving evidence is to be fully familiar with the content of his statement, as that will form the basis for the questioning that will come from the applicant's advocate. Just as with the drafting of the statement and the interaction with the Cafcass officer, the tone of the evidence given is as important as its content. The judge will be forming a view not just of the content of the answers but of the way in which they are given.

6.64 The court will assess the respondent's case in the round on the basis of the complete presentation in the witness box. Clear, succinct and straightforward answers are the order of the day. The ability to demonstrate a level of insight not only into the problems and downsides associated with the proposed relocation, but also for possible advantages which might flow from the applicant's proposal, will be watched for. It is clearly important that there is no hint of malice towards the applicant and a willing acceptance of the importance of her role in the children's lives. Again, this is not the opportunity to seek to undermine or criticise the applicant. It is important to remain positive. A repeated emphasis on the welfare of the children will be recognised.

6.65 In closing submissions, the respondent's advocate speaks first. This is the opportunity to finally argue for the most appropriate legal framework and persuade the court how the facts of a particular application fit within it so as to allow the desired relocation.

6.66 Counsel will already have included key authorities in the court bundle, and unless the judge indicates otherwise these can be taken as read. The main point which the respondent wishes the court to take from each of those cases, as applied to his case, will have usually been made clearly in the skeleton argument, and again the court need not be addressed on those matters unless the judge indicates that he or she would like to hear further submissions.

6.67 Counsel may, nonetheless, wish to highlight crucial aspects in the closing statement. If there has been any dispute about the existing care arrangements for the child, for example, then the respondent's counsel may be well advised to push for a finding that the child has a shared care arrangement, and therefore that the discipline of *Payne* needs to be modified as appropriate.[34] If the finding itself is not certain to be made, counsel will be well advised to highlight

---

[34] See further **2.22** *et seq.*

to the judge the factors from the authorities which are especially pertinent to the case, as well as pointing to other cases establishing the point in question if that is appropriate.

THE COURT ORDER

6.68   In general, court orders are drafted by counsel and approved or amended by the judge. Every case will have its own details, but in general the order will:

- give an indication of how the decision was reached, noting for example that the court has read the bundle and heard oral evidence from the parties and the Cafcass officer;

- record any undertakings given in relation to the case by either parent or, in some cases, by someone else such as a grandparent,[35] generally making provision for requirements that the court cannot order or that the parties agree are appropriate. It is not possible to be prescriptive here: undertakings are an opportunity to be creative to suit the particular circumstances of your case;

    (i)   if the relocation is being allowed, these may include things such as:

    — an agreement to keep the respondent informed about such details as are relevant (such as school progress, medical conditions, etc);

    — an agreement to promote a positive relationship between the child and the other parent;

    — an undertaking that the applicant parent will make a computer available so as to allow the child to use Skype and email to have indirect contact with the respondent parent;

    — details about any financial security being provided;

    — an agreement to return the child to the jurisdiction of the courts of England and Wales if so required by an order of the court;

    — an agreement about jurisdiction for future issues about the child's upbringing.

    (ii)   if the relocation is being refused, there may still be undertakings, which may include things such as:

    — an agreement to promote a positive relationship between the child and the other parent;

    — an agreement to allow one parent to take the child on holidays abroad, as agreed, at particular intervals in the future.

---

[35]   See, for example, the undertakings given by the mother and maternal grandfather in *Re A (Security for Return to Jurisdiction) (Note)* [1999] 2 FLR 1 (FD), albeit there in the context of a temporary relocation; see **Appendix 3.4**.

- make the actual orders, which will include things like:

  — whether or not the relocation is allowed; if it is, then in an international relocation case the order should state specifically that the applicant parent is authorised to remove the child permanently from the jurisdiction;

  — if the relocation is allowed, the order should specify when it may take place, especially if the relocation is not to take place before a specified date or event (such as the end of the school term);

  — whether earlier orders made in relation to the child remain in force or not;

  — what new orders are made in respect of residence and contact, or in relation to shared residence, which often include a very detailed contact schedule;

  — any supplemental orders relating to moving or not moving (such as a specific issue order about which school the child should attend, or specific orders about future holiday arrangements).

6.69 To reiterate, these are just examples. Every case has its own particular issues, and it is not possible to set out an exhaustive list of the issues that may need to be addressed in the court order.

6.70 It is standard practice, and we think very advisable, for there to be a detailed contact order in the event of relocation being allowed.[36] The detail varies depending on the destination:

- **internal relocations within England and Wales**: orders are enforceable like any other Children Act order;

- **internal relocations to Scotland or Northern Ireland**: the order will be recognised automatically in the new location, but needs to be registered before it becomes enforceable;[37]

- **international relocation within the EU (except Denmark)**: contact orders and other matters relating to parental responsibility are automatically

---

[36] But cf *Re R (Leave to Remove: Contact)* [2010] EWCA Civ 1137, [2011] 1 FLR 1336 at [22]: Wilson LJ indicated that, since a court order granting permission to remove a child from the jurisdiction amounted to 'surrendering [the court's] control over the child', it was 'contrary to principle' for a contact order to be attached to the grant of leave to remove. We note that it remains standard practice to make such orders and, with respect, we think that to be the better approach. Many international agreements (including the Brussels IIR Regulation, the 1996 Hague Convention, and the international understanding of mirror orders) work on the basis that the pre-relocation court will make orders about the child's upbringing which are then recognised and enforced, or mirrored, in the destination state. Indeed, Art 12(3) of Brussels IIR would enable the English court to retain jurisdiction after a relocation; see **2.38**. Even absent such considerations, it is hard to see any difficulty with the making of contact orders: the worst that could happen, so far as we can see, is that they might be ignored by the court in the destination country.

[37] Family Law Act 1986, ss 25 and 27.

recognised and enforceable in the destination country, once that country becomes the child's place of habitual residence (usually after three months);[38]

- **international relocation outside the EU but to a 1996 Hague Convention country**: contact orders and other matters relating to parental responsibility may be automatically recognised and enforceable, depending on the particular country's domestic laws implementing the Convention;[39]

- **international relocation to other countries**: mirror orders may be obtainable, but not all countries recognise this concept; either way, other measures to help safeguard contact may be required.[40]

AFTER THE FINAL HEARING

6.71   A respondent who is unhappy with the decision of the court and wishes to appeal a decision to allow relocation should apply to the trial judge for permission to appeal and a stay preventing the removal of the child pending the appeal. If permission and a stay are refused, the respondent must apply to the Court of Appeal. If the matter is very urgent (for example, if the move is to take place within days) then the proposed appellant should telephone the Court of Appeal on 0207 947 6000, or 0207 947 6260 out of hours. An out of hours application should only be made in cases of real need and urgency, when the matter cannot wait until the next working day. Appeals are dealt with in Chapter 8.

6.72   Assuming there is to be no appeal, whatever decision is made, the best thing is for the parents to tell the children together if that is possible and if the children are of an age where they will be wondering what is happening. Even in the most amicable of cases, that will be difficult for the parent who was unsuccessful, and in many cases it will be simply too hard. If the parents cannot tell the child together, then each of them will need to speak with the child about it.

6.73   So far as is possible, each parent should put the decision in the most positive light he or she can manage. Focus on what will be good about the decision, and about how things are going to be for the child in the coming

---

[38]   Brussels II Revised, Council Regulation (EC) No 2201/2003.

[39]   Hague Convention on Jurisdiction, Applicable Law, Recognition, Enforcement and Co-operation in Respect of Parental Responsibility and Measures for the Protection of Children 1996. We address this Convention here only briefly; for more detail, see N Lowe and M Nicholls QC, *The 1996 Hague Convention on the Protection of Children* (Bristol, Jordan Publishing, 2012). A list of signatory countries is found in **Appendix 6.2**, or online at www.hcch.net/index_en.php?act=conventions.status&cid=70.

[40]   See also the measures that we discuss at **7.7** *et seq*.

weeks and months. Avoid talking about the parent's disappointment and upset, and if possible try to take ownership of the decision by saying things like 'we have decided that...'.

If the relocation is allowed

6.74 If the relocation is allowed, the order will usually have specified a date after which the applicant is allowed to move. While relocations sometimes happen in very short order after the completion of a final hearing, it is more common for there to be a delay of a few weeks or even months.

6.75 There will be practicalities to sort out, but these will mostly be for the applicant to do. So far as the respondent is concerned, this will be an opportunity to have as much contact as possible before any move and to make arrangements for forthcoming holidays, Skype contact, and so on. It can be a good idea to start building in some Skype contact before the move goes ahead, so that the child starts to see the link between Skype and in-person contact.

If the relocation is refused

6.76 In many ways, there is less to do if the application is refused by the court. Very occasionally, the applicant parent has indicated that she herself will relocate whether or not the child goes. If such an indication has been given, this is crunch time – the applicant must now decide whether she is really going to go or not.

6.77 Most parents decide they will not, but if the parent does decide that she is going anyway then practical arrangements will have to be made for transferring the child's residence to the respondent parent. If there is time, the shift is best done gradually, slowly increasing the amount of time that the child spends at the respondent's house until that becomes the main base. Whatever the time period involved though, both parents will need to be astute to the child's needs, wishes and feelings. It would be advisable to get assistance from a professional (perhaps from the Cafcass officer or ISW, if they are willing) about the practicalities of the change.

6.78 If, as is far more common, the applicant decides not to move, the issues arising are minimal. Arrangements will need to be made for future contact and residence arrangements, but there is no reason in principle why these should be any different after the relocation case than they were before. On the other hand, the case may be seen as an opportunity to make changes in one way or another. Those matters are tangential to the relocation case itself.

6.79 In many cases, arrangements for holidays (sometimes lengthy holidays) to the proposed destination will be sought by the applicant if the relocation is refused. Most of the time, so long as there are no concerns about non-return,[41]

---

[41]   If there are concerns about non-return, the matters that we discuss at **7.7** *et seq* will be relevant.

these are readily agreed, but it may be a matter that can be dealt with before the judge in the immediate aftermath of the relocation decision being taken if it is apparent that there is any difficulty.

Longer term issues

6.80 If a move to another jurisdiction has taken place (which includes, for this purpose, a move to Scotland or Northern Ireland[42]), that will have significant long-term consequences for the child. While it remains reasonably common for applicant parents to give undertakings to the English court that they will return the child to the jurisdiction of the English courts if ordered to do so, in reality the child will very quickly become habitually resident in the new country and therefore subject to the domestic family law of that country. This means that decisions about their future are likely to be determined in the new country.

6.81 So far as a move to a country within the EU is concerned (except Denmark), the new country will acquire jurisdiction after a period of three months after the date of the move (unless the parties agree otherwise).[43] If the destination country is within the EU, a contact order will be directly enforceable there, subject to any application to vary it. If the country is not within the EU, subject to specialist legal advice that is likely to have been sought, and if it has been agreed that mirror orders be put in place before the move, now is the time to ensure that everything is in order before the departure.

6.82 Whatever the outcome, a court which has recently made orders – for residence, contact, preventing or allowing relocation – will expect them to be honoured unless there has been a change of circumstances or events have not turned out as would be expected. If there are difficulties with the orders that have been made, then the correct thing to do (assuming it is not possible to resolve matters by agreement) is to apply back to the judge who originally made the orders.

6.83 If matters proceed reasonably smoothly, and the need to vary arrangements arises only after a considerable amount of time, then the proper course (if matters cannot be agreed) is to apply to the court where the children are now living.

---

[42]   Family Law Act 1986; *Re W-B (Family Proceedings: Appropriate Jurisdiction within United Kingdom)* [2012] EWCA Civ 592, [2013] 1 FLR 394.
[43]   See further **2.36** *et seq*; Brussels II Revised, Council Regulation (EC) No 2201/2003, Art 9(1); *Re I (Contact Application: Jurisdiction)* [2009] UKSC 10, [2010] 1 FLR 361 at [35]; *VC v GC (Jurisdiction: Brussels II Revised Art 12)* [2012] EWHC 1246 (Fam), [2013] 1 FLR 244.

Chapter 7

TEMPORARY INTERNATIONAL RELOCATION

7.1   Temporary international relocation can mean almost anything from a holiday to a period of temporary residence abroad for a year or two for the purposes of work or study. This chapter should be read alongside the two which precede it, since we address here the main ways in which an application for a temporary relocation is likely to differ from an application for permanent relocation. We also focus here on safeguards and other measures which may help to ensure that a temporary relocation application is not abused as a means of covertly abducting the child.

7.2   A person who has a residence order in his or her favour does not need the permission of the court to remove a child for a period of less than a month.[1] A special guardian will be able to take a child abroad for up to three months.[2] If there is a residence order in force, those wishing to take a child abroad for longer or those who are not holders of the order will either have to obtain the written consent of everyone with parental responsibility or obtain the permission of the court.[3] If there is no residence order in force at all, then a parent wishing to prevent a removal should apply for a prohibited steps order.[4]

7.3   The ease with which an applicant parent is likely to obtain permission for the temporary relocation will usually depend on the length of time involved and the intended destination, as well as the reason for the trip. The court will of course be concerned with general welfare matters, but also, depending on the circumstances, with the risk of the child being retained out of the jurisdiction. If the destination is within the EU or is a signatory to the 1980 Hague Convention, the risk is usually considered minimal. Different considerations apply if it is not.

7.4   We divide this chapter into three main sections, which address, in turn:

- short temporary moves to EU and Hague Convention countries;

---

[1]   Children Act 1989, s 13(2); see **Appendix 1.1**.
[2]   Children Act 1989, s 14C(4).
[3]   Children Act 1989, s 13(1); see **Appendix 1.1**.
[4]   Children Act 1989, s 8; see **Appendix 1.1**. As we discussed at **2.8**, removal of the child may constitute abduction even when there is no residence or contact order in force, but remedies for abduction vary in their effectiveness depending on the country to which the child is taken: see generally N Lowe, M Everall QC and M Nicholls, *International Movement of Children: Law Practice and Procedure* (Bristol, Jordan Publishing, 2004).

- short temporary moves to non-EU and non-Hague Convention countries;

- longer temporary moves.

SHORT TEMPORARY MOVES TO EU AND HAGUE CONVENTION COUNTRIES

7.5   There is usually little difficulty in obtaining permission to take a child on a short trip to another EU country or to a country which is a signatory of the Hague Convention on the Civil Aspects of International Child Abduction 1980.[5] There are straightforward legal mechanisms in place to secure the return of a child retained unlawfully in these jurisdictions, and the courts generally assume that those legal remedies will provide adequate protection.

7.6   The courts will normally regard it as in the interests of children to go on holiday with one of their parents, unless the children are very young indeed or the parent can somehow not be trusted to ensure the children are safe and well cared for abroad. A holiday which does not interfere with schooling or exams, and which does not unduly affect the time the child will have with the other parent, will therefore usually be looked upon very favourably. Most parents recognise this, and disputes about holidays of this type are rare. It is common for both parents to wish to take the child on holiday and one parent is unlikely to object to something that they wish to do too.

SHORT TEMPORARY MOVES TO NON-EU AND NON-HAGUE CONVENTION COUNTRIES

7.7   Applications to take children outside the EU to a country which is not a signatory of the Hague Convention on the Civil Aspects of International Child Abduction 1980,[6] should be heard in the High Court (or, if the case is urgent and no High Court judge is available, before a senior circuit judge authorised to sit as a High Court judge under s 9 of the Senior Courts Act 1981).[7] The reason for having the case heard in the High Court is that it provides greater flexibility,[8] and a more potent judicial authority in case there is any difficulty regarding the child's return.

7.8   In particular, if the child is not returned, the respondent parent may have difficulty relying on the legal system in the destination country to enforce the child's return. Orders from the High Court regulating a child's residence and

---

5   A list of countries that have acceded to the Convention can be found in **Appendix 6.1**, or online at www.hcch.net/index_en.php?act=conventions.status&cid=24.
6   Pakistan is a slightly special case because of the UK-Pakistan Judicial Protocol on Child Abduction 2003.
7   See *Practice Direction: Allocation and Transfer of Proceedings* [2009] 1 FLR 365, para [5.2].
8   In particular, the possibility of making the child a ward of court is available only in the High Court; see **7.11**.

visit abroad are likely to carry more weight with a foreign court, and the wardship jurisdiction can be invoked to provide added security. Both within wardship and otherwise, the High Court may have greater flexibility to make orders which will have the effect of making it more difficult to retain the child abroad unlawfully.

7.9   Aside from the general welfare considerations involving an application to take a child abroad, the main issue in temporary international relocation cases is the risk of non-return. The court must assess not only the likelihood of the risk of abduction to (or more accurately, unlawful retention in) the foreign country, but also the consequences to the children and other parent if that does occur. If a child is not returned home and is thereby prevented from having contact with the remaining parent, possibly for many years, he or she is likely to suffer considerable harm.

7.10   Part of the assessment of risk involves an assessment of the applicant herself. The court will ask itself questions designed to answer the following points:

- does the applicant parent have a good record of reliability so far as contact or shared residence arrangements are concerned, and more generally?

- have the children been taken abroad before and, if so, were they returned on time and without difficulty?

- what are the ties that the applicant has with this country? If the applicant has a job here, property and family, then it will be less likely that she will abandon everything and remain abroad. Likewise the greater the connections the applicant has with the destination country, the greater the risk of retention.

7.11   The normal approach to these applications is for the court to require all practical safeguards to be first put in place before the removal is sanctioned.[9] Examples of safeguards which can be put in place include:

- **mirror orders** in the court of the destination country;[10]

- **notarised agreements** whereby family members agree to ensure that children are returned at the end of a holiday or visit;

---

[9]   See, eg, *Re K (Removal from Jurisdiction: Practice)* [1999] 2 FLR 1084 (CA).

[10]   A mirror order is where the local court in the foreign jurisdiction is asked to make an order there in identical terms to the order made in the English court. Many jurisdictions will happily do this, though sometimes not until the child is physically present in the new country, which of course makes this option far less use in the case of a short temporary move. It is also worth being aware that in some countries the idea of a mirror order is not recognised and therefore such an order cannot be obtained.

- **monetary bonds** whereby the applicant is required to deposit a sum of money in a bank account; the money is then not released until the child is returned, and is usually made available (after a court application) to the respondent parent to use to fund his efforts to secure the child's return;[11]

- **undertakings** given by the applicant to return the child;

- **solemn, witnessed declarations** by the applicant and by family members to ensure the return of the child;[12]

- **a written agreement** by an applicant to transfer an interest in property to the other parent if the child is not returned by a specified date;[13]

- **having the child made a ward of court** by a High Court judge.[14] Wardship is more commonly used as a way of getting a child returned after an unlawful removal or retention, but it is occasionally used pre-emptively, before a temporary move takes place, as an incentive for bringing the child back in a timely manner. There is an automatic restriction on any ward being removed from the jurisdiction of England and Wales without the court's permission,[15] so if this route is taken then express consent from the court will be required specifying when and to where the child may be removed.

7.12   In a high risk case it may be necessary for the court to have expert evidence as to the legal system in the country of destination in case the children are not returned. Mirror orders, if it is practical to obtain such, are considered an important safeguard, and expert evidence as to the ease of obtaining them and the likelihood of them being properly and speedily enforced will be invaluable in some cases. If the court can be reassured that the foreign legal system is likely to enforce a return, this will remove or limit an important hurdle for the applicant. As can be seen above, there are other safeguards that can be used, involving the applicant and wider family members giving relevant undertakings and providing financial security. The list above is not exhaustive and can be adapted to meet the particular circumstances of the case.

7.13   It is of course not always possible to obtain expert evidence about the legal system in the destination, or mirror orders, having regard to the expense and timescales involved. Depending on the circumstances of an individual case,

---

[11]   *Re L (Removal from Jurisdiction: Holiday)* [2001] 1 FLR 241 (FD); in that case the sum was of £50,000 when the destination was the United Arab Emirates.

[12]   See, for example, the order of Wall J in *Re A (Security for Return to Jurisdiction)* [1999] 2 FLR 1 (FD); see **Appendix 3.4**. Similar provisions were ordered in *Re L (Removal from Jurisdiction: Holiday)* [2001] 1 FLR 241 (FD): one of the preconditions of leave was that the applicant was required to swear on the Koran.

[13]   *Re S and O (Temporary Removal from Jurisdiction)* [2009] *Family Law* 114 (FD).

[14]   See Practice Direction 12D: Inherent Jurisdiction (Including Wardship) Proceedings.

[15]   Ibid, para [4.1]. Note that this restriction covers England and Wales and not, as under s 13 of the Children Act 1989, the United Kingdom.

the court will not inevitably require expert evidence or mirror orders;[16] however, it must be understood to be 'the normal practice' that expert evidence will be required, and a judge concluding that it is not should 'explain very clearly why [expert evidence] is not required in a particular case'.[17]

7.14 It is good practice for there to be a declaration that the children are habitually resident in England and Wales and that the children should be returned by a particular date. The applicant parent should be expected to provide the court and the other parent with proof that return tickets have been purchased, along with a full itinerary and contact details.

Case Example: *Re M (Removal from Jurisdiction: Adjournment)* **[2010] EWCA Civ 888, [2011] 1 FLR 1943**

The respondent mother appealed against a decision allowing the applicant father to take the child on holiday to Cameroon. The judge had refused an adjournment for the purposes of obtaining an expert's opinion on the legal situation in Cameroon and on ways in which the child could be recovered in the event that the father retained him there, and had authorised the father's holiday. The judge had initially thought the father could go to the High Commission of Cameroon in London and make a notarised agreement to return the child to the jurisdiction of the English court, which turned out to be incorrect.

Allowing the appeal, Black LJ said:

> '[24] Whilst I would not want to be thought to be saying that no application of this type can proceed without expert evidence to deal with the practicalities of the foreign legal system and how a return from a non Hague Convention country could proceed if the child were not returned, it is in my view incumbent on a judge to approach the matter in accordance with *Re K*[18] with an inclination that such expert evidence will be necessary and, if he or she concludes it is not necessary, to explain very clearly why what might be classed as the normal practice is not required in a particular case. The judge did not do that here.
>
> [26] As to the judge's approach to the mother having declined to give prospective consent to removal if the expert was able to deal with the practicalities, that was not, in my view, a factor that should have carried➡

---

[16] See, eg, *Re S (Leave to Remove from the Jurisdiction: Securing Return from Holiday)* [2001] 2 FLR 507 (FD), which concerned an application to take children on holiday to India, and *Re S and O (Temporary Removal from Jurisdiction)* [2009] *Family Law* 114 (FD), which concerned a holiday in Barbados.

[17] *Re M (Removal from Jurisdiction: Adjournment)* [2010] EWCA Civ 888, [2011] 1 FLR 1943 at [24]. The importance of this issue, and the consequences if it goes wrong, probably explains why expert evidence is 'the normal practice' in these cases, contrary to the general position as set out in *Re TG (Care Proceedings: Case Management: Expert Evidence)* [2013] EWCA Civ 5, [2013] 1 FLR forthcoming at [29]–[34].

[18] *Re K (Removal from Jurisdiction: Practice)* [1999] 2 FLR 1084 (CA).

> weight in determining whether to grant the adjournment for expert evidence. As the appellant argues, requiring prospective consent would have deprived the mother of the opportunity of evaluating the report, subjecting it to cross examination, exploring the options that the report contained, and seeking to put the advice into the context of the entire case as the judge would have had to do.'

7.15 Once the court has addressed the issue of safeguards, if it concludes that the risk of the child being retained in the foreign jurisdiction is minimal or has been adequately answered using those safeguards, the court will determine the application based on the child's welfare, informed by an analysis of the welfare checklist.[19]

LONGER TEMPORARY REMOVALS

7.16 The situation becomes different again if the temporary removal is still for a relatively long time. By 'longer temporary removals', we mean proposals for the child to be out of the country for longer than a normal holiday, but where the clear intention is that the child will return to this country in the foreseeable future (at most, say, three or four years).

7.17 These cases fall somewhere between the holiday cases discussed above and the permanent removal discussed in Chapters 5 and 6. In legal terms, the guidance from the permanent relocation cases is not necessarily applicable to applications for temporary removal,[20] but many of those considerations will have some bearing here in ways that they might not for a holiday or other short removal. In short, '[t]he more temporary the removal, the less regard should be paid to the principles stated in *Payne v Payne*'.[21]

7.18 In particular, the court will want to address the following points from the standard guidance:

- Is the application genuinely motivated? Usually longer temporary relocations arise because of a time-limited specific opportunity which the applicant parent or her new partner has been offered, such as a fixed-term job transfer. The way in which this opportunity arose, and the applicant parent's motivation in seeking to pursue it, should be assessed.

- Is the application well researched and planned? As with a permanent move, the court will be concerned to know the applicant parent's plans for things like housing, schooling and ongoing contact between the child and the respondent parent.[22]

---

[19]   Children Act 1989, s 1(3); see **Appendix 1.1**.
[20]   *Re A (Temporary Removal from Jurisdiction)* [2004] EWCA Civ 1587, [2005] 1 FLR 639.
[21]   Ibid at [13].
[22]   See further the list of considerations set out in **3.38–3.43**.

- What will the effect of refusing the application be on the applicant parent and/or on the child? The effect of losing the specific opportunity on the applicant parent's career may be a significant factor,[23] especially if, for example, there is pressure from her employer to accept a temporary transfer.

- What effect will the move have on the child's relationship with the respondent parent? The distance involved in the move and the opportunities for ongoing contact will, as always, be a very important consideration.

7.19 In some cases, the court will also want to know whether it would be viable for the child to remain with the respondent parent for the duration of the applicant parent's temporary relocation. If the child is at school and has a shared residence arrangement, there may be less disruption to the child in remaining with the respondent parent than in making the temporary move abroad. At the same time, though, it can be argued that living in another country for a period of time is, in itself, advantageous to the child, broadening his or her experiences. These are all factors which the judge will need to weigh in each case.

Case Example: *Re A (Temporary Removal from Jurisdiction)* **[2004] EWCA Civ 1587, [2005] 1 FLR 639**

The applicant mother sought permission to remove her four year old daughter to South Africa for a period of two years to enable her to carry out research. The mother was a research associate at Newcastle University in the department of Geography, Politics and Sociology. The mother's contract (which was designed to earn her a PhD) required her to work for two years in South Africa at the University of Pretoria and also in the field. If the mother was not able to go, she was likely to lose her research job and her career would be damaged as a result.

The child was the subject of a shared residence order, spending five nights a week with the mother and two with the father. The trial judge refused the mother permission to take the child on the trip, but the mother successfully appealed. The Court of Appeal was clear that the *Payne v Payne*[24] guidance should not have been applied without significant modification to account for the fact that the proposed move was not intended to be permanent: ➡

---

[23] See, eg, *Re A (Temporary Removal from Jurisdiction)* [2004] EWCA Civ 1587, [2005] 1 FLR 639 at [14]: 'I would simply put the point in terms of the importance of the mother's career development and fulfilment. Success is of great value to her, but it is also of value to [the child], who would benefit from the mother's secure and prestigious academic position in her home city on her return from the South African work.'

[24] *Payne v Payne* [2001] EWCA Civ 166, [2001] 1 FLR 1052; see **Appendix 3.1**.

'[10] The considerations relevant to an application for permission to relocate permanently are simply not automatically, or perhaps at all, applicable to applications for temporary removal. The consequence of the misdirection is that the judge's assessment of detriment to [the child] in the diminution of contact to his father and all that is familiar, was an assessment as though the diminution and loss would be permanent and not temporary. Similarly, the criticism of the mother for prioritising her career before the interests of [the child] again proceeded as though her plan was for a permanent removal.'

The Court of Appeal stressed the fact that whilst the child's contact with the father would be reduced during the visit abroad, it would still continue and he would be able to resume the relationship fully when she returned.

7.20 Although Thorpe LJ suggested in the passage quoted above that the *Payne* guidelines might not apply at all if the removal was temporary, it is clearly a matter of degree depending on the case.[25] For example, Thorpe LJ stated that if an application involved a six-week holiday or three-month placement, 'surely no-one' would seek to suggest that judicial discretion was to be exercised by following *Payne*;[26] but, on the facts of *Re A*, with a two-year move, the position was that the judge should have 'adjusted' the guidelines rather than disapplying them altogether.[27]

CONCLUSION

7.21 As in every other case where a decision is being made about a child, the court will apply the welfare test. Everything else is a matter of guidance. Where the risk of a child being kept abroad is minimal or has otherwise been addressed, the courts will generally favour a child spending a temporary period abroad if there are no other reasons which militate against the trip. The longer the trip, the more effect it will have and the more issues are likely to be put in the balance.

7.22 There is an interesting discussion to be had as to where a proposed removal moves from being temporary to permanent. In *Re A (Temporary Removal from Jurisdiction)*,[28] the removal for two years was characterised as temporary, but after the move it is likely that the mother and child would have become ordinarily resident in South Africa. If the mother later wished to remain in South Africa permanently, would she have applied there to stay? In practical terms, could the child have been brought back? It might be noted that some international relocation cases in England and Wales stem from a factual

---

[25]   Of course, this should be the position generally in relocation cases following *K v K (Relocation: Shared Care Arrangement)* [2011] EWCA Civ 793, [2012] 2 FLR 880 (see **Appendix 3.3**), and *Re F (Permission to Relocate)* [2012] EWCA Civ 1364, [2012] 3 FCR 443.
[26]   *Re A (Temporary Removal from Jurisdiction)* [2004] EWCA Civ 1587, [2005] 1 FLR 639 at [13].
[27]   Ibid at [5].
[28]   Ibid.

background where the parents came together to this jurisdiction, originally intending to stay for only a fixed period of time but where, after the parental separation, one of them wished to remain.[29] No doubt more cases such as this will be reported and time will tell how such cases will be treated by the courts.

---

[29] See, for example, the facts of *Re F (Permission to Relocate)* [2012] EWCA Civ 1364, [2012] 3 FCR 443. The parents came together from Spain when their child was 4, because the father had a good job offer in the United Kingdom. The move was originally to last two years; the father later extended his contract by three more years. Shortly after the renewal of the contract, the mother returned to Spain, and some time later initiated legal proceedings to have the child join her there.

Chapter 8

APPEALS

8.1 Many parents, with a relocation hearing ahead of them, will suggest that if the case goes against them they will appeal. However, while they can of course try to do so, the vast majority of appeals do not succeed. Most are not even granted formal permission to appeal, and even when a case is given permission to appeal the appellate tribunal frequently upholds the decision of the trial judge.

8.2 It was sometimes thought that this general approach to appeals was not applied with quite the same rigour to relocation cases. There was a view amongst both academics and practitioners in the mid-2000s that international relocation cases were routinely given permission to appeal, especially if the trial judge had refused the relocation application.[1] However, we would caution against such a view, since applications for permission to appeal relocation cases are turned down, both on paper and at renewed oral hearings, on a regular basis.

8.3 Indeed, research recently conducted by one of the authors suggests that applications to appeal relocation cases are usually refused permission to appeal.[2] While it is difficult to be sure whether all applications have been collected,[3] the research aimed to gather all applications for permission to appeal international relocation cases in 2012. The findings are set out in Table 8.1.

---

[1] See, eg, M Hayes, 'Relocation Cases: Is the Court of Appeal Applying the Correct Principles?' [2006] *Child and Family Law Quarterly* 351, pp 369–371; for some practitioners' views on this issue in 2008–2009, see R George, *Relocation Disputes: Law and Practice in England and New Zealand* (Oxford, Hart Publishing, 2013), Ch 4.

[2] Dr Rob George collected materials relating to relocation cases in 2012. While most of these materials related to decisions of first instance courts, he also collected documents relating to appeals, which form the basis of this discussion.

[3] Note that appeals from decisions of district judges in the county courts are heard by circuit judges, and those cases have not been collected as part of Dr George's study. That ought not to have affected many international relocation cases, since district judges in the court courts do not normally hear such cases; but it does mean that we cannot comment on applications for permission to appeal relocation decisions taken by district judges in the county courts.

Table 8.1: Table of applications for permission to appeal international relocation cases showing type of judge hearing the original case and the court hearing the appeal.

Decision of	*Appeal to*	*No of applications for PTA received*	*No of applications granted PTA*	*No of appeals then allowed*
High Court judge	Court of Appeal	2	0	-
Circuit judge	Court of Appeal	10	4	0
District judge (PRFD)	High Court	2	0	-

8.4   What this research shows is that, in 2012, out of 12 applications for permission to appeal international relocation cases to the Court of Appeal, only four were given permission to appeal. Three then proceeded to a full hearing, but not one appeal was successful.[4] There is no base-line data with which to compare the 2012 findings, so we cannot comment on whether there has been any change in practice from earlier years.[5] However, looking at cases which are in the public domain,[6] the Court of Appeal has not heard more than two or three relocation appeals in the last several years.[7] It seems certain that these numbers represent a small proportion of the number of applications for permission to appeal which the Court of Appeal received. Consequently, there is every reason to think that the trial judge's determination is likely to be the end of the matter, and the chances of appealing that decision successfully are slim.

---

[4]   The Court of Appeal cases, all dismissing the appeals, were: *Re F (Permission to Relocate)* [2012] EWCA Civ 1364, [2012] 3 FCR 443; *Re O (A Child)* [2012] All ER (D) 39 (Dec) (CA); *Re E (Children)* [2012] EWCA Civ 1893. The fourth case that was given leave to appeal, *Re B (A Child)* [2012] EWCA Civ 1317, settled before the appeal was heard. The Court of Appeal also heard (and dismissed) one internal relocation appeal (see *Re S (Residence Order: Internal Relocation)* [2012] EWCA Civ 1031, [2012] 3 FCR 153) and refused permission to appeal another 2012 internal relocation (see *Re C (A Child)* [2013] EWCA Civ 55). Most internal relocation cases are heard by district judges, and therefore appeals go to the Circuit Bench, which means that we are unable to tell how many such cases seek to appeal and how many appeals succeed. Anecdotally, we think the numbers to be small.

[5]   A limited comparison with 2011 is possible, since some Permission to Appeal applications were sent to Dr George that year in preparation for the 2012 research. Consequently, it can be said that while three cases were heard in the Court of Appeal that year, at least eight more were turned down at the permission stage.

[6]   That is, either formally reported or online (eg on www.bailii.org, on www.familylaw.co.uk, or on www.familylawhub.co.uk).

[7]   As best we can tell, the number of full hearings heard in the Court of Appeal for recent years are as follows: 2008, two cases; 2009, two cases; 2010, two cases; 2011, three cases (one of which was granted permission to appeal by the trial judge).

8.5   Given the rarity of a successful appeal, therefore, all the energies of the client, solicitor and counsel must be directed towards winning the case at first instance, and in particular in trying to persuade the judge to accept the facts put forward and to make clear findings upon them. Written submissions should be prepared, either at the beginning or the end of the case for the first instance judge, directing him towards the recent authorities and explaining the relevance of those authorities to the particular facts of the case. Nobody wishes to have to explain to the Court of Appeal that they failed to draw the judge's attention to a recent case, or that they did not give the assistance that he was entitled to expect.

8.6   It is only possible to appeal a relocation decision with the permission either of the trial judge or of the appeal court,[8] and permission must be sought from the court which made the original order before the appeal court is approached directly.[9] Permission to appeal will be given only where (a) the court considers the appeal would have a real prospect of success; or (b) there is some other compelling reason for the appeal to be heard.[10]

8.7   The first limb of this test requires the appeal court to ask 'whether there is a "realistic" as opposed to a "fanciful" prospect of success' if the court heard the appeal.[11] It does not mean that the appeal must be likely to succeed on the balance of probabilities.[12] Nonetheless, given the limited power of the appeal court to interfere with the original decision,[13] it is rare for permission to appeal to be granted. In practice the trial judge will almost always refuse permission unless the case has thrown up a new point of law, or there is something very unusual about the case.

8.8   Relying on an appeal to achieve the desired outcome must therefore be thought of as a last resort. Even if permission to appeal is granted, all that the court will do is to review the decision of the trial judge. We now set out the legal principles that apply to appeals once permission has been granted.

---

[8]   CPR 1998, rr 52.3(1) and (2).
[9]   FPR 2010, rr 30.3(3) and (4); Practice Direction 30A, para [4.2].
[10]   CPR 1998, r 52.3(6).
[11]   *Swain v Hillman* [2001] 1 All ER 91 (CA) at 92; see similarly *Tanfern v Cameron-MacDonald* [2000] 1 WLR 1311 (CA) at [21], and the recent discussion by Moor J in *AV v RM (Appeal)* [2012] EWHC 1173 (Fam), [2012] 2 FLR 709 at [8]–[11].
[12]   Such a threshold was suggested by Mostyn J in *NLW v ARC* [2012] EWHC 55 (Fam), [2012] 2 FLR 129, but we agree with Moor J that such an approach would amount to a judicial gloss on the Rules and, in any case, is contrary to the Court of Appeal authority in *Swain v Hillman* [2001] 1 All ER 91 (CA) and *Tanfern v Cameron-MacDonald* [2000] 1 WLR 1311 (CA): see *AV v RM (Appeal)* [2012] EWHC 1173 (Fam), [2012] 2 FLR 709 at [9].
[13]   See **8.10** *et seq*.

THE LAW ON APPEALS

8.9   Unless there are exceptional circumstances, the appeal tribunal will not hear oral evidence. The appeal will not be allowed unless the decision of the court below was wrong, or unjust because of a serious procedural or other irregularity in the proceedings.[14]

8.10   The power of the appeal court[15] in all children cases, including both international and internal relocation cases, is limited. The appeal is categorically not a second bite of the cherry for the party who is unhappy with the original decision: it must be shown that the original decision was in some way wrong.

Procedural error or error of law

8.11   One ground of appeal is procedural error. However, these cases are vanishingly rare (none of the reported relocation cases involves procedural error), and we do not consider it any further.

8.12   Another way in which the decision could be wrong is that the judge could have made an error of law. If true, this ground of appeal is quite straightforward. However, in the context of a relocation decision, that would usually mean that the judge had failed to regard the child's welfare as the paramount consideration,[16] and demonstrating that to be the case is so unlikely that we need not give it further consideration.

8.13   It might be argued that if the judge did not follow the relevant appellate guidance and did not explain his decision not to do so, that may suffice to bring an appeal. This is possible, but at the end of the day, the point of the guidance is to help the judge consider all the relevant matters when reaching a welfare decision,[17] so if he has done that without the guidance then his decision is likely to stand.

Overlooking relevant factors or considering irrelevant ones

8.14   The next possible ground of appeal is 'that [the judge] has failed to take into account some matter which he should have taken into account, [or] has taken into account some matter which he should have left out of account'.[18]

---

[14]   CPR 1998, r 52.11(3).
[15]   Where we refer in this section to 'the Court of Appeal', that should be understood as a convenient shorthand for any court hearing a first appeal: see **8.35**.
[16]   Children Act 1989, s 1(1). In *K v K (Relocation: Shared Care Arrangement)* [2011] EWCA Civ 973, [2012] 2 FLR 880, it was confirmed that the welfare principle was indeed the only legal principle applicable to relocation cases; see extracts in **Appendix 3.3**.
[17]   *K v K (Relocation: Shared Care Arrangement)* [2011] EWCA Civ 973, [2012] 2 FLR 880; see **Appendix 3.3**.
[18]   *Re C (Leave to Remove from Jurisdiction)* [2000] 2 FLR 457 (CA) at 464.

8.15 Three things that are not meant by this ground of appeal should be noted. One is that this is not an opportunity to challenge the factual findings made by the trial judge. The judge is responsible for making the relevant findings of fact (which includes judgments about the credibility and reliability of witnesses), and it will be a very unusual case where the appeal court feels able to interfere with these findings.[19]

8.16 For example, if the judge has decided that the applicant parent's motivation for seeking to relocate is to limit or destroy the child's relationship with the other parent, there is little that can be done about this unless the judge ignored glaring evidence to the contrary. Likewise, if the finding is that she does not have such a motivation, and the parent staying behind is convinced that the judge has been hoodwinked, the chances of convincing an appellate court to overturn the trial judge's findings are minimal.

8.17 The second point is that, once the judge has made those findings of fact, she is also responsible for giving each finding the weight that she considers that it deserves in the individual case. Almost every unsuccessful litigant believes that the trial judge placed too much or too little weight on one thing or another. This is very difficult to demonstrate in practice, however, as any lawyer will know.

8.18 The difficulty for would-be appellants is that the judge's balancing of the different factors in the case (whether arising from judicial guidance or from the particular eccentricities of the case) also forms part of the judicial discretion.[20] Consequently, so long as the balance which the judge makes is within 'the generous ambit within which reasonable disagreement is possible',[21] then it will not be open to appeal:[22]

> 'If there is indeed a discretion in which various factors are relevant, the evaluation and balancing of those factors is also a matter for the trial judge. Only if his decision is so plainly wrong that he must have given far too much weight to a particular factor is the appellate court entitled to interfere ... Too ready an interference by the appellate court ... risks robbing the trial judge of the discretion entrusted to him by the law.'

8.19 Finally, even if these hurdles are overcome, it needs to be understood that what is required to be shown is not only that the judge considered some irrelevant matter (or failed to consider some relevant matter), but that this error

---

[19] See, eg, *Piglowska v Piglowski* [1999] 2 FLR 763 (HL) at 784; *Re J (Child Returned Abroad: Convention Rights)* [2005] UKHL 40, [2005] 2 FLR 802 at [10]. Wholly exceptionally, if findings of fact fly in the face of clearly contrary evidence which has not been addressed by the judge, this may be a matter for the appeal court.

[20] See, eg, *Piglowska v Piglowski* [1999] 2 FLR 763 (HL) at 784: 'the appellate court must bear in mind the advantage which the first instance judge had in seeing the parties and the other witnesses. This is well understood on questions of credibility and findings of primary fact. But it goes further than that. It applies also to the judge's evaluation of those facts.'

[21] *Bellenden (Formerly Satterthwaite) v Satterthwaite* [1948] 1 All ER 343 (CA) at 345.

[22] *Re J (Child Returned Abroad: Convention Rights)* [2005] UKHL 40, [2005] 2 FLR 802 at [12].

led the judge to reach a decision which she would not otherwise have reached. In other words, if the error cannot be shown to have made a difference to the outcome, then the appeal will not succeed.

Decision 'plainly wrong'

8.20 The final basis for an appeal is, as a sort of catch-all backup provision, that 'for some other reason, [the judge] has reached a decision which is plainly wrong'.[23] As the Court of Appeal made clear as long ago as 1948:

> It is, of course, not enough for the [party seeking to appeal] to establish that [the appeal] court might, or would, have made a different order. We are here concerned with a judicial discretion, and it is of the essence of such a discretion that on the same evidence two different minds might reach widely different decisions without either being appealable. It is only where the decision exceeds the generous ambit within which reasonable disagreement is possible, and is, in fact, plainly wrong, that an appellate body is entitled to interfere.[24]

8.21 These comments have been quoted and approved many times.[25] However, it is important to understand fully what they mean. All of the points we made in the previous section regarding findings of fact and the weighing of factors apply here too.[26] The overall effect is that those cases where the judge could have gone either way, and which are therefore finely balanced, are often the most difficult to appeal: '[t]he more difficult the decision to be made, the more difficult it is for the appellate court to interfere with the exercise of discretion vested in the judge'.[27]

8.22 It is also important to bear in mind that the judgment given by the trial judge has to be read in its entirety. Every judgment contains points which could have been expressed more clearly or more fully, and these normal imperfections will not be enough to cause the appeal court to interfere. As Lord Hoffmann once explained:[28]

> The exigencies of daily courtroom life are such that reasons for judgment will always be capable of having been better expressed ... These reasons should be read on the assumption that, unless he has demonstrated the contrary, the judge knew how he should perform his functions and which matters he should take into account.

---

[23] *Re C (Leave to Remove from Jurisdiction)* [2000] 2 FLR 457 (CA) at 464.

[24] *Bellenden (Formerly Satterthwaite) v Satterthwaite* [1948] 1 All ER 343 (CA) at 345.

[25] See especially *G v G (Minors: Custody Appeal)* [1985] FLR 894 (HL) at 898, and *Piglowska v Piglowski* [1999] 2 FLR 763 (HL) at 784.

[26] See **8.15–8.18**.

[27] *Re L, V, M and H (Contact: Domestic Violence)* [2000] 2 FLR 334 (CA) at 349.

[28] *Piglowska v Piglowski* [1999] 2 FLR 763 (HL) at 784. This point has been repeated frequently in recent Court of Appeal judgments, showing its ongoing application: see, eg, *Re B (A Child)* [2012] EWCA Civ 1475 at [5]; *Re M (Children)* [2012] EWCA Civ 1710 at [47]; *Re TG (Care Proceedings: Case Management: Expert Evidence)* [2013] EWCA Civ 5, [2013] 1 FLR forthcoming at [38]; *Re H (A Child)* [2013] EWCA Civ 72 at [69].

8.23 The appeal court consequently has a very limited scope to interfere in relocation cases. The effect of that limited power is seen most clearly at the stage of applications for permission to appeal,[29] but any family lawyer with experience in the Court of Appeal knows that the same is true of those cases which are listed for a hearing.

APPLYING FOR PERMISSION TO APPEAL

Note:

In the following discussion, we refer to procedure as relates to appeals to the Court of Appeal, since most relocation cases are appealed to that court. However, it should be noted that appeals to circuit judges in the county courts, and appeals to High Court judges (which will apply only to appeals against decisions of district judges in the Principal Registry of the Family Division) are governed by a separate Practice Direction.[30] The principles upon which an appeal will be decided are the same wherever the appeal is heard, unless the appeal is a second appeal.[31]

8.24 The parent thinking about bringing an appeal needs to keep all of these issues in mind when making his or her decision. However, given the far-reaching nature of decisions in relocation cases, it may well be worth considering seeking advice about the merits of at least a paper application to appeal. If the appeal has no realistic chance of success, it will probably stop there, and the costs and time spent will be limited. At least that way the unsuccessful parent in the trial court will know that everything has been done that is reasonably possible to assess the decision of the trial judge.

8.25 That said, lawyers must be careful not to give false hope. If counsel's opinion is that permission to appeal is unlikely to be granted, the client should be told this clearly. While the decision whether or not to seek to appeal is, at the end of the day, for the parent to make (unless he or she is publicly funded, in which case funding will only be extended if there are reasonable prospects of success), the lawyer should do what he or she can to avoid pointless applications which waste costs and judicial time.

8.26 It should be noted that, unlike the usual rule in children's cases at first instance, parties may be required to pay the other side's costs in the Court of Appeal, even if there is no evidence of bad conduct or of a wasteful approach to the litigation.[32] Therefore, the unsuccessful appellant may be ordered to pay his or her own costs and those of the other side.

---

[29] See **8.2–8.4**.
[30] See CPR 1998, Practice Direction 52B.
[31] See **8.57–8.58**.
[32] There is some doubt about the rules for costs in family cases in the Court of Appeal because of the way that the rules are drafted. The general rule that costs follow the event is set out in

8.27 As this book is being written by lawyers, it should come as no surprise that we would advise any litigant to seek specialist advice about the prospects of an appeal, preferably from counsel experienced in the appellate courts. This can save time and money in the long run, and banish false hopes. Additionally, if the appeal is to be pursued, an experienced advocate can ensure that there is a proper focus on the key points in the case.

8.28 One further important point should considered before seeking to appeal. If the reason for a parent considering applying to appeal is that he or she considers the reasons given by the judge to be inadequate or incomplete then, before the order is drawn up, the judge should be invited to expand or clarify the reasons for the decision.[33] This is especially true of *ex tempore* judgments given immediately that a case has finished, but is also true of oral decisions given later and of reserved written judgments.[34]

8.29 Appeals in all cases about the upbringing of children, including both internal and international relocation, are governed by the same rules and principles. The procedure to be followed is set out in CPR 1998, Part 52. Practice Direction 52C applies to appeals to the Court of Appeal and Practice Direction 52B to appeals from a district judge to the county court or High Court.

Applying for a stay

8.30 If the appeal is against an order permitting an applicant to relocate with a child by a given date, the fact that the order is being appealed does not, in itself, operate as a stay against the order. Therefore it is imperative for an appellant in these circumstances to apply for a stay of the order to the trial judge, or if he refuses, to the Court of Appeal.[35]

8.31 If the first instance judge refuses a stay, and the situation is genuinely urgent, the prospective appellant may telephone the Court of Appeal on 0207 947 6000 (or 0207 947 6260 out of hours) to make an application.[36] The matter may then be referred to a Deputy Master and then a Lord or Lady Justice of

---

CPR 1998, r 44.3(2). CPR 1998, r 44.3(3) disapplies this to proceedings in the Court of Appeal in connection with proceedings in the Family Division. Then FPR 2010, r 28.2(1) disapplies the costs rules in CPR 1998, r 44.3(2) and (3) generally in family proceedings. So there is a double disapplication. In *Gojkovic v Gojkovic (No 2)* [1991] 2 FLR 233 (CA) and *Baker v Rowe* [2009] EWCA Civ 1162, [2010] 1 FLR 761 the Court of Appeal stated that the court has a 'clean sheet' with respect to costs, but needed to start somewhere – and that should be that 'costs follow the event'.

[33] FPR 2010, Practice Direction 30A, paras [4.6]–[4.8].

[34] See generally *English v Emery Reimbold* [2002] EWCA Civ 605, [2002] 1 WLR 2409 at [24]–[25], approved and applied in the family law context by *Re T (Contact: Alienation: Permission To Appeal)* [2002] EWCA Civ 1736, [2003] 1 FLR 531 at [40]. More recently, *Shirt v Shirt* [2012] EWCA Civ 1029, [2013] 1 FLR 232 at [32]–[40] has clarified that it is acceptable for a judge to amend the transcript of an oral judgment, so long as the effect of the amendment is to expand upon or clarify the original reasons (not to change those reasons, and not to add new reasons).

[35] CPR 1998, r 52.7.

[36] *Re S (Child Proceedings: Urgent Appeals)* [2007] EWCA Civ 958, [2007] 2 FLR 1044.

Appeal. An out-of-hours application should be made only in cases of real need and urgency, when the matter cannot wait until the next working day because, for example, the child is going to be removed immediately.

8.32 The appellant must put forward solid grounds as to why a stay should be granted, but generally a stay will be granted if it would preserve the status quo pending an appeal. If it is alleged that delay to the children will cause great inconvenience and difficulty then the Court of Appeal may be prepared to consider the issue of permission as a matter of urgency. It is very rare for relocation cases to require this degree of urgency however, and woe betide any litigant or lawyer who uses this procedure without proper justification.

General points

8.33 There are three points that are worth stressing straight away. First, the final hearing of an international relocation case will normally have been heard by either a High Court judge, a judge of the Principal Registry of the Family Division, or a circuit judge in a county court (not by a district judge in a county court).[37] In practice, international relocation cases are, from time to time, listed before a district judge in a county court, either because the individual judge has special expertise or because of pressure on the lists.

8.34 Internal relocation cases are normally not heard in the High Court (though they can be). They are mostly heard by circuit judges and district judges in the Principal Registry and in the county courts.

8.35 The relevance of this point is that the route of appeal is different depending on the tribunal which heard the case at first instance, as shown in Table 8.2. It is important to be aware of this point so as to file a notice of appeal before the correct tribunal.[38]

---

[37] See **3.15–3.16**. As usual, we include here deputy judges of the Family Division of the High Court, senior circuit judges sitting as High Court judges under s 9 of the Senior Courts Act 1981, and recorders.

[38] It is possible to transfer cases which would normally be appealed to a circuit judge or to a High Court judge to the Court of Appeal, if the appeal 'would raise an important point of principle or practice' or 'there is some other compelling reason for the Court of Appeal to hear it': FPR 2010, r 30.13. See also **8.57–8.58** on second appeals.

Table 8.2: Table setting out to which court or judge an appeal is made (subject to obtaining the necessary permissions)[39]

Decision of	Appeal to
High Court judge (or deputy)	Court of Appeal
Circuit judge (or recorder)	Court of Appeal
District judge of the Principal Registry of the Family Division	High Court judge
District judge of a county court	Circuit judge

8.36 The second point worth noting is that, regardless of the tribunal whose decision is being appealed, the first step in bringing an appeal is to ask the trial judge for permission.[40] It will be rare for such permission to be granted, so a party seeking to appeal should then renew their application before the relevant appeal court. If the appeal court considers the application to appeal on paper only and turns the application down, the party seeking to appeal can, as of right, renew their application at an oral hearing (usually but not necessarily heard without notice to the other side).[41] If permission is then refused, there is no further appeal possible.[42]

8.37 Thirdly, as with all child law cases, time limits are crucial. The maximum time limit for filing a notice of appeal is 21 days from the date of the decision being appealed, but it is not uncommon for a shorter time limit (usually of 14 days) to be imposed in an individual case by the judge whose decision is being appealed.[43] If the application for permission to appeal is turned down on paper, the person seeking to appeal has only 7 days to renew their application if they wish to have a further oral hearing of their application.[44]

8.38 The court which is to hear any appeal has a discretion to allow an extension of these time limits,[45] but will do so only where there is good reason for failure to comply with the original limit. The application for an extension must set out the reason for the delay and all steps taken prior to the application being submitted.[46]

8.39 Assuming permission to appeal is refused by the trial judge (and even if it is not) the proposed appellant must complete an appellant's notice and file it

---

[39]   See FPR 2010, Practice Direction 30A, para [2.1].
[40]   FPR 2010, r 30.3(3); Practice Direction 30A, para [4.2].
[41]   FPR 2010, r 30.3(4)–(5); Practice Direction 30A, para [4.3]–[4.5].
[42]   FPR 2010, Practice Direction 30A, para [4.5].
[43]   FPR 2010, Practice Direction 30A, para [5.35].
[44]   FPR 2010, r 30.3(6); Practice Direction 30A, para [4.13].
[45]   FPR 2010, r 4.1(3)(a).
[46]   FPR 2010, Practice Direction 30A, para [5.4].

within 21 days of the decision. This document is known as Form N161. The form is self-explanatory, though there is also a guidance leaflet (EX340) which is readily obtained online.

8.40 The grounds of appeal should be set out in the form or on a separate sheet. All applications for permission to appeal[47] should be accompanied by a skeleton argument which complies with Section V of CPR 1998 Practice Direction 52A, along with the relevant Practice Direction which applies to the particular type of appeal.[48] This should preferably be sent at the same time or, if that is not practicable, appended within 14 days of the filing of the notice.

8.41 The skeleton argument should consist of a list of numbered points which the party wishes to make. These should define and confine the areas of controversy and each point should be stated as concisely as the nature of the case allows.[49]

8.42 CPR 1998 Practice Direction 52C gives further guidance on the documents to be included in the Court of Appeal bundle,[50] together with guidance on the inclusion of authorities and time estimates.[51]

RESPONDING TO AN APPLICATION FOR PERMISSION TO APPEAL

8.43 In general terms, a respondent does not need to do anything at all unless and until he or she is informed by the Court of Appeal that the case is going to be listed for hearing. If the case is going to be listed for hearing, this is generally because permission to appeal has been granted, or that the court has decided to list the application for permission and the appeal together (this is very common). Occasionally the Court of Appeal will list an oral hearing where only the permission to appeal is being considered, in which case the respondent will not be required to attend. If permission is granted at this hearing, then the appeal will be heard on notice at a later date.

8.44 If the case is listed for a hearing, or for 'permission to appeal with appeal to follow if granted', then a respondent may file a respondent's notice.[52] If the respondent wishes to ask for permission to appeal as well, or if he wishes to ask the Court of Appeal to uphold the order of the lower court for different or additional reasons, then he must file a respondent's notice.[53] Unless the lower court directs otherwise, the notice must be filed within 14 days of either the

---

[47] While CPR Practice Direction 52B, para [8.3], states that skeleton arguments should be used in appeals to the High Court or within the County Court only where the facts or law justify them, that will almost inevitably be the case in an appeal relating to a relocation decision.

[48] For appeals to the Court of Appeal, that means CPR 1998, Practice Direction 52C, para [31].

[49] CPR 1998, Practice Direction 52A, para [5.1].

[50] CPR 1998, Practice Direction 52C, para [27].

[51] CPR 1998, Practice Direction 52C, paras [24] and [29].

[52] CPR 1998, r 52.5(1); Practice Direction 52C, Section III.

[53] CPR 1998, r 52.5(2); Practice Direction 52C, para [8].

lower court giving permission, or of receiving notification from the Court of Appeal that the case is going to be listed.[54]

8.45 Although a respondent's notice is not necessary save for the reasons above, if one is filed then a skeleton argument must follow within 14 days,[55] and must comply with the general provisions on skeleton arguments.[56] A skeleton argument will also be needed even if no respondent's notice was filed if the respondent is legally represented and proposes to address the court.[57] The old Practice Direction stated that the skeleton should be lodged with the court no less than seven days before the appeal hearing if there is no respondent's notice. The current Practice Direction refers only to the skeleton needing to be filed '42 days after the date of listing window notification' if there is no respondent's notice, and within 14 days of the service of the notice if there is.[58] The respondent's skeleton argument, like that of the appellant, is a very important document and will help to define the issues for the Court of Appeal and to determine how long the case will take.

8.46 It follows from what has been said above that the position of the respondent is often a happier one than that of the appellant. It is generally easier to persuade the Court of Appeal that the judge was acting within the proper bounds of his discretion than otherwise. It is unwise to be complacent, however, because the fact that a case is listed at all will be significant. It will be important to scrutinise the comments of the Court of Appeal judge who listed the case for appeal, as they are often indicate the aspects of the judgment of the court below which are going to be the focus at the appeal hearing, and where there may be weaknesses.

8.47 It is important to limit the number of documents in the bundle for the Court of Appeal as much as possible. Apart from the judgment, notice(s) and skeleton arguments, it will usually be necessary to include all the statements and any expert and Cafcass reports. Exhibits are usually unnecessary.

8.48 Practice Directions 52A–E contain detailed information about the preparation and contents of the bundle, and also as to the citation of authorities, and the Court of Appeal has emphasised the need to follow this guidance.[59]

8.49 If the Court of Appeal refuses permission to appeal then after the application has been renewed at an oral hearing, is the end of the matter. There is no appeal against a decision to refuse permission to appeal.[60]

---

[54]   CPR 1998, rr 52.5(4) and (5); Practice Direction 52C, para [21].
[55]   CPR 1998, Practice Direction 52C, para [9].
[56]   CPR 1998, Practice Direction 52C, para [31].
[57]   CPR 1998, Practice Direction 52C, para [13].
[58]   CPR 1998, Practice Direction 52C, paras [9] and [21].
[59]   *TW v A City Council* [2011] EWCA Civ 17, [2011] 1 FLR 1597.
[60]   See Access to Justice Act 1999, s 54(4); FPR 2010, Practice Direction 30A, para [4.5].

THE HEARING OF APPEALS

8.50 Every appeal is limited to a review of the decision of the lower court unless the court considers that it would be in the interests of justice to hold a re-hearing. If the appeal is allowed, a remission back to the High Court or county court with all the delay and expense that would involve is often the last thing that the parties want. If the Court of Appeal can identify a specific point which the trial judge did not take into account, or placed too much weight upon, and if by putting that right the answer is obvious, then the appeal will be overturned and a new decision substituted. On the other hand, if there remain too many uncertainties and the answer is not obvious then remitting the case, either to the judge who originally heard it or to a different judge for a retrial, will be the only solution.[61]

8.51 The Court of Appeal will not generally accept fresh evidence, unless the rules in *Ladd v Marshall* apply.[62] These are:

(a) the evidence could not have been obtained with reasonable diligence for use at the trial;

(b) the evidence must be such that, if given, it would probably have an important influence on the result of the case, although it need not be decisive; and

(c) the evidence must be such as it is presumably to be believed; it must be apparently credible although it need not be incontrovertible.

In children's cases, the rules are less strictly applied,[63] and in any event the court must give effect to the overriding objective which is to do justice.[64] If a decision is taken to allow the appeal after reviewing the judgment below, then the Court of Appeal may receive fresh evidence to help decide how to dispose of the appeal, though it would be more common for the case to be remitted to a trial judge.

8.52 An oral hearing in the Court of Appeal will begin with the appellant's submissions. Sometimes the appellant's counsel will be left to develop the arguments contained in the skeleton argument at some length; but it is more common for the appeal judges, who will have read all the documents in the case, to ask questions of counsel straight away, and to challenge them on various propositions that have been set out in writing, or on weaknesses in the appeal. Counsel can expect to have to have to deal with difficult points and to concentrate on the best points in the case rather than on every point.

---

[61] See, for example, *K v K (Relocation: Shared Care Arrangement)* [2011] EWCA Civ 793, [2012] 2 FLR 880; see **Appendix 3.3**.

[62] See *Ladd v Marshall* [1954] 1 WLR 1489 (CA).

[63] *Webster v Norfolk County Council* [2009] EWCA Civ 59, [2009] 1 FLR 1378.

[64] *Sharab v Al Saud* [2009] EWCA Civ 353, [2009] 2 Lloyd's Rep 160 at [52(iii)].

8.53 It is very important for counsel to know when to stop and sit down. This is almost always sooner rather than later. It can be a hard thing to judge, and most advocates will have got this wrong at one time or another. Young or inexperienced advocates and litigants in person will be given a certain amount of leeway, but those who are experienced (and particularly those who are in silk) are rightly expected to put their points across with economy and moderation.

8.54 After the appellant's submissions have been completed, the Court of Appeal will call upon any other party who supports the appeal to ask them if they wish to add anything. Then they may call upon the respondent to make submissions. If, as is often the case, they have already decided to dismiss the appeal they will not call upon the respondent but will simply proceed to give judgment. Otherwise, the respondent will be put through a similar exercise (depending on the strength or otherwise of the case) as the appellant. Then, the Court of Appeal may proceed to judgment straight away, or reserve judgment to a later date depending on the complexity of the issues.

8.55 If the Court of Appeal hears the full appeal, regardless of the outcome, then there is a theoretical possibility of taking the case to the Supreme Court.[65] Permission to appeal to the Supreme Court should first be sought from the Court of Appeal. If this is refused, then an application can be made to the Supreme Court for permission. The time limit is 28 days from the date of the decision of the Court of Appeal. Permission will not be given unless it is considered that the proposed appeal raises an arguable point of law of general public importance which ought to be considered by the Supreme Court.[66] The Supreme Court Rules 2009 contain all the rules with respect to appeals.

8.56 The Supreme Court has yet to entertain an appeal with respect to a relocation case, and for most litigants an appeal beyond the Court of Appeal is vanishingly unlikely.

SECOND APPEALS

8.57 If the relocation decision has been taken by a district judge (whether sitting at the Principal Registry or in a county court) and has been taken on appeal to a High Court or circuit judge, then any appeal to the Court of Appeal thereafter will be a second appeal. Different principles apply to the consideration of second, as opposed to first appeals.[67]

---

[65] In the case of an appeal to a circuit judge from a district judge in a county court, or an appeal to a High Court judge from a district judge in the Principal Registry, the renewed appeal would be to the Court of Appeal: see **8.57–8.58**.

[66] UKSC Practice Direction 3, para [3.3.3].

[67] CPR 1998, r 52.13.

8.58 Permission can only be given by the Court of Appeal to appeal a decision which is itself an appeal.[68] Permission will only be given if the appeal would raise an important point of principle or practice, or if there is some compelling reason for the Court of Appeal to hear it.[69] An important point of principle or practice will only be something which has not yet been established, and must of course be on a point or points that would be relevant in other cases. 'Some other compelling reason' is a reserve power, enabling the court to hear an appeal if the circumstances warrant it, for example if there has been a procedural irregularity rendering the hearings below unfair, or some other point upon which the court should intervene.[70] It is rare for second appeals to be allowed.

---

[68] CPR 1998, r 52.13(1); Practice Direction 52A, para [4.7].

[69] CPR 1998, rr 52.13(2)(a) and (b).

[70] See *Uphill v BRB (Residuary) Ltd* [2005] EWCA Civ 60, [2005] 1 WLR 2070. There is some suggestion that 'the effect of a decision relating to the welfare or future upbringing of a child may itself constitute a compelling reason for hearing a second appeal' (see *Re B (Residence: Grandparents)* [2009] EWCA Civ 545, [2009] 2 FLR 632 at [14]; rev'd on other grounds *Re B (A Child)* [2009] UKSC 5, [2010] 1 FLR 551), but this is far from clear and the authors are not aware of any second appeal being heard on this basis.

Appendix 1

EXTRACTS FROM KEY LEGISLATIVE PROVISIONS

1.1

CHILDREN ACT 1989

A1.1

Authors' Note

At time of writing, the government was proposing legislation which would replace 'residence orders' and 'contact orders' under s 8 of the Children Act 1989 with 'child arrangements orders'. The proposed legislation envisages two types of child arrangements order: an order regulating with whom a child should live and when; and an order regulating with whom a child should spend time or otherwise have contact and when. It further envisages that s 13 of the Children Act 1989 be amended so that (i) no person may remove the child from the UK if there is a child arrangements order in place regulating with whom the child concerned is to live and / or when the child is to live with any person, without the written consent of every person with parental responsibility for the child or permission from the court and (ii) a person who is named in a child arrangements order as a person with whom the child is to live may remove the child from the United Kingdom for up to one month.

Separately, a proposed new s 1(2A) would instruct the court to presume, unless the contrary were shown, that the involvement of each of a child's parents in the child's life would further the child's welfare. It is difficult to predict what effect (if any) such a provision would have on relocation law.

The Act as produced here was correct at time of going to press.

1 Welfare of the child

(1) When a court determines any question with respect to –

    (a) the upbringing of a child; or
    (b) the administration of a child's property or the application of any income arising from it,

the child's welfare shall be the court's paramount consideration.

(2) In any proceedings in which any question with respect to the upbringing of a child arises, the court shall have regard to the general principle that any delay in determining the question is likely to prejudice the welfare of the child.

(3) In the circumstances mentioned in subsection (4), a court shall have regard in particular to –

(a)   the ascertainable wishes and feelings of the child concerned (considered in the light of his age and understanding);

(b)   his physical, emotional and educational needs;

(c)   the likely effect on him of any change in his circumstances;

(d)   his age, sex, background and any characteristics of his which the court considers relevant;

(e)   any harm which he has suffered or is at risk of suffering;

(f)   how capable each of his parents, and any other person in relation to whom the court considers the question to be relevant, is of meeting his needs;

(g)   the range of powers available to the court under this Act in the proceedings in question.

(4) The circumstances are that –

(a)   the court is considering whether to make, vary or discharge a section 8 order, and the making, variation or discharge of the order is opposed by any party to the proceedings; or

(b)   the court is considering whether to make, vary or discharge [a special guardianship order or] an order under Part IV.

(5) Where a court is considering whether or not to make one or more orders under this Act with respect to a child, it shall not make the order or any of the orders unless it considers that doing so would be better for the child than making no order at all.

8 Residence, contact and other orders with respect to children

(1) In this Act –

'a contact order' means an order requiring the person with whom a child lives, or is to live, to allow the child to visit or stay with the person named in the order, or for that person and the child otherwise to have contact with each other;

'a prohibited steps order' means an order that no step which could be taken by a parent in meeting his parental responsibility for a child, and which is of a kind specified in the order, shall be taken by any person without the consent of the court;

'a residence order' means an order settling the arrangements to be made as to the person with whom a child is to live; and

'a specific issue order' means an order giving directions for the purpose of determining a specific question which has arisen, or which may arise, in connection with any aspect of parental responsibility for a child.

(2) In this Act 'a section 8 order' means any of the orders mentioned in subsection (1) and any order varying or discharging such an order.

9 Restrictions on making section 8 orders

(5) No court shall exercise its powers to make a specific issue order or prohibited steps order –

(a)   with a view to achieving a result which could be achieved by making a residence or contact order

11 General principles and supplementary provisions

(7) A section 8 order may –

(a)   contain directions about how it is to be carried into effect;
(b)   impose conditions which must be complied with by any person—
    (i)   in whose favour the order is made;
    (ii)   who is a parent of the child concerned;
    (iii)   who is not a parent of his but who has parental responsibility for him; or
    (iv)   with whom the child is living,
    and to whom the conditions are expressed to apply;
(c)   be made to have effect for a specified period, or contain provisions which are to have effect for a specified period;
(d)   make such incidental, supplemental or consequential provision as the court thinks fit.

13 Change of child's name or removal from jurisdiction

(1) Where a residence order is in force with respect to a child, no person may –

(a)   …
(b)   remove him from the United Kingdom;

without either the written consent of every person who has parental responsibility for the child or the leave of the court.

(2) Subsection (1)(b) does not prevent the removal of a child, for a period of less than one month, by the person in whose favour the residence order is made.

(3) In making a residence order with respect to a child the court may grant the leave required by subsection (1)(b), either generally or for specified purposes.

Appendix 2

EXTRACTS FROM KEY PRACTICE DIRECTIONS

2.1

PRACTICE DIRECTION 3A
PRE-APPLICATION PROTOCOL FOR
MEDIATION INFORMATION AND
ASSESSMENT

A2.1

This Practice Direction supplements FPR Part 3 (Pre-Application Protocol for Mediation Information and Assessment)

Introduction

1.1 This Practice Direction applies where a person is considering applying for an order in family proceedings of a type specified in Annex B (referred to in this Direction as "relevant family proceedings").

1.2 Terms used in this Practice Direction and the accompanying Pre-action Protocol have the same meaning as in the FPR.

1.3 This Practice Direction is supplemented by the following Annexes:

(i)   Annex A: The Pre-application Protocol ("the Protocol"), which sets out steps which the court will normally expect an applicant to follow before an application is made to the court in relevant family proceedings;

(ii) Annex B: Proceedings which are "relevant family proceedings" for the purposes of this Practice Direction; and

(iii) Annex C: Circumstances in which attendance at a Mediation Information and Assessment Meeting is not expected.

Aims

2.1 The purpose of this Practice Direction and the accompanying Protocol is to:

(a)   supplement the court's powers in Part 3 of the FPR to encourage and facilitate the use of alternative dispute resolution;

(b)   set out good practice to be followed by any person who is considering making an application to court for an order in relevant family proceedings; and

(c)   ensure, as far as possible, that all parties have considered mediation as an alternative means of resolving their disputes.

Rationale

3.1 There is a general acknowledgement that an adversarial court process is not always best suited to the resolution of family disputes, particularly private law disputes between parents relating to children, with such disputes often best resolved through discussion and agreement, where that can be managed safely and appropriately.

3.2 Litigants who seek public funding for certain types of family proceedings are (subject to some exceptions) already required to attend a meeting with a mediator as a pre- condition of receiving public funding.

3.3 There is growing recognition of the benefits of early information and advice about mediation and of the need for those wishing to make an application to court, whether publicly funded or otherwise, to consider alternative means of resolving their disputes, as appropriate.

3.4 In private law proceedings relating to children, the court is actively involved in helping parties to explore ways of resolving their dispute. The Private Law Programme, set out in Practice Direction 12B, provides for a first hearing dispute resolution appointment ('FHDRA'), at which the judge, legal advisor or magistrates, accompanied by an officer from Cafcass (the Children and Family Court Advisory and Support Service), will discuss with parties both the nature of their dispute and whether it could be resolved by mediation or other alternative means and can give the parties information about services which may be available to assist them. The court should also have information obtained through safeguarding checks carried out by Cafcass, to ensure that any agreement between the parties, or any dispute resolution process selected, is in the interests of the child and safe for all concerned.

3.5 Against that background, it is likely to save court time and expense if the parties take steps to resolve their dispute without pursuing court proceedings. Parties will therefore be expected to explore the scope for resolving their dispute through mediation before embarking on the court process.

The Pre-application Protocol

4.1 To encourage this approach, all potential applicants for a court order in relevant family proceedings will be expected, before making their application, to have followed the steps set out in the Protocol. This requires a potential applicant except in certain specified circumstances, to consider with a mediator whether the dispute may be capable of being resolved through mediation. The court will expect all applicants to have compiled with the Protocol before commencing proceedings and (except where any of the circumstances In Annex C applies) will expect any respondent to have attended a Mediation Information and Assessment Meeting, if invited to do so. If court proceedings are taken, the court will wish to know at the first hearing whether mediation has been considered by the parties. In considering the conduct of any relevant family proceedings, the court will take into account any failure to comply with the Protocol and may refer the parties to a meeting with a mediator before the proceedings continue further.

4.2 Nothing in the Protocol is to be read as affecting the operation of the Private Law Programme, set out in Practice Direction 12B, or the role of the court at the first hearing in any relevant family proceedings.

Annex A – The Pre-application Protocol

1 This Protocol applies where a person ("the applicant") is considering making an application to the court for an order in relevant family proceedings.

2 Before an applicant makes an application to the court for an order in relevant family proceedings, the applicant (or the applicant's legal representative) should contact a family mediator to arrange for the applicant to attend an information meeting about family mediation and other forms of alternative dispute resolution (referred to in this Protocol as "a Mediation Information and Assessment Meeting").

3 An applicant is not expected to attend a Mediation Information and Assessment Meeting where any of the circumstances set out in Annex C applies.

4 Information on how to find a family mediator may be obtained from local family courts, from the Community Legal Advice Helpline – CLA Direct (0845 345 4345) or at www.direct.gov.uk.

5 The applicant (or the applicant's legal representative) should provide the mediator with contact details for the other party or parties to the dispute ("the respondent(s)"), so that the mediator can contact the respondent(s) to discuss that party's willingness and availability to attend a Mediation Information and Assessment Meeting.

6 The applicant should then attend a Mediation Information and Assessment Meeting arranged by the mediator. If the parties are willing to attend together, the meeting may be conducted jointly, but where necessary separate meetings may be held. If the applicant and respondent(s) do not attend a joint meeting, the mediator will invite the respondent(s) to a separate meeting unless any of the circumstances set out in Annex C applies.

7 A mediator who arranges a Mediation Information and Assessment Meeting with one or more parties to a dispute should consider with the party or parties concerned whether public funding may be available to meet the cost of the meeting and any subsequent mediation. Where none of the parties is eligible for, or wishes to seek, public funding, any charge made by the mediator for the Mediation Information and Assessment Meeting will be the responsibility of the party or parties attending, in accordance with any agreement made with the mediator.

8 If the applicant then makes an application to the court in respect of the dispute, the applicant should at the same time file a completed Family Mediation Information and Assessment Form (Form FM1) confirming attendance at a Mediation Information and Assessment Meeting or giving the reasons for not attending.

9 The Form FM1, must be completed and signed by the mediator, and countersigned by the applicant or the applicant's legal representative, where either:

(a) the applicant has attended a Mediation Information and Assessment Meeting; or

(b) the applicant has not attended a Mediation Information and Assessment Meeting and

(i) the mediator is satisfied that mediation is not suitable because another party to the dispute is unwilling to attend a Mediation Information and Assessment Meeting and consider mediation;

(ii) the mediator determines that the case is not suitable for a Mediation Information and Assessment Meeting; or

(iii) a mediator has made a determination within the previous four months that the case is not suitable for a Mediation Information and Assessment Meeting or for mediation.

10 In all other circumstances, the Form FM1 must be completed and signed by the applicant or the applicant's legal representative.

11 The form may be obtained from magistrates' courts, county courts or the High Court or from www.direct.gov.uk.

Annex B – Proceedings which are "relevant family proceedings" for the purposes of this Practice Direction

1 Private law proceedings relating to children, except:

- proceedings for an enforcement order, a financial compensation order or an order under paragraph 9 or Part 2 of Schedule A1 to the Children Act 1989;
- any other proceedings for enforcement of an order made in private law proceedings; or
- where emergency proceedings have been brought in respect of the same child(ren) and have not been determined.

("Private law proceedings" and "emergency proceedings" are defined in Rule 12.2)

2 Proceedings for a financial remedy, except:

- Proceedings for an avoidance of disposition order or an order preventing a disposition;
- Proceedings for enforcement of any order made in financial remedy proceedings.

("Financial remedy" is defined in Rule 2.3(1) and "avoidance of disposition order" and "order preventing a disposition" are defined in Rule 9.3(1))

Annex C – A person considering making an application to the court in relevant family proceedings is not expected to attend a Mediation Information and Assessment Meeting before doing so if any of the following circumstances applies:

1 The mediator is satisfied that mediation is not suitable because another party to the dispute is unwilling to attend a Mediation Information and Assessment Meeting and consider mediation.

2 The mediator determines that the case is not suitable for a Mediation Information and Assessment Meeting.

3 A mediator has made a determination within the previous four months that the case is not suitable for a Mediation Information and Assessment Meeting or for mediation.

4 *Domestic abuse*

Any party has, to the applicant's knowledge, made an allegation of domestic violence against another party and this has resulted in a police investigation or the issuing of civil proceedings for the protection of any party within the last 12 months.

5 *Bankruptcy*

The dispute concerns financial issues and the applicant or another party is bankrupt.

6 The parties are in agreement and there is no dispute to mediate.

7 The whereabouts of the other party are unknown to the applicant.

8 The prospective application is for an order in relevant family proceedings which are already in existence and are continuing.

9 The prospective application is to be made without notice to the other party.

10 *Urgency*

The prospective application is urgent, meaning:

    (a)   there is a risk to the life, liberty or physical safety of the applicant or his or her family or his or her home; or

    (b)   any delay caused by attending a Mediation Information and Assessment Meeting would cause a risk of significant harm to a child, a significant risk of a miscarriage of justice, unreasonable hardship to the applicant or irretrievable problems in dealing with the dispute (such as an Irretrievable loss of significant evidence).

11 There is current social services involvement as a result of child protection concerns in respect of any child who would be the subject of the prospective application.

12 A child would be a party to the prospective application by virtue of Rule 12.3(1).

13 The applicant (or the applicant's legal representative) contacts three mediators within 15 miles of the applicant's home and none is able to conduct a Mediation Information and Assessment Meeting within 15 working days of the date of contact.

2.2

PRACTICE DIRECTION 12B
THE REVISED PRIVATE LAW
PROGRAMME

A2.2

This Practice Direction supplements FPR Part 12.

1 Introduction

1.1 The Private Law Programme has achieved marked success in enabling the resolution of the majority of cases by consent at the First Hearing Dispute Resolution Appointment ("FHDRA"). It has been revised to build on the successes of the initial programme and to take account of recent developments in the law and practice associated with private family law.

1.2 In particular, there have been several legislative changes affecting private family law. The Allocation and Transfer of Proceedings Order 2008 (the "Allocation Order"), requires the transfer of cases from the County Court to the Family Proceedings Court (FPC). Sections 1 to 5 and Schedule 1 of the Children and Adoption Act 2006 which came into force on 8 December 2008, amends the Children Act 1989 by introducing Contact Activity Directions, Contact Activity Conditions, Contact Monitoring Requirements, Financial Compensation Orders and Enforcement Orders.

1.3 There has been growing recognition of the impact of domestic violence and abuse, drug and alcohol misuse and mental illness, on the proper consideration of the issues in private family law; this includes the acceptance that Court orders, even those made by consent, must be scrutinised to ensure that they are safe and take account of any risk factors. Coupled with this is the need to take account of the duty on Cafcass, pursuant to s 16A Children Act 1989, to undertake risk assessments where an officer of the Service ("Cafcass Officer") suspects that a child is at risk of harm. (References to Cafcass include CAFCASS CYMRU and references to the Cafcass Officer include the Welsh family proceedings officer in Wales).

1.4 There is awareness of the importance of involving children where appropriate in the decision making process.

1.5 The Revised Programme incorporates these developments. It also retains the essential feature of the FHDRA as the forum for the parties to be helped to reach agreement as to, and understanding of, the issues that divide them. It recognises that having reached agreement parties may need assistance in putting it into effect in a co-operative way.

1.6 The Revised Programme is designed to provide a framework for the consistent national approach to the resolution of the issues in private family law whilst enabling local practices and initiatives to be operated in addition and within the framework.

1.7 The Revised Programme is designed to assist parties to reach safe agreements where possible, to provide a forum in which to find the best way to resolve issues in each individual case and to promote outcomes that are sustainable, that are in the best interests of children and that take account of their perspectives.

2 Principles

2.1 Where an application is made to a court under Part II of the Children Act 1989, the child's welfare is the court's paramount concern. The court will apply the principle of the "Overriding Objective" to enable it to deal with a case justly, having regard to the welfare principles involved. So far as practicable the Court will –

(a) Deal expeditiously and fairly with every case;
(b) Deal with a case in ways which are proportionate to the nature, importance and complexity of the issues;
(c) Ensure that the parties are on an equal footing;
(d) Save unnecessary expense;
(e) Allot to each case an appropriate share of the court's resources, while taking account of the need to allot resources to other cases.

2.2 The court will give effect to the overriding objective when applying this programme and when exercising its powers to manage cases.

The parties are required to help the court further the overriding objective and promote the welfare of the child by the application of the welfare principle, pursuant to s 1(1) of the Children Act 1989.

This Programme provides that consideration and discussion of all issues will not take place until the FHDRA when parties are on an equal footing and can hear what is said to and by each other. This excludes the safety checks and enquiries carried out by Cafcass before the first hearing that are required for that hearing and deal only with safety issues.

At the **FHDRA** the Court shall consider in particular –

(a) Whether and the extent to which the parties can safely resolve some or all of the issues with the assistance of the Cafcass Officer and any available mediator.
(b) Risk identification followed by active case management including risk assessment, and compliance with the Practice Direction 14 January 2009: "Residence and Contact Orders: Domestic Violence and Harm".
(c) Further dispute resolution.

(d) The avoidance of delay through the early identification of issues and timetabling, subject to the Allocation Order.
(e) Judicial scrutiny of the appropriateness of consent orders.
(f) Judicial consideration of the way to involve the child.
(g) Judicial continuity.

3 Practical arrangements before the FHDRA

3.1 Applications shall be issued on the day of receipt in accordance with the appropriate Rules of Procedure. It is important that the form C100 is fully completed, especially on pages 1, 2, 3 and 5 otherwise delay may be caused by requests for information.

3.2 If possible at the time of issue, and in any event by no later than 24 hours after issue, or in courts where applications are first considered on paper, by no later than 48 hours after issue, the court shall

(i) send or hand to the Applicant
(ii) send to Cafcass

the following:

(a) a copy of the Application Form C100, (together with Supplemental Information Form C1A) (if provided) (references to form C1A are to be read as form C100A following the introduction of this replacement form),
(b) the Notice of Hearing
(c) the Acknowledgment Form C7,
(d) a blank Form C1A,
(e) the Certificate of Service Form C9,
(f) information leaflets for the parties.

3.3 Save in urgent cases that require an earlier listing, the fully effective operation of this Practice Direction requires the FHDRA to take place within **4** weeks of the application. Where practicable, the first hearing must be listed to be heard in this period and in any event no later than within **6** weeks of the application. Where, at the time of introduction of this Programme, the Designated Family Judge/Justices' Clerk determines that it is not practicable to list the first hearing within 4 weeks, they should, in consultation with HMCS and Cafcass, formulate a timetable for revisiting the position and managing to list the FHDRA within 4 weeks.

3.4 Copies of each Application Form C100 and Notice of Hearing shall be sent by the court to Cafcass in accordance with 3.2 above.

3.5 The Respondent shall have at least 14 days notice of the hearing where practicable, but the court may abridge this time.

3.6 The Respondent should file a response on the Forms C7/C1A no later than 14 days before the hearing.

3.7 A copy of Forms C7/C1A shall be sent by the court to Cafcass on the day of receipt.

3.8 **NOTE:** This provision relates to cases that are placed in the FHDRA list for hearing other than by direct application in accordance with the procedure referred to in paragraph 3.1. Such listing may follow an application under the Family Law Act 1996, or a direction by the Court in other proceedings. In all such cases, or where the Court adjourns proceedings to a 'dispute resolution hearing' (sometimes called 'conciliation'), this will be treated as an adjournment to a FHDRA, and the documents referred to in para 3.2 must be filed and copied to parties and Cafcass for safety checks and enquiries, in the same way.

3.9 Before the FHDRA Cafcass shall identify any safety issues by the steps outlined below. Such steps shall be confined to matters of safety. Neither Cafcass nor a Cafcass Officer shall discuss with either party before the FHDRA any matter other than relates to safety. The Parties will not be invited to talk about other issues, for example relating to the substance of applications or replies or about issues concerning matters of welfare or the prospects of resolution. If such issues are raised by either party they will be advised that such matters will be deferred to the FHDRA when there is equality between the parties and full discussion can take place which will also be a time when any safety issues that have been identified also can be taken into account.

(a)   In order to inform the court of possible risks of harm to the child in accordance with its safeguarding framework Cafcass will carry out safeguarding enquiries, including checks of local authorities and police, and telephone risk identification interviews with parties.

(b)   If risks of harm are identified, Cafcass may invite parties to meet separately with the Cafcass Officer before the FHDRA to clarify any safety issue.

(c)   Cafcass shall record and outline any safety issues for the court.

(d)   The Cafcass Officer will not initiate contact with the child prior to the FHDRA. If contacted by a child, discussions relating to the issues in the case will be postponed to the day of the hearing or after when the Cafcass officer will have more knowledge of the issues.

(e)   At least 3 days before the hearing the Cafcass Officer shall report the outcome of risk identification work to the court by completing the Form at Schedule 2.

4 The First Hearing Dispute Resolution Appointment

4.1 The parties and Cafcass Officer shall attend this hearing. A mediator may attend where available.

4.2 At the hearing, which is not privileged, the court should have the following documents:

(a)   C100 application, and C1A if any
(b)   Notice of Hearing
(c)   C7 response and C1A if any
(d)   Schedule 2 safeguarding information

4.3 The detailed arrangements for the participation of mediators will be arranged locally. These will include:

(a) Arrangements for the mediator to ask the parties in a particular case to consent to the mediator seeing the papers in the case where it seems appropriate to do so.

(b) Arrangements for the mediator to ask the parties to waive privilege for the purpose of the first hearing where it seems to the mediator appropriate to do so in order to assist the work of the mediator and the outcome of the first hearing.

(c) In all cases it is important that such arrangements are put in place in a way that avoids any pressure being brought to bear in this connection on the parties that is inconsistent with general good mediation practice.

4.4 At the FHDRA the Court, in collaboration with the Cafcass Officer, and with the assistance of any mediator present, will seek to assist the parties in conciliation and in resolution of all or any of the issues between them. Any remaining issues will be identified, the Cafcass Officer will advise the court of any recommended means of resolving such issues and directions will be given for the future resolution of such issues. At all times the decisions of the Court and the work of the Cafcass Officer will take account of any risk or safeguarding issues that have been identified.

4.5 The Cafcass Officer shall, where practicable, speak separately to each party at court and before the hearing.

4.6 In the County Court, the Court shall have available a telephone contact to the Family Proceedings Court listing manager, diary dates for the appropriate Family Proceedings Court, or other means by which the County Court, at the time of the hearing, will be able to list subsequent hearings in the Family Proceedings Court.

5 Conduct of the Hearing

The following matters shall be considered

5.1 *Safeguarding*:

(a) The court shall inform the parties of the content of any screening report or other information which has been provided by Cafcass, unless it considers that to do so would create a risk of harm to a party or the child. The court may need to consider whether and how any information contained in the checks should be disclosed to the parties if Cafcass have not disclosed it.

(b) Whether a risk assessment is required and when.

(c) Whether a fact finding hearing is needed to determine allegations whose resolution is likely to affect the decision of the court.

5.2 *Dispute Resolution*:

(a) There will be at every FHDRA a period in which the Cafcass Officer, with the assistance of any Mediator and in collaboration with the

Court, will seek to conciliate and explore with the parties the resolution of all or some of the issues between them. The procedure to be followed in this connection at the hearing will be determined by local arrangements between the Cafcass manager, or equivalent in Wales, and the Designated Family Judge or the Justices' Clerk where appropriate.

(b) What is the result of any such meeting at Court?

(c) What other options there are for resolution e.g. may the case be suitable for further intervention by Cafcass; mediation by an external provider; collaborative law or use of a parenting plan?

(d) Would the parties be assisted by attendance at Parenting Information Programmes or other activities, whether by formal statutory provision under section 11 Children Act 1989 as amended by Children and Adoption Act 2006 or otherwise?

5.3 *Consent Orders*:

Where agreement is reached at any hearing or submitted in writing to the court, no order will be made without scrutiny by the court. Where safeguarding checks or risk assessment work remain outstanding, the making of a final order may be deferred for such work. In such circumstances the court shall adjourn the case for no longer than 28 days to a fixed date. A written notification of this work is to be provided by Cafcass in accordance with the timescale specified by the court. If satisfactory information is then available, the order may be made at the adjourned hearing in the agreed terms without the need for attendance by the parties. If satisfactory information is not available, the order will not be made, and the case will be adjourned for further consideration with an opportunity for the parties to make further representations.

5.4 *Reports*:

(a) Are there welfare issues or other specific considerations which should be addressed in a report by Cafcass or the Local Authority? Before a report is ordered, the court should consider alternative ways of working with the parties such as are referred to in paragraph 5.2 above. If a report is ordered in accordance with Section 7 of the Children Act 1989, it should be directed specifically towards and limited to those issues. General requests should be avoided and the Court should state in the Order the specific factual and other issues that are to be addressed in a focused report. In determining whether a request for a report should be directed to the relevant local authority or to Cafcass, the court should consider such information as Cafcass has provided about the extent and nature of the local authority's current or recent involvement with the subject of the application and the parties, and any relevant protocol between Cafcass and the Association of Directors of Children's Services.

(b) Is there a need for an investigation under S 37 Children Act 1989?

(c) A copy of the Order requesting the report and any relevant court documents are to be sent to Cafcass or, in the case of the Local

Authority, to the Legal Adviser to the Director of the Local Authority Children's Services and, where known, to the allocated social worker by the court forthwith.

(d)   Is any expert evidence required in compliance with the Experts' Practice Direction?

5.5 *Wishes and feelings of the child*:

(a)   Is the child aware of the proceedings? How are the wishes and feelings of the child to be ascertained (if at all)?

(b)   How is the child to be involved in the proceedings, if at all, and whether at or after the FHDRA?

(c)   If consideration is given to the joining of the child as a party to the application, the court should consider the current Guidance from the President of the Family Division. Where the court is considering the appointment of a guardian ad litem, it should first seek to ensure that the appropriate Cafcass manager has been spoken to so as to consider any advice in connection with the prospective appointment and the timescale involved. In considering whether to make such an appointment the Court shall take account of the demands on the resources of Cafcass that such appointment would make.

(d)   Who will inform the child of the outcome of the case where appropriate?

5.6 *Case Management*:

(a)   What, if any, issues are agreed and what are the key issues to be determined?

(b)   Are there any interim orders which can usefully be made (e.g. indirect, supported or supervised contact) pending final hearing?

(c)   What directions are required to ensure the application is ready for final hearing – statements, reports etc?

(d)   List for final hearing, consider the need for judicial continuity (especially if there has been or is to be a fact finding hearing or a contested interim hearing).

5.7 *Transfer to FPC*:

The case should be transferred to the FPC, pursuant to the Allocation and Transfer of Proceedings Order 2008 unless one of the specified exceptions applies. The date should be fixed at court and entered on the order.

6 The Order

6.1 The Order shall set out in particular:

(a)   The issues about which the parties are agreed.

(b)   The issues that remain to be resolved.

(c)   The steps that are planned to resolve the issues.

(d)   Any interim arrangements pending such resolution, including arrangements for the involvement of children.

(e)   The timetable for such steps and, where this involves further hearings, the date of such hearings.

(f)   A statement as to any facts relating to risk or safety; in so far as they are resolved the result will be stated and, in so far as not resolved, the steps to be taken to resolve them will be stated.

(g)   If it be the case, the fact of the transfer of the case to the Family Proceedings Court with the date and purpose of the next hearing.

(h)   If it be the case, the fact that the case cannot be transferred to the Family Proceedings Court and the reason for the decision. Jordan Publishing www.familylaw.co.uk

(i)   Whether in the event of an order, by consent or otherwise, or pending such an order, the parties are to be assisted by participation in mediation, Parenting Information Programmes, or other types of parenting intervention, and to detail any contact activity directions or conditions imposed by the court.

PRACTICE DIRECTION 16A
REPRESENTATION OF CHILDREN

A2.3

This Practice Direction supplements FPR Part 16.

. . .

Part 4

Appointment of Children's Guardian under Rule 16.4

Section 1 – When a child should be made a party to proceedings

7.1 Making the child a party to the proceedings is a step that will be taken only in cases which involve an issue of significant difficulty and consequently will occur in only a minority of cases. Before taking the decision to make the child a party, consideration should be given to whether an alternative route might be preferable, such as asking an officer of the Service or a Welsh family proceedings officer to carry out further work or by making a referral to social services or, possibly, by obtaining expert evidence.

7.2 The decision to make the child a party will always be exclusively that of the court, made in the light of the facts and circumstances of the particular case. The following are offered, solely by way of guidance, as circumstances which may justify the making of such an order –

(a) where an officer of the Service or Welsh family proceedings officer has notified the court that in the opinion of that officer the child should be made a party;

(b) where the child has a standpoint or interest which is inconsistent with or incapable of being represented by any of the adult parties;

(c) where there is an intractable dispute over residence or contact, including where all contact has ceased, or where there is irrational but implacable hostility to contact or where the child may be suffering harm associated with the contact dispute;

(d) where the views and wishes of the child cannot be adequately met by a report to the court;

(e) where an older child is opposing a proposed course of action;

(f) where there are complex medical or mental health issues to be determined or there are other unusually complex issues that necessitate separate representation of the child;

(g)   where there are international complications outside child abduction, in particular where it may be necessary for there to be discussions with overseas authorities or a foreign court;

(h)   where there are serious allegations of physical, sexual or other abuse in relation to the child or there are allegations of domestic violence not capable of being resolved with the help of an officer of the Service or Welsh family proceedings officer;

(i)   where the proceedings concern more than one child and the welfare of the children is in conflict or one child is in a particularly disadvantaged position;

(j)   where there is a contested issue about scientific testing.

7.3 It must be recognised that separate representation of the child may result in a delay in the resolution of the proceedings. When deciding whether to direct that a child be made a party, the court will take into account the risk of delay or other facts adverse to the welfare of the child. The court's primary consideration will be the best interests of the child.

7.4 When a child is made a party and a children's guardian is to be appointed –

(a)   consideration should first be given to appointing an officer of the Service or Welsh family proceedings officer. Before appointing an officer, the court will cause preliminary enquiries to be made of Cafcass or CAFCASS CYMRU. For the relevant procedure, reference should be made to the practice note issued by Cafcass in June 2006 and any modifications of that practice note.

(b)   If Cafcass or CAFCASS CYMRU is unable to provide a children's guardian without delay, or if for some other reason the appointment of an officer of the Service of Welsh family proceedings officer is not appropriate, rule 16.24 makes further provision for the appointment of a children's guardian.

7.5 The court may, at the same time as deciding whether to join a child as a party, consider whether the proceedings should be transferred to another court taking into account the provisions of Part 3 of the Allocation and Transfer of Proceedings Order 2008.

2.4

PRACTICE DIRECTION 25A
EXPERTS – EMERGENCIES AND
PRE-PROCEEDINGS INSTRUCTIONS

A2.4

This Practice Direction supplements FPR Part 25.

. . .

Emergency and urgent cases

2.1 In emergency or urgent cases – for example, where, before formal issue of proceedings, a without-notice application is made to the court during or out of business hours; or where, after proceedings have been issued, a previously unforeseen need for (further) expert evidence arises at short notice – a party may wish to put expert evidence before the court without having complied with all or any part of Practice Directions 25B to E. In such circumstances, the party wishing to put the expert evidence before the court must apply forthwith to the court – where possible or appropriate, on notice to the other parties – for directions as to the future steps to be taken in respect of the expert evidence in question.

Pre-application instruction of experts

3.1 When experts' reports are commissioned before the commencement of proceedings, it should be made clear to the expert that he or she may in due course be reporting to the court and should therefore consider himself or herself bound by the duties of an expert set out in Practice Direction 25B (*The Duties of An Expert, the Expert's Report and Arrangements for An Expert To Attend Court*). In so far as possible the enquiries of the expert and subsequent letter of instruction should follow either Practice Direction 25C (*Children Proceedings -the Use of Single Joint Experts and the Process Leading to an Expert Being Instructed or Expert Evidence Being Put Before The Court*) or 25D (*Financial Remedy Proceedings and other Family Proceedings (except Children Proceedings) – the Use of Single Joint Experts and the Process Leading to Expert Evidence Being Put Before The Court*).

3.2 In particular, a prospective party to children proceedings (for example, a local authority) should always write a letter of instruction when asking a potential witness for a report or an opinion, whether that request is within proceedings or pre-proceedings (for example, when commissioning specialist assessment materials, reports from a treating expert or other evidential materials); and the letter of instruction should conform to the principles set out in Practice Direction 25C.

3.3 It should be noted that the court's permission is required to put expert evidence (in any form) before the court in all family proceedings (see FPR 25.4(1)). In children proceedings, the court's permission is also required for an expert to be instructed and for a child to be medically or psychiatrically examined or otherwise assessed for the purposes of the provision of expert evidence in the proceedings (FPR 25.4(2)). Where the court's permission has not been given in accordance with FPR 25.4(2), evidence resulting from such instructions or examination or other assessment is inadmissible unless the court rules otherwise (FPR 25.4(3) and (4)). The court's permission will be needed to put any expert evidence before the court which was obtained before proceedings have started.

2.5

PRACTICE DIRECTION 25B
THE DUTIES OF AN EXPERT, THE
EXPERT'S REPORT AND
ARRANGEMENTS FOR AN EXPERT TO
ATTEND COURT

A2.5

This Practice Direction supplements FPR Part 25.

. . .

The expert's overriding duty

3.1 An expert in family proceedings has an overriding duty to the court that takes precedence over any obligation to the person from whom the expert has received instructions or by whom the expert is paid.

Particular duties of the expert

4.1 An expert shall have regard to the following, among other, duties:

  (a) to assist the court in accordance with the overriding duty;
  (b) to provide advice to the court that conforms to the best practice of the expert's profession;
  (c) to answer the questions about which the expert is required to give an opinion (in children proceedings, those questions will be set out in the order of the court giving permission for an expert to be instructed, a child to be examined or otherwise assessed or expert evidence to be put before the court);
  (d) to provide an opinion that is independent of the party or parties instructing the expert;
  (e) to confine the opinion to matters material to the issues in the case and in relation only to the questions that are within the expert's expertise (skill and experience);
  (f) where a question has been put which falls outside the expert's expertise, to state this at the earliest opportunity and to volunteer an opinion as to whether another expert is required to bring expertise not possessed by those already involved or, in the rare case, as to whether a second opinion is required on a key issue and, if possible, what questions should be asked of the second expert;

(g)   in expressing an opinion, to take into consideration all of the material facts including any relevant factors arising from ethnic, cultural, religious or linguistic contexts at the time the opinion is expressed;

(h)   to inform those instructing the expert without delay of any change in the opinion and of the reason for the change.

The requirement for the court's permission

5.1 The general rule in family proceedings is that the court's permission is required to put expert evidence (in any form) before the court (FPR25.4(1)). The court is under a duty to restrict expert evidence to that which in the opinion of the court is necessary to assist the court to resolve the proceedings. The overriding objective in FPR1.1 applies when the court is exercising this duty. In children proceedings, the court's permission is required to instruct an expert and for a child to be medically or psychiatrically examined or otherwise assessed for the purposes of the provision of expert evidence in the proceedings (FPR25.4(2)).

Preliminary enquiries which the expert should expect to receive

6.1 In good time for the information requested to be available for –

(a)   **the court hearing** when the court will decide whether to give permission for the expert evidence to be put before the court (or also in children proceedings, for the expert to be instructed or the child to be examined or otherwise assessed); or

(b)   **the advocates' meeting or discussion** where one takes place before such a hearing, the party or parties intending to instruct the expert shall approach the expert with some information about the case.

6.2 The details of the information to be given to the expert are set out in Practice Direction 25C, paragraph 3.2 and Practice Direction 25D paragraph 3.3 and include the nature of the proceedings, the questions for the expert, the time when the expert's report is likely to be required, the timing of any hearing at which the expert may have to give evidence and how the expert's fees will be funded.

6.3 Children proceedings are confidential which means in those proceedings parties raising preliminary enquiries of an expert who has not yet been instructed can only tell the expert information which he or she will need about the case to be able to answer the preliminary questions raised.

Balancing the needs of the court and those of the expert

7.1 It is essential that there should be proper co-ordination between the court and the expert when drawing up the case management timetable: the needs of the court should be balanced with the needs of the expert whose forensic work is undertaken as an adjunct to his or her main professional duties.

The expert's response to preliminary enquiries

8.1 In good time for the court hearing when the court will decide whether or not to give permission for the expert evidence to be put before the court (or also in children proceedings, for the expert to be instructed or the child to be examined or otherwise assessed) or for the advocates' meeting or discussion where one takes place before that hearing, the party or parties intending to instruct the expert will need confirmation from the expert—

    (a)   that acceptance of the proposed instructions will not involve the expert in any conflict of interest;

    (b)   that the work required is within the expert's expertise;

    (c)   that the expert is available to do the relevant work within the suggested time scale;

    (d)   when the expert is available to give evidence, of the dates and times to avoid and, where a hearing date has not been fixed, of the amount of notice the expert will require to make arrangements to come to court (or to give evidence by telephone conference or video link) without undue disruption to his or her normal professional routines;

    (e)   of the cost, including hourly or other charging rates, and likely hours to be spent attending experts' meetings, attending court and writing the report (to include any examinations and interviews);

    (f)   of any representations which the expert wishes to make to the court about being named or otherwise identified in any public judgment given by the court.

Content of the expert's report

9.1 The expert's report shall be addressed to the court and prepared and filed **in accordance with the court's timetable** and must –

    (a)   give details of the expert's qualifications and experience;

    (b)   include a statement identifying the document(s) containing the material instructions and the substance of any oral instructions and, as far as necessary to explain any opinions or conclusions expressed in the report, summarising the facts and instructions which are material to the conclusions and opinions expressed;

    (c)   state who carried out any test, examination or interview which the expert has used for the report and whether or not the test, examination or interview has been carried out under the expert's supervision;

    (d)   give details of the qualifications of any person who carried out the test, examination or interview;

    (e)   answer the questions about which the expert is to give an opinion and which relate to the issues in the case;

    (f)   in expressing an opinion to the court –

        (i)   take into consideration all of the material facts including any relevant factors arising from ethnic, cultural, religious or linguistic contexts at the time the opinion is expressed, identifying the facts, literature and any other material, including research material, that the expert has relied upon in forming an opinion;

(ii)   describe the expert's own professional risk assessment process and process of differential diagnosis, highlighting factual assumptions, deductions from the factual assumptions, and any unusual, contradictory or inconsistent features of the case;

(iii)   indicate whether any proposition in the report is an hypothesis (in particular a controversial hypothesis), or an opinion deduced in accordance with peer-reviewed and tested technique, research and experience accepted as a consensus in the scientific community;

(iv)   indicate whether the opinion is provisional (or qualified, as the case may be), stating the qualification and the reason for it, and identifying what further information is required to give an opinion without qualification;

(g)   where there is a range of opinion on any question to be answered by the expert –

(i)   summarise the range of opinion;

(ii)   identify and explain, within the range of opinions, any "unknown cause", whether arising from the facts of the case (for example, because there is too little information to form a scientific opinion) or from limited experience or lack of research, peer review or support in the relevant field of expertise;

(iii)   give reasons for any opinion expressed: the use of a balance sheet approach to the factors that support or undermine an opinion can be of great assistance to the court;

(h)   contain a summary of the expert's conclusions and opinions;

(i)   contain a statement that the expert –

(i)   has no conflict of interest of any kind, other than any conflict disclosed in his or her report;

(ii)   does not consider that any interest disclosed affects his or her suitability as an expert witness on any issue on which he or she has given evidence;

(iii)   will advise the instructing party if, between the date of the expert's report and the final hearing, there is any change in circumstances which affects the expert's answers to (i) or (ii) above;

(iv)   understands their duty to the court and has complied with that duty; and

(v)   is aware of the requirements of FPR Part 25 and this practice direction;

(j)   be verified by a statement of truth in the following form – "I confirm that I have made clear which facts and matters referred to in this report are within my own knowledge and which are not. Those that are within my own knowledge I confirm to be true. The opinions I have expressed represent my true and complete professional opinions on the matters to which they refer." (FPR Part 17 deals with statements of truth.

Rule 17.6 sets out the consequences of verifying a document containing a false statement without an honest belief in its truth.)

Arrangements for experts to give evidence

Preparation

10.1 Where the court has directed the attendance of an expert witness, the party who instructed the expert or party responsible for the instruction of the expert shall, **by a date specified by the court prior to the hearing at which the expert is to give oral evidence ("the specified date") or, where in care or supervision proceedings an Issues Resolution Hearing ("the IRH") is to be held, by the IRH**, ensure that –

(a) a date and time (if possible, convenient to the expert) are fixed for the court to hear the expert's evidence, substantially in advance of the hearing at which the expert is to give oral evidence and no later than a specified date prior to that hearing or, where an IRH is to be held, than the IRH;

(b) if the expert's oral evidence is not required, the expert is notified as soon as possible;

(c) the witness template accurately indicates how long the expert is likely to be giving evidence, in order to avoid the inconvenience of the expert being delayed at court;

(d) consideration is given in each case to whether some or all of the experts participate by telephone conference or video link, or submit their evidence in writing, to ensure that minimum disruption is caused to professional schedules and that costs are minimised.

Experts attending court

10.2 Where expert witnesses are to be called, all parties shall, **by the specified date or, where an IRH is to be held, by the IRH**, ensure that –

(a) the parties' advocates have identified (whether at an advocates' meeting or by other means) the issues which the experts are to address;

(b) wherever possible, a logical sequence to the evidence is arranged, with experts of the same discipline giving evidence on the same day;

(c) the court is informed of any circumstance where all experts agree but a party nevertheless does not accept the agreed opinion, so that directions can be given for the proper consideration of the experts' evidence and opinion;

(d) in the exceptional case the court is informed of the need for a witness summons.

PRACTICE DIRECTION 25C
CHILDREN PROCEEDINGS – THE USE OF
SINGLE JOINT EXPERTS AND THE
PROCESS OF LEADING TO AN EXPERT
BEING INSTRUCTED OR EXPERT
EVIDENCE BEING PUT BEFORE THE
COURT

A2.6

This Practice Direction supplements FPR Part 25.

Scope of this Practice Direction

1.1 This Practice Direction applies to children proceedings and contains guidance on –

(a)   the use of single joint experts;
(b)   how to prepare for the hearing at which the court will consider whether to give permission for an expert to be instructed, a child to be medically or psychiatrically examined or otherwise assessed for the purposes of provision of expert evidence in the proceedings or for putting expert evidence (in any form) before the court including–
  (i)   preliminary enquiries of experts;
  (ii)   the content of an application for the court's permission in addition to matters mentioned in FPR 25.7;
  (iii)   matters to be set out in the draft order to be attached to the application for permission; and
(c)   the letter of instruction to the expert.

1.2 "Children proceedings" includes proceedings under Schedule 1 to the 1989 Act as those proceedings are proceedings which relate wholly or mainly to the maintenance or upbringing of a minor referred to in FPR 25.2(1).

Single joint experts

2.1 FPR 25.4 applies to a single joint expert ("SJE") in addition to an expert instructed by one party. This means that the court's permission is required to put expert evidence from an SJE (in any form) before the court (FPR 25.4(1)). The court's permission is also required to instruct an SJE and for a child to be medically or psychiatrically examined or otherwise assessed for the purposes of provision of evidence from an SJE (FPR 25.4(2)). Wherever possible, expert evidence should be obtained from an SJE instructed by both or all the parties. To that end, a party wishing to instruct an expert should as soon as possible after the start of the proceedings first give the other party or parties a list of the names of one or more experts in the relevant speciality whom they consider suitable to be instructed.

2.2 **Within 5 business days after receipt of the list of proposed experts,** the other party or parties should indicate any objection to one or more of the named experts and, if so, supply the name(s) of one or more experts whom they consider suitable.

2.3 Each party should disclose whether they have already consulted any of the proposed experts about the issue(s) in question.

2.4 Where the parties cannot agree on the identity of the expert, each party should think carefully before seeking the permission of the court to instruct their own expert because of the costs implications. Disagreements about the use and identity of an expert may be better managed by the court in the context of the application for the court's permission to instruct the expert and for directions for the use of an SJE (see paragraph 2.6 below).

Instructing separate experts

2.5 If the parties seek the permission of the court to instruct separate experts,-

(a)   they should agree in advance that the reports will be disclosed; and
(b)   the instructions to each expert should comply, so far as appropriate, with paragraphs 4.1 and 6.1 below (*Letter of instruction*).

Where two or more parties wish to instruct an SJE

2.6 If two or more parties wish to instruct an SJE, before applying to the court for permission and directions for the use of an SJE, the parties should-

(a)   so far as appropriate, comply with the guidance in paragraphs 3.2 (Preliminary enquires of the expert) and paragraphs 3.10 and 3.11 below;
(b)   receive the expert's confirmation in response to preliminary enquires referred to in paragraph 8.1 of Practice Direction 25B;
(c)   have agreed in what proportion the SJE's fee is to be shared between them (at least in the first instance) and when it is to be paid; and
(d)   if applicable, have obtained agreement for public funding.

2.7 The instructions to the SJE should comply, so far as appropriate, with paragraphs 4.1 and 6.1 below (*Letter of instruction*).

Preparation for the permission hearing

3.1 Paragraphs 3.2 to 3.11 give guidance on how to prepare for the hearing at which the court will consider whether to give permission for an expert to be instructed, a child to be examined or otherwise assessed or expert evidence to be put before the court. The purpose of the preparation is to ensure that the court has the information required to enable it to exercise its powers under FPR 25.4 and 25.5.

Preliminary enquiries of the expert

3.2 **In good time for the information requested to be available for the hearing** at which the court will consider whether to give permission for an expert to be instructed, a child to be examined or otherwise assessed or expert evidence to be put before the court or for the advocates' meeting or discussion where one takes place before that hearing, the party or parties intending to instruct the expert shall approach the expert with the following information—

(a)   the nature of the proceedings and the issues likely to require determination by the court;

(b)   the issues in the proceedings to which the expert evidence is to relate;

(c)   the questions about which the expert is to be asked to give an opinion (including any ethnic, cultural, religious or linguistic contexts) and which relate to the issues in the case;

(d)   the date when the court is to be asked to give permission for the instruction (or if – unusually – permission has already been given, the date and details of that permission);

(e)   whether permission is to be asked of the court for the instruction of another expert in the same or any related field (that is, to give an opinion on the same or related questions);

(f)   the volume of reading which the expert will need to undertake;

(g)   whether or not permission has been applied for or given for the expert to examine the child;

(h)   whether or not it will be necessary for the expert to conduct interviews – and, if so, with whom;

(i)   the likely timetable of legal and social work steps;

(j)   in care and supervision proceedings, any dates in the Timetable for the Child which would be relevant to the proposed timetable for the assessment;

(k)   when the expert's report is likely to be required;

(l)   whether and, if so, what date has been fixed by the court for any hearing at which the expert may be required to give evidence (in particular the Final Hearing); and whether it may be possible for the expert to give evidence by telephone conference or video link: see paragraphs 10.1 and 10.2 (*Arrangements for experts to give evidence*) of Practice Direction 25B;

(m)   the possibility of making, through their instructing solicitors, representations to the court about being named or otherwise identified in any public judgment given by the court;

(n)   whether the instructing party has public funding and the legal aid rates of payment which are applicable.

Confidentiality of children proceedings and making preliminary enquiries of an expert

3.3 For the purposes of the law of contempt of court, information relating to children proceedings (whether or not contained in a document filed with the court or recorded in any form) may be communicated only to an expert whose instruction by a party has been permitted by the court (see FPR 12.73(1)(a)(vii) and 14.14(c)(vii)) as children proceedings are confidential.

3.4 Before permission is obtained from the court to instruct an expert in children proceedings, the party seeking permission needs to make the enquiries of the expert referred to above in order to provide the court with information to enable it to decide whether to give permission. In practice, enquiries may need to be made of more than one expert for this purpose. This will in turn require each expert to be given sufficient information about the case to decide whether or not he or she is in a position to accept instructions. Such preliminary enquiries, and the disclosure of information about the case which is a necessary part of such enquiries, will not require the court's permission and will not amount to a contempt of court.

Expert's response to preliminary enquiries

3.5 In good time for the hearing at which the court will consider whether to give permission for an expert to be instructed, a child to be examined or otherwise assessed or expert evidence to be put before the court, **the party or parties** intending to instruct the expert must obtain the confirmations from the expert referred to in paragraph 8.1 of Practice Direction 25B. These confirmations include that the work is within the expert's expertise, the expert is available to do the work within the relevant timescale and the expert's costs.

3.6 Where the parties **cannot agree who should be the single joint expert** before the hearing at which the court will consider whether to give permission for an expert to be instructed, a child to be examined or otherwise assessed or expert evidence to be put before the court, they should obtain the above confirmations in respect of all experts whom they intend to put to the court for the purposes of FPR 25.11(2)(a) as candidates for the appointment.

The application for the court's permission mentioned in FPR 25.4

Timing and oral applications for the court's permission mentioned in FPR 25.4

3.7 An application for the court's permission for an expert to be instructed, a child to be examined or otherwise assessed or expert evidence to be put before the court should be made as soon as it becomes apparent that it is necessary to make it. FPR 25.6 makes provision about the time by which applications for the court's permission should be made.

3.8 Applications should, wherever possible, be made so that they are considered at any directions hearing or other hearing for which a date has been fixed or for which a date is about to be fixed. It should be noted that one application notice can be used by a party to make more than one application for an order or direction at a hearing held during the course of proceedings. An application for the court's permission for an expert to be instructed, a child to be examined or otherwise assessed or expert evidence to be put before the court may therefore be included in an application notice requesting other orders to be made at such a hearing.

3.9 Where a date for a hearing has been fixed, a party who wishes to make an application at that hearing but does not have sufficient time to file an application notice should as soon as possible inform the court (if possible in writing) and, if possible, the other parties of the nature of the application and the reason for it. The party should provide the court and the other party with as much as possible of the information referred to in FPR 25.7 and paragraph 3.10 below. That party should then make the application orally at the hearing. An oral application of this kind should be the exception and reserved for genuine cases where circumstances are such that it has only become apparent shortly before the hearing that an expert opinion is necessary.

The application

3.10 In addition to the matters specified in FPR 25.7(2)(a) and (3), an application for the court's permission for an expert to be instructed, a child to be examined or otherwise assessed or expert evidence to be put before the court, must state –

(a)   the discipline, qualifications and expertise of the expert (by way of C.V. where possible);
(b)   the expert's availability to undertake the work;
(c)   the timetable for the report;
(d)   the responsibility for instruction;
(e)   whether the expert evidence can properly be obtained by only one party (for example, on behalf of the child);
(f)   why the expert evidence proposed cannot properly be given by an officer of the service, Welsh family proceedings officer or the local authority (social services undertaking a core assessment) in accordance with their respective statutory duties or any other party to the proceedings or an expert already instructed in the proceedings;
(g)   the likely cost of the report on an hourly or other charging basis;
(h)   the proposed apportionment (at least in the first instance) of any jointly instructed expert's fee; when it is to be paid; and, if applicable, whether public funding has been approved.

The terms of the draft order to be attached to the application for the court's permission

3.11 FPR 25.7(2)(b) provides that a draft of the order giving the court's permission as mentioned in FPR 25.4 is to be attached to the application for the court's permission. That draft order must set out the following matters –

(a)   the issues in the proceedings to which the expert evidence is to relate and which the court is to identify;
(b)   the questions relating to the issues in the case which the expert is to answer and which the court is to approve ensuring that they

    (i)   are within the ambit of the expert's area of expertise;

    (ii)   do not contain unnecessary or irrelevant detail;

    (iii) are kept to a manageable number and are clear, focused and direct;

(c)   the party who is responsible for drafting the letter of instruction and providing the documents to the expert;

(d)   the timetable within which the report is to be prepared, filed and served;

(e)   the disclosure of the report to the parties and to any other expert;

(f)   the organisation of, preparation for and conduct of any experts' discussion (*see Practice Direction 25E – Discussions between Experts in Family Proceedings*);

(g)   the preparation of a statement of agreement and disagreement by the experts following an experts' discussion;

(h)   making available to the court at an early opportunity the expert reports in electronic form;

(i)   the attendance of the expert at court to give oral evidence (alternatively, the expert giving his or her evidence in writing or remotely by video link), whether at or for the Final Hearing or another hearing; unless agreement about the opinions given by the expert is reached at or before the Issues Resolution Hearing ("IRH") or, if no IRH is to be held, by a date specified by the court prior to the hearing at which the expert is to give oral evidence.

Letter of instruction

4.1 The party responsible for instructing the expert shall prepare (in agreement with the other parties where appropriate), a letter of instruction to the expert and shall –

(a)   set out the context in which the expert's opinion is sought (including any ethnic, cultural, religious or linguistic contexts);

(b)   set out the questions approved by the court and which the expert is required to answer and any other linked questions ensuring that they –

    (i)   are within the ambit of the expert's area of expertise;

    (ii)   do not contain unnecessary or irrelevant detail;

    (iii) are kept to a manageable number and are clear, focused and direct; and

    (iv) reflect what the expert has been requested to do by the court (Annex A to this *Practice Direction* sets out suggested questions in letters of instruction to (1) child mental health professionals or paediatricians, and (2) adult psychiatrists and applied psychologists, in Children Act 1989 proceedings);

(c)   list the documentation provided, or provide for the expert an indexed and paginated bundle which shall include –

    (i)   an agreed list of essential reading; and

    (ii)   a copy of this Practice Direction and Practice Directions 25B and E and where appropriate Practice Direction 15B;

(d)   identify any materials provided to the expert which have not been produced either as original medical (or other professional) records or in response to an instruction from a party, and state the source of that material (such materials may contain an assumption as to the standard of proof, the admissibility or otherwise of hearsay evidence, and other important procedural and substantive questions relating to the different purposes of other enquiries, for example, criminal or disciplinary proceedings);

(e)   identify all requests to third parties for disclosure and their responses in order to avoid partial disclosure, which tends only to prove a case rather than give full and frank information;

(f)   identify the relevant people concerned with the proceedings (for example, the treating clinicians) and inform the expert of his or her right to talk to them provided that an accurate record is made of the discussions;

(g)   identify any other expert instructed in the proceedings and advise the expert of their right to talk to the other experts provided that an accurate record is made of the discussions;

(h)   subject to any public funding requirement for prior authority, define the contractual basis upon which the expert is retained and in particular the funding mechanism including how much the expert will be paid (an hourly rate and overall estimate should already have been obtained), when the expert will be paid, and what limitation there might be on the amount the expert can charge for the work which they will have to do. In cases where the parties are publicly funded, there may also be a brief explanation of the costs and expenses excluded from public funding by Funding Code criterion 1.3 and the detailed assessment process.

. . .

Asking the court to settle the letter of instruction to a single joint expert

6.1 Where possible, the written request for the court to consider the letter of instruction referred to in rule 25.12(2) should be set out in an e-mail to the court and copied by e-mail to the other instructing parties. The request should be sent to the relevant court or (by prior arrangement only) directly to the judge dealing with the proceedings. In the magistrates' court, the request should be sent to the relevant court or (by prior arrangement only) to any district judge (magistrates' courts) hearing the proceedings (and copied to the legal adviser) or to the legal adviser. The court will settle the letter of instruction, usually without a hearing to avoid delay; and will send (where practicable, by e-mail) the settled letter to the lead solicitor for transmission

ANNEX A
(drafted by the Family Justice Council)

Suggested questions in letters of instruction to child mental health professional or paediatrician in Children Act 1989 proceedings

A. The Child(ren)

1. Please describe the child(ren)'s current health, development and functioning (according to your area of expertise), and identify the nature of any significant changes which have occurred

- Behavioural
- Emotional
- Attachment organisation
- Social/peer/sibling relationships
- Cognitive/educational
- Physical
  — Growth, eating, sleep
  — Non-organic physical problems (including wetting and soiling)
  — Injuries
  — Paediatric conditions

2. Please comment on the likely explanation for/aetiology of the child(ren)'s problems/difficulties/injuries

- History/experiences (including intrauterine influences, and abuse and neglect)
- Genetic/innate/developmental difficulties
- Paediatric/psychiatric disorders

3. Please provide a prognosis and risk if difficulties not addressed above.

4. Please describe the child(ren)'s needs in the light of the above

- Nature of care-giving
- Education
- Treatment

in the short and long term (subject, where appropriate, to further assessment later).

B. The parents/primary carers

5. Please describe the factors and mechanisms which would explain the parents' (or primary carers) harmful or neglectful interactions with the child(ren) (if relevant).

6. What interventions have been tried and what has been the result?

7. Please assess the ability of the parents or primary carers to fulfil the child(ren)'s identified needs now.

8. What other assessments of the parents or primary carers are indicated?

- Adult mental health assessment

- Forensic risk assessment
- Physical assessment
- Cognitive assessment

9. What, if anything, is needed to assist the parents or primary carers now, within the child(ren)'s time scales and what is the prognosis for change?

- Parenting work
- Support
- Treatment/therapy

C. Alternatives

10. Please consider the alternative possibilities for the fulfilment of the child(ren)'s needs

- What sort of placement
- Contact arrangements

Please consider the advantages, disadvantages and implications of each for the child(ren).

Suggested questions in letters of instruction to adult psychiatrists and applied psychologists in Children Act 1989 proceedings

1. Does the parent/adult have – whether in his/her history or presentation – a mental illness/disorder (including substance abuse) or other psychological/emotional difficulty and, if so, what is the diagnosis?

2. How do any/all of the above (and their current treatment if applicable) affect his/her functioning, including interpersonal relationships?

3. If the answer to Q1 is yes, are there any features of either the mental illness or psychological/emotional difficulty or personality disorder which could be associated with risk to others, based on the available evidence base (whether published studies or evidence from clinical experience)?

4. What are the experiences/antecedents/aetiology which would explain his/her difficulties, if any, (taking into account any available evidence base or other clinical experience)?

5. What treatment is indicated, what is its nature and the likely duration?

6. What is his/her capacity to engage in/partake of the treatment/therapy?

7. Are you able to indicate the prognosis for, time scales for achieving, and likely durability of, change?

8. What other factors might indicate positive change?

(It is assumed that this opinion will be based on collateral information as well as interviewing the adult).

Appendix 3

EXTRACTS FROM KEY INTERNATIONAL RELOCATION CASES

3.1

PAYNE V PAYNE
[2001] EWCA CIV 166, [2001] 1 FLR 1052

A3.1

Court of Appeal

Dame Elizabeth Butler-Sloss P, Thorpe and Robert Walker LJJ

THORPE LJ:

[16] The modern law regulating applications for the emigration of children begins with the decision of this court in *Poel v Poel* [1970] 1 WLR 1469. I doubt that the judges deciding the case recognised how influential it would prove to be. Whilst emphasising that the court should have regard primarily to the welfare of the child, both Sachs LJ and Winn LJ emphasised the importance of recognising and supporting the function of the primary carer. That consideration was most clearly expressed by Sachs LJ when he said (at 1473):

> 'When a marriage breaks up, a situation normally arises when the child of that marriage, instead of being in the joint custody of both parents, must of necessity become one who is in the custody of a single parent. Once that position has arisen and the custody is working well, this court should not lightly interfere with such reasonable way of life as is selected by that parent to whom custody has been rightly given. Any such interference may, as my Lord has pointed out, produce considerable strains which would not only be unfair to the parent whose way of life is interfered with but also to any new marriage of that parent. In that way it might well in due course reflect on the welfare of the child. The way in which the parent who properly has custody of a child may choose in a reasonable manner to order his or her way of life is one of those things which the parent who has not been given custody may well have to bear, even though one has every sympathy with the latter on some of the results.'

[17] In the later case of *Nash v Nash* [1973] 2 All ER 704, Davies LJ said (at 706G):

> 'But I emphasise once more that when one parent has been given custody it is a very strong thing for this court to make an order which will prevent the following of a chosen career by the parent who has custody.'

[18] The subsequent development of this approach was achieved by Ormrod LJ. In *A v A (Child: Removal from Jurisdiction)* (1980) 1 FLR 380, it appears that the decision in *Poel v Poel* was cited by counsel for the father appealing the grant of leave to the mother by the Family Division judge. For at 381-382 he said:

> 'It is always difficult in these cases when marriages break up where a wife who, as this one is, is very isolated in this country feels the need to return to her own family and her own country; and, although Mr Swift has argued persuasively for the test which was suggested in the case of *Poel v Poel* [1970] 1 WLR 1469, the test which is often put on the basis of whether it is reasonable for the mother to return to her own country with the child, I myself doubt whether it provides a satisfactory answer to this question. The fundamental question is what is in the best interest of the child; and once it has been decided with so young a child as this that there really is no option so far as care and control are concerned, then one has to look realistically at the mother's position and ask oneself the question: where is she going to have the best chance of bringing up this child reasonably well? To that question the only possible answer in this case is Hong Kong. It is true that it means cutting the child off to a large extent – almost wholly perhaps – from the father; but that is one of the risks which have to be run in cases of this kind. If it is wholly unreasonable, as I think it is in this case, to require the mother to remain in England, assuming even the court ought to put her in the position of choosing between staying very unhappily and uncomfortably in England and going home to her own country, then I still think the answer is that where she can best bring up this child is the proper solution to this case.'

[19]   He adopted the same approach in the unreported case of *Moodey v Field* (13 February 1981) when he said: 'The question therefore in each case is, is the proposed move a reasonable one from the point of view of the adults involved? If the answer is yes, then leave should only be refused if it is clearly shown beyond any doubt that the interests of the children and the interests of the custodial parent are incompatible.'

[20]   This approach was questioned in the Family Division by Balcombe J in the case of *Chamberlain v de la Mare* (1983) 4 FLR 434. He emphasised that his duty was to regard the welfare of the child as the first and paramount consideration and that each factor should be weighed one against another no factor taking priority against another. His decision was reversed in the Court of Appeal. Ormrod LJ held that Balcombe J had misdirected himself in questioning whether the decisions in *Poel v Poel* [1970] 1 WLR 1469 and *Nash v Nash* [1973] 2 All ER 704 were consistent with the statute. Ormrod LJ emphasised that the court in *Poel* had not weighed the interests of the adults against the interests of the children but rather had weighed the effect on the children of imposing unreasonable restraints on the adults. Having cited his earlier decision in *Moodey v Field* ((unreported) 13 February 1981) he said at 443:

> 'The reason why the court should not interfere with the reasonable decision of the custodial parent, assuming, as this case does, that the custodial parent is still going to be responsible for the children, is, as I have said, the almost inevitable bitterness which such an interference by the court is likely to produce. Consequently, in

ordinary sensible human terms the court should not do something which is, prima facie, unreasonable unless there is some compelling reason to the contrary. That I believe to be the correct approach.'

[21]   In the case of *Lonslow v Hennig (Formerly Lonslow)* [1986] 2 FLR 378, Dillon LJ reviewed and applied these authorities in allowing a mother's appeal from the refusal of her application to emigrate with the children to New Zealand. Having reminded himself that so far as the law was concerned the first point was that the welfare of the children was the paramount consideration and secondly that previous cases decided on other facts could only provide guidelines, he noted that there was a consistent line of guidance throughout the decisions of this court since 1970.

[22]   In *Belton v Belton* [1987] 2 FLR 343, Purchas LJ in allowing a mother's appeal against the refusal of her application to emigrate to New Zealand said (at 349):

'I sympathize and understand, where a lay person such as a father is concerned, the difficulty of reconciliation with the concept of such a separation being in the paramount interests of the child in the long term, but the long-term interests of the child revolve around establishing, as Griffiths LJ (as he then was) said in *Chamberlain* , a sound, secure family unit in which the child should go forward and develop. If that can be supported by contact with the father, that is an immense advantage, but, if it cannot, then that is no reason for diverting one's concentration from the central and paramount issue in the case.'

[23]   He summarised the authorities by saying (at 349-350):

'… the authorities and the law which dictate the hard and difficult decision which must be made once it is established that the custodial parent genuinely desires to emigrate and, in circumstances in which there is nothing adverse to be found in the conditions to be expected, those authorities are quite clear in the course that the court must take, whatever the hardship and distress that may result.'

[24]   In *Tyler v Tyler* [1989] 2 FLR 158, Kerr LJ, having been referred to virtually all the reported cases in which an issue of this kind had arisen, offered this summary (at 160-161):

'I also accept that this line of authority shows that where the custodial parent herself, it was the mother in all those cases, has a genuine and reasonable desire to emigrate then the court should hesitate long before refusing permission to take the children.'

[25]   In more recent times both at first instance and in this court I have sought to apply this line of authority to a series of cases giving rise to differing facts and circumstances. We have been referred to *MH v GP (Child: Emigration)* [1995] 2 FLR 106, *Re H (Application to Remove from Jurisdiction)* [1998] 1 FLR 848 and *Re C (Leave to Remove from Jurisdiction)* [2000] 2 FLR 457. However in the first case I referred to the ratio in *Chamberlain v de la Mare*

(1983) 4 FLR 434 as creating 'a presumption in favour of the reasonable application of the custodial parent'. Equally in the last case I said at 459 that:

> '... a balance then had to be struck to determine whether or not the resulting risk of harm to S was such as to outweigh the presumption that reasonable proposals from the custodial parent should receive the endorsement of the court.'

In both passages I was using the word presumption in the non-legal sense. But with the advantage of hindsight I regret the use of that word. Generally in the language of litigation a presumption either casts a burden of proof upon the party challenging it or can be said to be decisive of outcome unless displaced. I do not think that such concepts of presumption and burden of proof have any place in Children Act 1989 litigation where the judge exercises a function that is partly inquisitorial. In the context of applications for contact orders I expressed my misgivings in the use of the language of presumptions: see in *Re L (Contact: Domestic Violence); Re V (Contact: Domestic Violence); Re M (Contact: Domestic Violence); Re H (Contact: Domestic Violence)* [2000] 2 FLR 334.

[26]   In summary a review of the decisions of this court over the course of the last 30 years demonstrates that relocation cases have been consistently decided upon the application of the following two propositions:

(a)   the welfare of the child is the paramount consideration; and

(b)   refusing the primary carer's reasonable proposals for the relocation of her family life is likely to impact detrimentally on the welfare of her dependent children. Therefore her application to relocate will be granted unless the court concludes that it is incompatible with the welfare of the children.

The value of the guidance

[27]   Few guidelines for the determination of individual cases, the facts of which are never replicated, have stood so long in our family law. Where guidelines can be formulated there are obvious benefits. The opportunity for practitioners to give clear and confident advice as to outcome helps to limit the volume of contested litigation. Of the cases that do proceed to a hearing clear guidance from this court simplifies the task of the trial judge and helps to limit the volume of appeals. The opportunity for this court to give guidance capable of general application is plainly circumscribed by the obvious consideration that any exercise of discretion is fact dependent and no two cases are identical. But in relocation cases there are a number of factors that are sufficiently commonplace to enhance the utility of guidelines. I instance:

(a)   the applicant is invariably the mother and the primary carer;

(b)   generally the motivation for the move arises out of her remarriage or her urge to return home; and

(c)   the father's opposition is commonly founded on a resultant reduction in contact and influence.

[28]   Furthermore, guidance of this sort is significant in the wider field of international family law. There is a clear interaction between the approach of courts in abduction cases and in relocation cases. If individual jurisdictions adopt a chauvinistic approach to applications to relocate then there is a risk that the parent affected will resort to flight. Conversely, recognition of the respect due to the primary carer's reasonable proposals for relocation encourages applications in place of unilateral removal. Equally as this case demonstrates, a return following a wrongful retention allows a careful appraisal of welfare considerations on a subsequent application to relocate. Accordingly it is very desirable that there should be conformity within the international community. At the international common law judicial conference arranged in Washington in September 2000 by the US an additional session was allocated to the discussion of the approach adopted by the seven delegate jurisdictions to relocation cases. That discussion demonstrated that for all jurisdictions the welfare of the child is the paramount consideration. However some jurisdictions afford greater weight than others to the harm that the refusal of the primary carer's reasonable proposal is likely to cause to the children. In my judgment there is some prospect that standardisation at a point close to the approach adopted in this jurisdiction is achievable. There may be an opportunity for evaluation across a much wider range at the Fourth Special Commission to review the operation of the Hague Convention on the Civil Aspects of International Child Abduction 1980 in March 2001.

The foundation of the guidance

[29]   A review of the Court of Appeal authorities over the last 30 years demonstrates that although not the originator of the guidance, Ormrod LJ was its principal exponent. He rationalises it and its strongest statement comes in his judgment in *Moodey v Field* ((unreported) 13 February 1981) as well perhaps in the judgment of Purchas LJ in *Belton v Belton* [1987] 2 FLR 343. Since the direction has stood for 30 years and since its amplification by Ormrod LJ, first in *A v A (Child: Removal from Jurisdiction)* (1980) 1 FLR 380 over 20 years ago, it is perhaps necessary to question whether changing perceptions of child development and welfare in the interim undermine or erode his exposition. That exposition, as he himself said, was very much based on common sense. But even generally accepted perceptions can shift within a generation. The shift upon which Mr Cayford relies is in the sphere of contact. He asserts that over the last 30 years the comparative importance of contact between the child and the absent parent has greatly increased. No authority for the proposition is demonstrated. Without some proof of the proposition I would be doubtful of accepting it. Throughout my professional life in this specialist field contact between child and absent parent has always been seen as

an important ingredient in any welfare appraisal. The language may have shifted but the proposition seems to have remained constant. I believe that conviction is demonstrated by the review of the contact cases over much the same period to be found in my judgment in *Re L (Contact Domestic Violence), Re V (Contact Domestic Violence), Re M (Contact Domestic Violence), Re H (Contact Domestic Violence)* [2000] 2 FLR 334, cited above, at (25). Furthermore practicalities are all against this submission. International travel is comparatively cheaper and more competitive than ever before. Equally communication is cheaper and the options more varied.

[30]   Quite apart from [counsel for the father's] submission, I do not believe that the evaluation of welfare within the mental health professions over this period calls into any question the rationalisation advanced by Ormrod LJ in his judgments. In a broad sense the health and well-being of a child depends upon emotional and psychological stability and security. Both security and stability come from the child's emotional and psychological dependency upon the primary carer. The extent of that dependency will depend upon many factors including its duration and the extent to which it is tempered by or shared with other dependencies. For instance is the absent parent an important figure in the child's life? What is the child's relationship with siblings and/or grandparents and/or a step-parent? In most relocation cases the judge will need to make some evaluation of these factors.

[31]   Logically and as a matter of experience the child cannot draw emotional and psychological security and stability from the dependency unless the primary carer herself is emotionally and psychologically stable and secure. The parent cannot give what she herself lacks. Although fathers as well as mothers provide primary care I have never myself encountered a relocation application brought by a father and for the purposes of this judgment I assume that relocation applications are only brought by maternal primary carers. The disintegration of a family unit is invariably emotionally and psychologically turbulent. The mother who emerges with the responsibility of making the home for the children may recover her sense of well-being simply by coping over a passage of time. But often the mother may be in need of external support, whether financial, emotional or social. Such support may be provided by a new partner who becomes stepfather to the child. The creation of a new family obviously draws the child into its quest for material and other fulfilment. Such cases have given rise to the strongest statements of the guidelines. Alternatively the disintegration of the family unit may leave the mother in a society to which she was carried by the impetus of family life before its failure. Commonly in that event she may feel isolated and driven to seek the support she lacks by returning to her homeland, her family and her friends. In the remarriage cases the motivation for relocation may well be to meet the stepfather's career needs or opportunities. In those cases refusal is likely to destabilise the new family emotionally as well as to penalise it financially. In the case of the isolated mother, to deny her the support of her family and a return to her roots may have an even greater psychological detriment and she may have no one who might share her distress or alleviate her depression ...

[32] Thus in most relocation cases the most crucial assessment and finding for the judge is likely to be the effect of the refusal of the application on the mother's future psychological and emotional stability.

[35] I am in broad agreement with the views expressed by Ward LJ to the effect that the advent of the [European Convention on Human Rights] within our domestic law [when the Human Rights Act 1998 entered force] does not necessitate a revision of the fundamental approach to relocation applications formulated by this court and consistently applied over so many years. The reason that I hold this opinion is that reduced to its fundamentals the court's approach is and always has been to apply child welfare as the paramount consideration. The court's focus upon supporting the reasonable proposal of the primary carer is seen as no more than an important factor in the assessment of welfare. In a united family the right to family life is a shared right. But once a family unit disintegrates the separating members' separate rights can only be to a fragmented family life. Certainly the absent parent has the right to participation to the extent and in what manner the complex circumstances of the individual case dictate.

[36] But despite the fact that this appeal has raised only the asserted Art 8 rights of the secondary caring parent, we should not lose sight of the Art 8 rights of the primary carer, although not specifically asserted in argument. However an appeal may well arise in which a disappointed applicant will contend that s 13(1)(b) of the Children Act 1989 imposes a disproportionate restriction on a parent's right to determine her place of habitual residence. This right was recognised by the decision of this court in *Re E (Residence: Imposition of Conditions)* [1997] 2 FLR 638 within the confines of the jurisdiction of the court and indeed beyond within the UK. But why should the same right not extend to anywhere within the European Union (having regard to Art 48 of the Treaty of Rome) or, beyond that, within wider Europe? From that point to a right to world-wide mobility seems but a short step.

[39] . . . As early as 1988, the House of Lords stated that the European Convention for the Protection of Human Rights and Fundamental Freedoms 1950 in no way conflicted with the requirements in English law that in all matters concerning the upbringing of a child, welfare was paramount (*Re KD (A Minor) (Access: Principles)* [1988] 2 FLR 139). This has been restated recently in *Dawson v Wearmouth* [1999] 1 FLR 1167, *Re A (Adoption: Mother's Objections)* [2000] 1 FLR 665 and *Re N (Leave to Withdraw Care Proceedings)* [2000] 1 FLR 134 . . .

[40] However there is a danger that if the regard which the court pays to the reasonable proposals of the primary carer were elevated into a legal presumption then there would be an obvious risk of the breach of the respondent's rights not only under Art 8 but also his rights under Art 6 to a fair trial. To guard against the risk of too perfunctory an investigation resulting from too ready an assumption that the mother's proposals are necessarily compatible with the child's welfare I would suggest the following discipline as a prelude to conclusion:

(a) Pose the question: is the mother's application genuine in the sense that it is not motivated by some selfish desire to exclude the father from the child's life? Then ask is the mother's application realistic, by which I mean founded on practical proposals both well researched and investigated? If the application fails either of these tests refusal will inevitably follow.

(b) If however the application passes these tests then there must be a careful appraisal of the father's opposition: is it motivated by genuine concern for the future of the child's welfare or is it driven by some ulterior motive? What would be the extent of the detriment to him and his future relationship with the child were the application granted? To what extent would that be offset by extension of the child's relationships with the maternal family and homeland?

(c) What would be the impact on the mother, either as the single parent or as a new wife, of a refusal of her realistic proposal? [Where the mother cares for the child or proposes to care for the child within a new family, the impact of refusal on the new family and on the stepfather or prospective stepfather must also be carefully calculated.[1]]

(d) The outcome of the second and third appraisals must then be brought into an overriding review of the child's welfare as the paramount consideration, directed by the statutory checklist insofar as appropriate.

[41] In suggesting such a discipline I would not wish to be thought to have diminished the importance that this court has consistently attached to the emotional and psychological well-being of the primary carer. In any evaluation of the welfare of the child as the paramount consideration great weight must be given to this factor.

DAME ELIZABETH BUTLER-SLOSS P:

[77] The implementation of the Children Act 1989 in 1991 gave the courts a larger menu of possible orders and a greater flexibility. The Children Act 1989 gave to the majority of parents the new concept of parental responsibility, (see ss 2 and 4) and diminished the impact of a former custody order and the perceived control of the custodial parent over the decision-making with regard to the children of the family. In s 8 residence orders replaced custody orders and the non-residential parent had greater responsibility and rights over the child during periods of access, now called contact. The earlier emphasis upon the rights of the custodial parent had therefore to be reconsidered in the light

---

[1] Authors' note: this sentence was added to the discipline by Thorpe LJ in *Re B (Removal from Jurisdiction), Re S (Removal from Jurisdiction)*[2003] EWCA Civ 1149, [2003] 2 FLR 1043 at [11].

of the philosophy of the Children Act 1989. In *MH v GP (Child: Emigration)* [1995] 2 FLR 106 Thorpe J was asked to approve the application of a single mother to remove permanently to New Zealand with her 4-year-old son. The father had regular contact with his son. Thorpe J said at 110:

> '... in approaching the first question, whether or not there should be leave for permanent removal, I apply the principles which have stood largely unchanged since the decision of the Court of Appeal in *Poel v Poel* [1970] 1 WLR 1469. In the later case of *Chamberlain v de la Mare* (1983) 4 FLR 434, a strong Court of Appeal stated that, in considering whether to give leave, the welfare of the child was the first and paramount consideration, but that leave should not be withheld unless the interests of the children and those of the custodial parent were clearly shown to be incompatible.
>
> That statement of principle creates a presumption in favour of the reasonable application of the custodial parent, but in weighing whether the reasonable application is or is not incompatible with the welfare of D, I have to assess the importance of the relationship between D and his father, not only as it is but as it should develop. The relationship with the father is the doorway through which D relates to other members of the family, particularly his half-sister L, his paternal grandmother, and his paternal first cousins. That is the crux of this case.'

[79] In *Re H (Application to Remove from Jurisdiction)* [1998] 1 FLR 848, the mother remarried and wished to move to the US with her new husband, an American. The father had played an unusually large role in caring for the child as a baby and continued to keep closely in touch with her. The judge said that it was a finely balanced case but gave the mother leave to remove the child permanently from the jurisdiction. The father appealed. Thorpe LJ, (as he became), referred to *Poel v Poel* [1970] 1 WLR 1469 and subsequent reported cases in his judgment and said at 853:

> '... these applications for leave are always difficult cases that require very profound investigation and judgment. But not a lot is to be gained by seeking support from past decisions, however superficially similar the factual matrix may appear to be. In my judgment, the approach that the court must adopt in these cases has not evolved or developed in any way since the decision of this court in *Poel v Poel*.'

[80] In *Re C (Leave to Remove from Jurisdiction)* [2000] 2 FLR 457 this court (Morritt, Thorpe and Chadwick LJJ) took the same approach, citing *Poel v Poel* [1970] 1 WLR 1469, *Chamberlain v de la Mare* (1983) 4 FLR 434 and *MH v GP (Child: Emigration)* [1995] 2 FLR 106, although they differed on the outcome.

[81] The Human Rights Act 1998 came into force in October 2000 and all the previous decisions have to be scrutinised in the light of the European Convention for the Protection of Human Rights and Fundamental Freedoms 1950 ...

[82] All those immediately affected by the proceedings, that is to say the mother, the father and the child have rights under Art 8(1). Those rights inevitably in a case such as the present appeal are in conflict and, under Art 8(2), have to be balanced against the rights of the others. In addition and of the greatest significance is the welfare of the child which, according to European jurisprudence, is of crucial importance, and where in conflict with a parent is overriding (see *Johansen v Norway* (1996) 23 EHRR 33 at 67 and 72). Article 8(2) recognises that a public authority, in this case the court, may interfere with the right to family life where it does so in accordance with the law, and where it is necessary in a democratic society for, inter alia, the protection of the rights and freedoms of others and the decision is proportionate to the need demonstrated. That position appears to me to be similar to that which arises in all child-based family disputes and the European case-law on children is in line with the principles set out in the Children Act 1989. I do not, for my part, consider that the Convention has affected the principles the courts should apply in dealing with these difficult issues. Its implementation into English law does however give us the opportunity to take another look at the way the principles have been expressed in the past and whether there should now be a reformulation of those principles. I think it would be helpful to do so, since they may have been expressed from time to time in too rigid terms. The judgment of Thorpe J in *MH v GP (Child: Emigration)* [1995] 2 FLR 106 was the first time to my knowledge that the word 'presumption' had been used in the reported cases, and I would respectfully suggest that it over-emphasised one element of the approach in the earlier cases. I can understand why the word was used, since in *Tyler v Tyler* [1989] 2 FLR 158 the reformulation by Purchas LJ of the principles in *Poel v Poel* [1970] 1 WLR 1469 and *Chamberlain v de la Mare* (1983) 4 FLR 434 may itself have been expressed unduly firmly.

[83] Section 13(1)(b) of the Children Act 1989 does not create any presumption and the criteria in s 1 clearly govern the application. The underlying principles in *Poel* (above), as explained in *Chamberlain* (above), have stood the test of time and give valuable guidance as to the approach the court should adopt in these most difficult cases. It is, in my view, helpful to go back to look again at the reasons given in both those decisions. They were based upon the welfare of the child which was the first and paramount consideration by virtue of s 1 of the Guardianship of Minors Act 1971. The view of both courts was well-summarised by Griffiths LJ in *Chamberlain* (above), that the welfare of young children was best met by bringing them up in a happy, secure family atmosphere. Their happiness and security, after the creation of a new family unit, will depend on becoming members of the new family. Reasonable arrangements made by the mother or stepfather to relocate should not in principle be frustrated, since it would be likely to have an adverse effect upon the new family. It might reflect upon the stability of the new relationship. The stress upon the second family would inevitably have a serious adverse effect upon the children whose welfare is paramount. Even if there is not a new relationship, the effect upon the parent with the residence order of the frustration of plans for the future might have an equally bad effect upon the children. If the arrangements are sensible and the proposals are genuinely important to the applicant parent and the effect of refusal of the application would be seriously adverse to the new family, eg mother and child, or the mother, stepfather and child, then this would be, as Griffiths LJ said, a factor that had to be given great weight when weighing up the various factors in the balancing exercise.

[84] The strength of the relationship with the other parent, usually the father, and the paternal family will be a highly relevant factor, see *MH v GP (Child: Emigration)* [1995] 2 FLR 106. The ability of the other parent to continue contact with the child and the financial implications need to be explored. There may well be other relevant factors to weigh in the balance, such as, with the elder child, his/her views, the importance of schooling or other ties to the current home area. The state of health of the child and availability of specialist medical expertise or other special needs may be another factor. There are, of course, many other factors which may arise in an individual case. I stress that there is no presumption in favour of the applicant, but reasonable proposals made by the applicant parent, the refusal of which would have adverse consequences upon the stability of the new family and therefore an adverse effect upon the welfare of the child, continue to be a factor of great weight. As in every case in which the court has to exercise its discretion, the reasonableness of the proposals, the effect upon the applicant and upon the child of refusal of the application, the effect of a reduction or cessation of contact with the other parent upon the child, the effect of removal of the child from his/her current environment are all factors, among others which I have not enumerated, which have to be given appropriate weight in each individual case and weighed in the balance. The decision is always a difficult one and has not become less so over the last 30 years.

Summary

[85] In summary I would suggest that the following considerations should be in the forefront of the mind of a judge trying one of these difficult cases. They are not and could not be exclusive of the other important matters which arise in the individual case to be decided. All the relevant factors need to be considered, including the points I make below, so far as they are relevant, and weighed in the balance. The points I make are obvious but in view of the arguments presented to us in this case, it may be worthwhile to repeat them:

(a) The welfare of the child is always paramount.

(b) There is no presumption created by s 13(1)(b) in favour of the applicant parent.

(c) The reasonable proposals of the parent with a residence order wishing to live abroad carry great weight.

(d) Consequently the proposals have to be scrutinised with care and the court needs to be satisfied that there is a genuine motivation for the move and not the intention to bring contact between the child and the other parent to an end.

(e) The effect upon the applicant parent and the new family of the child of a refusal of leave is very important.

(f) The effect upon the child of the denial of contact with the other parent and in some cases his family is very important.

(g) The opportunity for continuing contact between the child and the parent left behind may be very significant.

[86] All the above observations have been made on the premise that the question of residence is not a live issue. If, however, there is a real dispute as to which parent should be granted a residence order, and the decision as to which parent is the more suitable is finely balanced, the future plans of each parent for the child are clearly relevant. If one parent intends to set up home in another country and remove the child from school, surroundings and the other parent and his family, it may in some cases be an important factor to weigh in the balance. But in a case where the decision as to residence is clear as the judge in this case clearly thought it was, the plans for removal from the jurisdiction would not be likely to be significant in the decision over residence.

3.2

J V S (LEAVE TO REMOVE)
[2010] EWHC 2098 (FAM), [2011] 1 FLR 1694

A3.2

Family Division

ELEANOR KING J:

[10] This is a truly international family. The boys are Japanese and Swedish nationals and passport holders, but have spent all their lives in London. As is commonplace with bi-lingual families, in the early days at home the mother spoke to the children in her mother-tongue (Japanese) and the father spoke to them in English. When the children were at nursery school they attended a Japanese nursery school full time.

[75] A starting point of any consideration of authorities is *Payne v Payne* [2001] EWCA Civ 166, [2001] 1 FLR 1052 . . .

[77] In *Re G (Leave to Remove)* [2007] EWCA Civ 1497, [2008] 1 FLR 1587, the appellant in that case launched a wholesale attack on the *Payne* discipline. It was suggested that the *Payne* approach is outdated and heavily criticised by judges, academics and practitioners and that, in modern times, when joint or shared residence orders have become commonplace, judges in applying the principles in *Payne* were applying them on the basis of a status of sole residence order and sole primary carer. The Court of Appeal, having considered those submissions, disagreed and declined to re-visit the guidance in *Payne*. Thorpe LJ said in *Re G* at para [19]:

> 'These cases are particularly traumatic for the parties, since each of them conceives so much as being at stake. They are very, very difficult cases for the trial judges. Often the balance is very fine between grant and refusal. The judge is only too aware of how heavily invested each of the parents is in the outcome for which they contend. The judges are very well aware of how profoundly the decision will affect the future lives of the children and how difficult it will be for the disappointed parent to adjust to the outcome. Despite the difficulties that these cases present, certainly from the perspective of this court, the principles enunciated in *Payne v Payne* are well understood and have been of evident assistance to trial judges in the difficult task that they perform. The Court of Appeal therefore recognises that relocation cases are by, their very nature, difficult and frequently finely balanced.'

[78] In the recent case of *Re D (Leave to Remove: Appeal)* Wall LJ acknowledged the criticisms that there had been in the *Payne* approach. He said at para [33]:

> '... there is a perfectly respectable argument for the proposition that it places too great an emphasis on the wishes and feelings of the relocating parent, and ignores or relegates the harm done of children by a permanent breach of the relationship which children have with the left behind parent.'

The President, however, concluded in that case that all the facts had been fully and properly considered by the judge and that the case was not one where there should be consideration of the principles contained in *Payne*.

. . .

[80]   Finally, Mostyn J has recently refused a mother's application to relocate in *Re AR (A Child: Relocation)* [2010] EWHC 1346 (Fam), [2010] 2 FLR 1577 and, in doing so, analysed the emphasis on the effect on the primary carer and the criticisms which have been made of that approach.

[81]   [Counsel for the father] properly and appropriately accepted in submissions that this court is bound by the Court of Appeal decision in *Payne*. I have, therefore, to decide this case on the basis of the *Payne* discipline regardless of whatever a growing tide of opinion may or may not say about that approach. What [counsel] says is that, at the end of the day, *Payne* says one thing namely that the welfare of these two children is paramount. I agree. This court, he submits, must be careful not to allow itself to become confined in a strait-jacket, with the series of questions presenting the only test. Care, he says, must be taken to ensure that the question of the impact of refusal of the mother is but one component of an assessment of the best interests of the boys and not the only feature. I unhesitatingly agree.

[82] The welfare of these boys is paramount. In conducting the balancing exercise I am bound by the discipline of *Payne*, not limited to the questions set out by Thorpe LJ, but also with the judgment of Lady Butler-Sloss P (as she then was) at the forefront of my mind. I consider *Payne* only under the umbrella of the paramountcy rule and using the welfare checklist as a tool to assist me, whilst always bearing in mind the Art 8 rights of these children.

[94]   Although there may be mounting criticism of *Payne* in some quarters, it should be remembered that Thorpe LJ gave his guidance in the context of two types of case namely the primary carer who wished to relocate following a new partner to a different part of the world and, secondly, the foreign national who wishes to return home. In the context of this case parts of Thorpe's LJ judgment resonate as strongly now as when it was written ...

[95] Mostyn J in his recent decision of *Re AR (A Child: Relocation)* recorded his views on how the impact of refusal on a parent should be regarded in these cases. He says at para [8]:

'Indeed there is a strong view that the heavy emphasis on the emotional reaction of the thwarted primary carer represents an illegitimate gloss on the purity of the paramountcy principle. Moreover, some argue that it promotes selfishness and detracts from the importance of co-parenting.'

At para [12], commenting on Wilson LJ in *Re H (Leave to Remove)* [2010] EWCA Civ 915, [2010] 2 FLR 1875:

'Certainly the factor of the impact on the thwarted primary carer deserves its own berth and as such deserves its due weight, no more, no less. The problem with the attribution of great weight to this particular factor is that, paradoxically, it appears to penalise selflessness and virtue, while rewarding selfishness and uncontrolled emotions.'

[96] I endorse Mostyn J's analysis of the potential paradox that the assessment of impact can throw up namely that, if disproportionate weight is given to the impact on the mother, it can be seen to penalise the mother who sets aside her own personal wishes for the sake of her children. With respect to Mostyn J and Wilson LJ, I think that the use of the expression 'thwarted primary carer' is not helpful. It seems to me that such an expression carries with it pejorative overtones which may have the effect of obscuring the fact that any court before moving to consider the impact of refusal as a primary concern will, under the *Payne* discipline, already have considered the motive of that primary carer in making the application. If the court has not been satisfied in that regard, the application will already have been dismissed prior to any consideration being given to the impact of refusal on the applicant.

[99] It is important that no court dealing with these cases shrinks from examining what the children involved will lose if the application is granted. For my part, I do not subscribe to the view that email and Skype are tolerable substitutes for lying around on a sofa on a Saturday evening, eating pizza and watching a DVD with your dad, or being taken into school by him every other Monday. Often, even on the most restrictive application of the *Payne* discipline, the loss of frequent informal contact between father and child will be considered to be too high a price to pay to satisfying a primary carer's desire to relocate. In such circumstances even the knowledge that the mother will be bitterly disappointed and resentful will not drive a court to the conclusion that the children's interests lie in allowing relocation.

[103] The court has had the benefit of the jointly instructed expert, Mikiko Otani. Ms Otani has prepared three reports, all of which I have read more than once with care. There is no concept of a mirror order in Japan. Jurisdiction passes to Japan upon change of residence. The suggestion is that a mediation agreement should be put in place to put before the Japanese court in the event of dispute. The reality is that such an agreement would be open to alteration.

The mother is willing to enter into a mediation agreement. The father's case is that, with no disrespect intended to Japan, there is in fact no comity and no regard for orders made in foreign jurisdictions. I remind myself that this is not a child abduction case but a relocation case where orders are to be made in circumstances where the court has found, and the Cafcass officer has accepted, that the mother wishes and intends to promote the relationship between the father and the children into the future. It would be more comfortable for the court, and more importantly for the father, if Japan were a signatory to the Hague Convention on the Civil Aspects of International Child Abduction 1980, but it is not and I have, therefore, to pay particular regard to my assessment of the mother and my view as to whether she can be trusted. I form the view that she can be trusted. The father is seeking the most draconian security in the event of relocation, far more than what is usually required even where there has been an earlier abduction. I have had, however, the clear impression that he does trust the mother and that his fear (and his justified fear) is that the bond with his children will inevitably slacken when they are living so far away and he, quite simply, does not want them to go.

[104] This mother has a very heavy burden resting upon her shoulders as a result of the decision I make today to allow her to relocate. This court is trusting her, but, more importantly, her children are trusting her to honour the trust that I am placing in her today. Her duty must now be to make sure that these very young children who are to be taken so far away from this unimpeachable and loving father have as much contact as can be achieved and that, at all stages of their day-to-day life, their relationship is nurtured and progressed with their father. The mother is the one who will most often find that she must be flexible, both as to arrangements and as to contact. She must be the one that has the tedium and difficulty of rearranging arrangements or having to alter things to allow for the father to take up contact and more important to allow the children to spend as much time as possible with their father. That is not to say that the father can be unreasonable, inconsistent or unpredictable as that too would adversely impact on the boys but rather that the mother show a generosity of nature and flexibility to ensure that contact takes place as she has promised it will. If the mother does not do this she will have herself to reproach for any loss of the relationship these children are entitled to have with their father as they grow up. I hope very much that one of the first things she will do is think about whether or not there could be some compromise as to the schooling of the children when they move to live in Japan.

3.3

K V K (RELOCATION: SHARED CARE ARRANGEMENT) [2011] EWCA CIV 793, [2012] 2 FLR 880

A3.3

Court of Appeal

Thorpe, Moore-Bick and Black LJJ

THORPE LJ:

Family background

[12]   The mother is of Canadian origin. The father is Polish although he spent childhood years in Canada. He moved to England in 1993 and the mother arrived here 10 years later.

[13]   The parents married in London on 27th July 2004. They have two daughters, I born 16th November 2006 and A born on 8th January 2009. Later in that year the marriage became unhappy and in July 2010 divorce proceedings were filed and the mother moved out of the matrimonial home, renting a flat in Pimlico.

[14]   Both are employed in the banking world and both work less than full time to enable them to be more involved with the children. A shared residence order was made by the District Judge on 23rd August 2010. Under its terms the girls spend five nights with their father and nine nights with their mother in every fourteen day period.

[15]   However, as [counsel for the father] explained, the father is released from work on Friday and Monday. Thus he has six consecutive days with his daughters. During this period he cares for the girls unaided.

[16]   The mother does not work on Wednesday. On that day, and at the weekends, she is with the children. Otherwise she relies upon the nanny who moved with her when she left the home. Thus although the mother has more nights the girls spend more daylight hours in the company of their father. So . . . this is a case in which there is not only a shared residence order but also an arrangement for the sharing of care under which the father's part is not inferior to the mother's.

[27]   Both counsel in their submissions have taken us through the line of authorities in this field. [Counsel for the father] began at the beginning with the judgments of this court in *Poel v Poel* [1971] WLR 1460, then followed *A v A* (1980) 1 FLR 380, *Payne v Payne* [2001] 1 FLR 1052, *Re Y* [2004] 2 FLR 330 and *C v C (International Relocation: Shared Care Arrangement)* [2011] EWHC 335 (Fam), [2011] 2 FLR 701.

[28]   The purpose of this journey was to demonstrate how reliant the line of authority is on the primary carer status of the applicant. Since the judgment of Hedley J in *Re Y* there is clear authority that the *Payne v Payne* line is not to be applied in cases where the applicant shares the care of the children more or less equally with the respondent.

[29]   [Counsel for the mother] also draws attention to *Payne* and particularly paragraph 11 which establishes that the children were in the physical care of the respondent for just over 40% of their routine. He then referred us to the decision of this court in *Re L* [2009] 1 FLR 1157 from which he seeks to extract the proposition that the same principles apply whether the applicant is a primary carer or a parent with shared residence order. For completeness he also drew our attention to the very recent decision of this court in *Re W (Relocation: Removal Outside Jurisdiction)* [2011] EWCA Civ 345, [2011] 2 FLR 409.

[35]   . . . Given the extent to which the father was providing daily care, the judge should have considered and applied the dicta of Hedley J in *Re Y* rather than those of the President in Payne. Unfortunately it appears that the case of *Re Y* was not cited and the judge can surely be excused from overlooking it.

The Law

[38]   Given the full and careful citation of authority it is necessary to make some further observation on the state of the case law.

[39]   As my Lord, Moore-Bick LJ, pointed out in argument, the only principle to be extracted from *Payne v Payne* is the paramountcy principle. All the rest, whether in paragraphs 40 and 41 of my judgment or in paragraphs 85 and 86 of the President's judgment is guidance as to factors to be weighed in search of the welfare paramountcy.

[40]   In family law principles are scarce and generally the more important function of this court is to state guidance. Guidance that directs the exercise of the welfare discretion is equivalent to a statutory checklist. It is valuable if it renders outcomes more predictable and if it supports judges in reaching and explaining discretionary conclusions in a way that is not open to appellate challenge.

[41]   I am in no doubt at all that the guidance in *Payne* is posited on the premise that the applicant is the primary carer. It so states in terms.

[42] It also reflects the fact that its foundation is the judgment of this court in *Poel*.

[43] In 1970, when *Poel* was decided, the court's statutory power was to make custody orders, care and control orders and access orders. Granting custody to one parent and care and control to the other was judicially criticised. Equally it was said that custody should not be awarded jointly to both parents, save in exceptional circumstances. So the ratio of the court was that, whilst the welfare of the child was paramount, the custodial parent should be supported in her choice of habitual residence. As Sachs LJ put it in his judgment, post separation a child 'instead of being in the joint custody of both parents, must of necessity, become one who is in the custody of a single parent.'

[44] Of course that all now seems archaic given our shift from parental power to parental responsibility introduced by the Children Act 1989 and given the more recent emphasis on the value to children of shared parenting where the parental relationship and the circumstances are favourable.

. . .

[46] Thus the survival of the authority of *Poel* into this century, in my judgment depends crucially upon the primacy of the applicant's care. As [counsel for the father] put it, if she is supplying so much she must be supported in her task precisely because the children are so dependent on her stability and wellbeing. Once the care is shared there is not the same dependency and the role of each parent may be equally important. The judgments in *Poel* consider only the position of the primary carer and an earlier position where there is a pending contest as to who should be the primary carer. Payne does not anywhere consider what should be the court's approach to an application where there is no primary carer.

[47] Another factor not considered in *Payne* is the mobility of the respondent: could he, should he also move? That is a factor which has risen in prominence over the last decade.

[48] Despite a considerable degree of criticism, the decision in *Payne* has been consistently applied over the last decade in cases in which the applicant is a primary carer. The continuity of that proposition is demonstrated by the judgment of the President in the case of *Re W (Relocation: Removal Outside Jurisdiction)* [2011] EWCA Civ 345, [2011] 2 FLR 409 ...

[56] Finally I must deal with the authority which I consider the judge should have applied namely *Re Y*. Having cited Payne and the President's guidance at paragraph 85, Hedley J continued:

'[14] Now, the court clearly contemplates two different states of affairs. The one, the more common and in some ways the more obvious, is where the child is clearly living with one parent, and it is that parent that wishes to leave the jurisdiction, for whatever reason. The other, and much less common state of affairs, is where that does not exist and either there is a real issue about where the child should live, or there is in place an arrangement which demonstrates that the child's home is equally with both parents. In those circumstances, which are the ones that apply in this case, many of the factors to which the court drew attention in *Payne v Payne* [2001] EWCA Civ 166, [2001] Fam 473, [2001] 1 FLR 1052 whilst relevant may carry less weight than otherwise they commonly do.

[15] The father does not have an application for a residence order in this case, but it was raised only in response to the mother's application for permission to remove, and the father's actual proposal is for a continuation of the present position.

[16] This case accordingly falls outside the main run of cases that one encounters where this problem is raised, and certainly within my own experience is unique. What it seems to me I must do is to remind myself of the opening provisions of the Children Act 1989. Section 1(1) says that when a court determines any question with respect to the upbringing of a child, the child's welfare shall be the court's paramount consideration, and in considering these issues I have to take a number of matters into account as required by s 1(3). It seems to me that of those matters, the ones that are important in this case are the educational and emotional needs of Y, the likely effect on him of any change in his circumstances, and his age and background so far as his life is presently concerned. It seems to me that I need to remind myself that the welfare of this child is the lodestar by which the court at the end of the day is guided.'

[57] I fully concur with the reasoning and conclusion of Hedley J. What is significant is not the label 'shared residence' because we see cases in which for a particular reason the label is attached to what is no more than a conventional contact order. What is significant is the practical arrangements for sharing the burden of care between two equally committed carers. Where each is providing a more or less equal proportion and one seeks to relocate externally then I am clear that the approach which I suggested in paragraph 40 in *Payne v Payne* should not be utilised. The judge should rather exercise his discretion to grant or refuse by applying the statutory checklist in section 1(3) of the Children Act 1989.

[58] An excellent example of this approach is to be seen in the recent judgment of Mrs Justice Theis in the case of *C v C (International Relocation: Shared Care Arrangement)* [2011] EWHC 335 (Fam), [2011] 2 FLR 701. Under the sub-heading 'Welfare check list' she turns in paragraph 64 to a detailed consideration of its subparagraphs over the course of three pages of judgment. That exercise leads her to her conclusion stated in paragraphs 65 and 67.

[59] The adjustment in judicial approach signalled by Hedley J is unlikely to affect many orders. A recent national survey, 'Understanding Society', puts the proportion of equal shared care at 3.1% of the total.

MOORE-BICK LJ:

[77]   *Payne v Payne* was in one sense a less complicated case than the present in as much as the mother had a residence order in her favour and was treated for practical purposes as the sole carer of the child, even though the father also provided a significant amount of care. There was evidence that continuing to live in England rather than being able to return to her family in New Zealand was having an adverse effect on her mental well-being and thus on the welfare of the child. No doubt the guidance which the judgments contain is of great value, but it must be read and understood in the particular context in which it was given.

[78]   In *Re Y (Leave to Remove from the Jurisdiction)* [2004] 2 FLR 330 the circumstances were different in some material respects. In particular, the child was the subject of an informal arrangement between his parents under which they shared his care almost equally and he had become integrated into the culture of Wales where he and both his parents lived. Having considered *Payne v Payne*, Hedley J held that many of the factors to which the court there drew attention carried less weight than might otherwise have been the case because of the particular circumstances of the parties before him. He declined to allow the mother to take the child with her to the United States, even though there was evidence that she felt isolated and distressed living in the United Kingdom and wished to return to her own country. The judge reminded himself, rightly in my view, that the welfare of the child was 'the lodestar by which the court at the end of the day is guided' and which in the last analysis 'overbears all other considerations, however powerful and reasonable they may be.'

[79]   If matters had remained there, I doubt whether the decision in *Payne v Payne* would have attracted much, or indeed any, criticism, but they did not. In *Re G (Leave to Remove)* [2007] EWCA Civ 1497, [2008] 1 FLR 1587 the father sought to challenge an order giving the mother permission to remove the children to Germany on the grounds that the guidance in *Payne v Payne* had become outdated and was being wrongly applied in cases where there were shared residence orders. In that case the children were in fact spending almost half their time with him. When refusing permission to appeal Thorpe LJ expressed the view that the court was bound by the decision in *Payne v Payne* as long as there had been no clear social change that required its reconsideration and that there had been none ... The court's attention does not appear to have been drawn to *Re Y (Leave to Remove from the Jurisdiction)* and the decision appears to have been treated as reinforcing the view that the detailed guidance given in *Payne v Payne* is to be followed regardless of the particular circumstances of the case.

[80]   Counsel also sought to refer us to the decision in *Re D (Leave to Remove: Appeal)* [2010] EWCA Civ 50, [2010] 2 FLR 1605, another case in which the father of a child sought permission to appeal on the grounds that the guidance in *Payne v Payne* placed too much emphasis on the wishes and feelings of the relocating parent and ignored the harm done by severing the child's relationship with the parent left behind. Wall LJ refused the application and in doing so expressed the view that the principles and guidelines in *Payne v Payne* could be altered only by legislation or by a decision of the Supreme Court ...

[81] In *Re H (Leave to Remove)* [2010] EWCA Civ 915, [2010] 2 FLR 1875 a further attempt was made to challenge what was seen as a too rigid application of Payne v Payne. Wilson LJ said (paragraph 21):

> 'In this court we are well aware of the criticisms made, both domestically and internationally, of its decision in Payne. Nevertheless one must beware of endorsing a parody of the decision. Both Thorpe LJ, at [26(a)], and the President, Dame Elizabeth Butler Sloss, at [85(a)], stressed that, in the determination of applications for permission to relocate, the welfare of the child was the paramount consideration. It is only against the subsidiary guidance to be collected from Payne that criticisms can perhaps more easily be levelled.'

[82] He then referred to paragraphs 26(b), 32 and 40 of the judgment of Thorpe LJ which, he said, had given rise to some controversy among family lawyers. He also referred to the Washington Declaration and rejected the submission that this court should replace the guidance given in Payne v Payne with that contained in paragraphs 3 and 4 of the Declaration, describing it as 'lacking elementary legal discipline'.

. . .

[86] I accept, of course, that the decision in *Payne v Payne* is binding on this court, as it is on all courts apart from the Supreme Court, but it is binding in the true sense only for its ratio decidendi. Nonetheless, I would also accept that where this court gives guidance on the proper approach to take in resolving any particular kind of dispute, judges at all levels must pay heed to that guidance and depart from it only after careful deliberation and when it is clear that the particular circumstances of the case require them to do so in order to give effect to fundamental principles. I am conscious that any views I express on this subject will be seen as coming from one who has little familiarity with family law and practice. Nonetheless, having considered *Payne v Payne* itself and the authorities in which it has been discussed, I cannot help thinking that the controversy which now surrounds it is the result of a failure to distinguish clearly between legal principle and guidance. In my view Wilson L.J. was, with respect, quite right to warn against endorsing a parody of the decision. As I read it, the only principle of law enunciated in *Payne v Payne* is that the welfare of the child is paramount; all the rest is guidance. Such difficulty as has arisen is the result of treating that guidance as if it contained principles of law from which no departure is permitted. Guidance of the kind provided in *Payne v Payne* is, of course, very valuable both in ensuring that judges identify what are likely to be the most important factors to be taken into account and the weight that should generally be attached to them. It also plays a valuable role in promoting consistency in decision-making. However, the circumstances in which these difficult decisions have to be made vary infinitely and the judge in each case must be free to weigh up the individual factors and make whatever decision he or she considers to be in the best interests of the child. As Hedley J said in *Re Y*, the welfare of the child overbears all other considerations, however powerful and reasonable they may be. I do not think that the court in *Payne v Payne* intended to suggest otherwise.

BLACK LJ:

[94] I have arrived at the same conclusion as my Lord, Lord Justice Thorpe, and my Lord, Lord Justice Moore-Bick and agree that permission must be granted and the appeal allowed.

[95] However, as I have come to this conclusion by a route that is not entirely the same as Thorpe LJ's, I should explain how my reasoning differs.

. . .

[141] The first point that is quite clear is that, as I have said already, the principle – the only authentic principle – that runs through the entire line of relocation authorities is that the welfare of the child is the court's paramount consideration. Everything that is considered by the court in reaching its determination is put into the balance with a view to measuring its impact on the child.

[142] Whilst this is the only truly inescapable principle in the jurisprudence, that does not mean that everything else – the valuable guidance – can be ignored. It must be heeded for all the reasons that Moore-Bick LJ gives but as guidance not as rigid principle or so as to dictate a particular outcome in a sphere of law where the facts of individual cases are so infinitely variable.

[143] Furthermore, the effect of the guidance must not be overstated. Even where the case concerns a true primary carer, there is no presumption that the reasonable relocation plans of that carer will be facilitated unless there is some compelling reason to the contrary, nor any similar presumption however it may be expressed. Thorpe LJ said so in terms in *Payne* and it is not appropriate, therefore, to isolate other sentences from his judgment, such as the final sentence of paragraph 26 ('Therefore her application to relocate will be granted unless the court concludes that it is incompatible with the welfare of the children') for re-elevation to a status akin to that of a determinative presumption. It is doubly inappropriate when one bears in mind that the judgments in *Payne* must be read as a whole, with proper weight given to what the then President said. She said that she wished to reformulate the principles since they may have been expressed from time to time in too rigid terms with the word 'presumption' over-emphasising one element of the approach (paragraph 82) whereas the criteria in s 1 Children Act govern the application (paragraph 83) and there is no presumption in favour of the applicant (paragraph 84). Dame Elizabeth referred, of course, to the effect on the parent with residence (paragraphs 83 and 84) but she also stressed that the relationship with the other parent is highly relevant and that there are many other factors which may arise in an individual case (paragraph 84). I detect in her discussion of the factors and in her summary at paragraph 85 no weighting in favour of any particular factor. She said that the reasonable proposals of the parent with a residence order wishing to live abroad carry 'great weight' whereas the effect on the child of denying contact with the other parent is 'very important' but I do not infer from that phraseology any loading in favour of the reasonable proposals as opposed to the effect of the loss of contact.

[144] *Payne* therefore identifies a number of factors which will or may be relevant in a relocation case, explains their importance to the welfare of the child, and suggests helpful disciplines to ensure that the proper matters are considered in reaching a decision but it does not dictate the outcome of a case. I do not see Hedley J's decision in *Re Y* as representative of a different line of authority from *Payne*, applicable where the child's care is shared between the parents as opposed to undertaken by one primary carer; I see it as a decision within the framework of which *Payne* is part. It exemplifies how the weight attached to the relevant factors alters depending upon the facts of the case.

[145] Accordingly, I would not expect to find cases bogged down with arguments as to whether the time spent with each of the parents or other aspects of the care arrangements are such as to make the case 'a *Payne* case' or 'a *Re Y* case', nor would I expect preliminary skirmishes over the label to be applied to the child's arrangements with a view to a parent having a shared residence order in his or her armoury for deployment in the event of a relocation application. The ways in which parents provide for the care of their children are, and should be, infinitely varied. In the best of cases they are flexible and responsive to the needs of the children over time. When a relocation application falls to be determined, all of the facts need to be considered.

3.4

RE A (SECURITY FOR RETURN TO JURISDICTION) (NOTE) [1999] 2 FLR 1 (FD)

A3.4

Family Division

WALL J:

ORDER:

Children Act 1989

Upon hearing leading counsel for the applicant mother and counsel for the father;

And upon reading the bundle lodged with the court;

And upon hearing the oral evidence of the mother, the father […]

And upon the mother undertaking:

(1) to return the child, A, to the jurisdiction of England and Wales not later than 3 September 1996;

(2) prior to her and the said child's departure from England to make a declaration on the Quran, if possible before the Head of the Muslim College, Dr Zaki Badawi, or before the Imam of the Regent's Park Mosque or before an Islamic law official in London that she will return A to the jurisdiction of England and Wales not later than 3 September 1996;

(3) to deliver, by her solicitors, to the court prior to her departure copies of sworn declarations by her father and her brother, such declarations to be:

    (i) sworn on the Holy Quran before a Shariah court;
    (ii) in Arabic, accompanied by a certified translation in English;
    (iii) in substantially the same terms as the draft declaration for her father annexed hereto, with such necessary amendments as may be required in the case of the declaration by her brother;

provided that in the case of the declaration by the mother's father, and the requirement that the declaration shall be made and sworn before a Shariah court the mother shall have liberty to apply to Wall J prior to 26 July 1996 on short notice in the event that her father declines to make such declaration and/or it is impracticable to make the said declarations before the Shariah court.

IT IS ORDERED THAT:

(1)   The applicant mother have leave to remove the child A (born 4 December 1990) from the jurisdiction of England and Wales for the purpose of a holiday in the Kingdom of Saudi Arabia, such holiday:

(i)   to commence on or after 3 August 1996;
(ii)   to be for not more than 28 days;
(iii)   to end not later than 3 September 1996.

(2)   Save for para 4 of the order of Singer J on 10 June 1996, all previous orders and undertakings in relation to the passports of the applicant mother and the said child shall be discharged.

(3)   The applicant mother's passport shall be held by her solicitors, Hecht & Co, until 1 August 1996 or until the documents referred to in the mother's undertakings recorded above have been delivered to the court, whichever shall be the later, and thereafter the said firm may release the mother's passport to her.

(4)   The child's passport (when issued by the Passport Office):

(i)   shall be delivered to and retained by the mother for the purpose of the holiday provided for herein;
(ii)   shall be delivered by the mother to her said solicitors within 5 days of her and the child's return to England and Wales after the said holiday and in any event not later than 2.00 pm on Monday, 9 September 1996;
(iii)   shall thereafter be held by the said firm and not released without the leave of the court.

(5)   All previous orders for contact shall be discharged.

(6)   The respondent father shall have the following contact to the said child:

(i)   on alternate weekends from Friday at 5.00 pm until Sunday at 6.00 pm;
(ii)   for one half of the school spring and winter holidays and of each half-term holiday;
(iii)   for one half of each school summer holiday in tranches not to exceed 14 days at any one time unless otherwise agreed provided that in the

summer holidays of 1996 the father shall have staying contact to A from end of the school term (19 or 20 July 1996 at his option) until 6.00 pm on 2 August 1996;

(iv)   on 25 December each year;

(v)   for one half of Eid El-Adha each year;

(vi)   by telephone at least twice each week, with at least one of the calls being initiated by the child (whether with her mother's assistance or not);

(vii)   on such other occasions as the parties shall from time to time freely agree; such orders being upon the basis that there shall be no special provisions in relation to the child's Gregorian and Islamic birthdays which shall be spent with the parent with whom the child would be in accordance with the foregoing provisions.

(7)   All further applications relating to leave to remove A from the jurisdiction be reserved to Wall J, if available.

(8)   The parties be at liberty to bespeak a transcript of the judgment of Wall J.

(9)   The mother be at liberty to disclose copies of this order to the persons and bodies referred to in her aforesaid undertakings.

(10)   There be no order for costs, save that the costs of the applicant and respondent shall be taxed pursuant to the provisions of the Legal Aid Act 1988.

Ordered by the Honourable Wall J on 4 July 1996.

DECLARATION BY THE GRANDFATHER

I make this declaration as head of my family and guardian of my daughter, and my granddaughter and in the absence of my daughter's husband.

And I acknowledge that my daughter and granddaughter are intending to visit Saudia Arabia, with the permission of the High Court of England, for a temporary period of up to 28 days and that they fully intend to (and must in accordance with the requirements of the English court) return to England at the end of the period to resume their continued residence in that country.

AND I SWEAR AND MAKE OATH ON THE HOLY QURAN

That I will put no impediment or obstacle in the way of my daughter and granddaughter being free to enter and/or leave Saudia Arabia according to my daughter's own wishes for the purposes of such visit.

Moreover, I will facilitate to the full extent of my powers the wishes of my daughter to enter and/or leave Saudi Arabia, together with my granddaughter for the purposes of such visit.

And particularly:

(1) I promise to facilitate and help my daughter to obtain an exit visa from Saudia Arabia and put no obstacle or impediment in her way to obtaining an exit visa;

(2) I promise to give my agreement and/or signature to any official document or official permission necessary in the obtaining of such a visa;

(3) I promise not to seek to change the civil status of my daughter or my granddaughter during the period of the visit;

(4) I promise not to put any undue influence or pressure (moral or financial) on or to dictate to my daughter that she should remain in Saudia Arabia against her wishes at the end of the period of the visit;

(5) Further, I promise, so far as it is within my powers, to facilitate and help my daughter's husband to obtain an entry and/or exit visa to Saudia Arabia in the event it should be necessary and that I will put no obstacles or impediments in the way of his obtaining such visas;

(6) I know of legal undertakings given by my daughter to the honourable High Court in England and I promise to do all in my power to ensure that my daughter complies and acts in conformity with such undertakings and that she respects the decision of the said honourable court.

And I further make oath that this declaration is to be irrevocable and not subject to variation for whatever reason by me (or by anyone who possesses power of attorney for me) from the date of this declaration and during the whole time of the said visit up until the time when my daughter and granddaughter have returned safely to England following the said visit when they will then come again under the English court's jurisdiction.

And I further make oath that if I fail to abide by any of the provisions of this declaration then I understand the Shariah court may charge me with making false witness and that my daughter's husband may bring such a charge against me.

Appendix 4

EXTRACTS FROM KEY INTERNAL RELOCATION CASES

B V B (RESIDENCE: CONDITION LIMITING GEOGRAPHIC AREA) [2004] 2 FLR 979 (FD)

A4.1

Family Division

Deputy High Court Judge Sally Bradley QC

BRADLEY QC:

[9]　The mother has indicated that she wishes to move to Newcastle. She has no particular part of Newcastle pinpointed as an ideal location for her. She has selected two schools for the children . . .

[11]　The mother has no links with Newcastle save for a 'friendship' with a family she met on holiday. She has very little knowledge of the area.

[12]　The father opposes the mother's plans. He wishes DB to remain at school in the area in which she is currently living. She has to leave her current school in July 2004 because of her age. She is a bright child, he says, who would have no difficulty in getting a place (subject of course to the usual problem of availability) at any number of good independent day-schools in the same area. CB's schooling (paid for by the father) could also be provided for in a good school locally, says the father.

[13]　His case is that the mother is proposing to move so that she can create as much distance as possible between him and DB and ultimately cause difficulties in the contact arrangements. He claims that her two attempts to move, with leave, to Australia were based upon the same bad motive. He also suggests that such a move would be bad for DB from a number of perspectives and ultimately it would not be in her best interests.

[16]　The mother's evidence was unimpressive. At the conclusion of her oral evidence I formed the clear view that not only was she at times blatantly untruthful but she was so hostile to the father that she often lost all sense of reality. Such was her determination to cause difficulty for the father she became incapable of recognising DB's needs at all.

[20] There is no doubt that the mother could buy a suitable house for herself, DB and CB and that the schools (X School for CB and Y School for DB) are appropriate. The children will, as children do, make friends locally and probably adapt to a new environment. The mother may be able to open a business in Newcastle and prosper financially (although it has to be said that her plans were vague and she seemed to have done very little research about the market for fitness teaching in the north east of England).

[21] The mother's proposal to move is characterised by a lack of clarity and lack of purpose. I have no doubt that her plans to move to Australia were partly motivated by a wish to make a fresh start after a marriage breakdown. But I also believe that a strong motivating factor for the mother has been her wish to create as much physical and emotional distance between her and the father and between DB and the father.

[24] With DB's welfare as my paramount consideration and having regard to all the items on the welfare checklist I am of the view that a move to a school out of the geographical area where she now lives would not be in her best interests. It would be in her best interests to remain in an area where good and appropriate schooling is available and, importantly, where there is a greater prospect of contact continuing.

[25] I have the power under s 11(7) of the Children Act 1989 to impose conditions upon any residence order which I made. There is currently no residence order in force. I propose to make such an order in favour of the mother that reflects the current situation. To achieve DB remaining in the area in which she currently lives I could elect to attach a condition to a s. 8 residence order or, as was originally sought by the father, make a specific issue order relating to DB's schooling. I am concerned to be as straightforward as possible. I have decided this case by examining the merits of the proposed move and the impact upon DB's welfare. The real issue is the move rather than the competing merits of different schools. I, therefore, propose to attach to the residence order a condition that DB and her mother should reside, until further order, within an area bounded by the A4 to the north, the M25 to the west and the A3 to the south and east. This is not to be taken to be a permanent prohibition on relocation. It is what is needed now. The future may bring many changes for the mother and allow her to make other proposals which would obtain the agreement of the father and the court. I will provide for the mother to have liberty to apply on this matter should she wish to relocate to an area which is perhaps not quite within the boundaries I have stated.

[26] In reaching my decision I have not overlooked the fact that historically there has been a reluctance by the courts to interfere with the decisions of a parent to relocate to another part of the UK. The mother does not need leave, as she would under s. 13(1)(b), if this was an application to permanently remove from the jurisdiction. She does, however, have to satisfactorily establish a case which will defeat an application by the father for a prohibited steps order or a s. 11(7) condition. It must be the case that a court will not ordinarily seek to dictate the primary carer's place of residence. The case of *Re S (A Child) (Residence Order: Condition)* [2001] EWCA Civ 847, [2001] 3 FCR 154 and in particular the judgment of Thorpe LJ makes it clear that I should not approach this issue as if I have a general discretion to restrict the mother's movements if I believe her plans are less than ideal. I have not done that. I am conscious that *Re S (A Child) (Residence Order: Condition)* and the well-known decision of *Re E (Residence: Imposition of Conditions)* [1997] 2 FLR 638 emphasise that s. 11(7) conditions should only be attached in exceptional circumstances. Indeed, Thorpe LJ would suggest that the cases should be 'highly exceptional'.

[27] I am going to impose a condition because I am firmly of the view that it is in DB's interests so to do. Suggesting that contact might be adversely affected if the move takes place is not speculative. It is, in my judgment, a very real possibility. If the move takes place and the contact then falters the consequences for DB will not be favourable.

[28] This case can be regarded as highly exceptional. This mother has made two applications to go to Australia with, I am satisfied, her prime motive being to get away from the father. This followed the pattern of what she did with CB and his father. Having been advised that the applications would fail she told me in her oral evidence that she planned to live in Devon or Cornwall. She had gone to the lengths of inquiring about schools. She had no links with Devon or Cornwall at all but told me that it was 'like Australia'. It is no coincidence that the proposed destination at the most extreme southwesterly aspect of the country would create the same practical and logistical difficulties for contact as would a move to Newcastle. She is determined to find a way to reduce, if not delete entirely, the amount of contact which takes place.

4.2

RE L (INTERNAL RELOCATION: SHARED RESIDENCE ORDER) [2009] EWCA CIV 20, [2009] 1 FLR 1157

A4.2

Court of Appeal

Wall, Aikens LJJ and Bennett J

WALL LJ:

Introduction

[2] . . . [T]he real issue between the parties was the mother's wish to relocate with L from North London, where both parents were living, to Chew Magna in Somerset, where she had obtained employment. The judge refused the mother permission to relocate. He did so, not by imposing conditions under s 11(7) of the Children Act 1989 (the 1989 Act), but by varying the shared residence order: (1) to extend the periods L spent with her father at weekends 'from after school on Fridays until the beginning to the school day on Tuesdays on alternate weeks'; and (2) 'from after school on Tuesdays until the beginning of the next school day being the Tuesdays in the weeks following the Tuesdays in (1)'.

The law

[11] . . . [T]his is, so far as I am aware, the first case to reach this court in which the question of a parent's proposed relocation with a child within England and Wales has arisen where there is already in existence a shared residence order in favour of the parents in relation to the same child. Several questions therefore arise. In particular: (1) what effect, if any, does such an order have? And; (2) what weight should a judge give to the existence of such an order?

[12] Both [counsel] submitted that it would be a powerful disincentive to parties entering into shared residence orders if either felt that the consequence of so doing was to place a fetter on any subsequent application to relocate. I agree. However, this provides only a partial answer to the questions posed in the previous paragraph, and it is, therefore, necessary to look at the authorities on internal relocation. They are, I think, the following (I list them in chronological order):

(1)   *Re E (Residence: Imposition of Conditions)* [1997] 2 FLR 638 (Re E).

(2)   *Re H (Children) (Residence Order: Condition)* [2001] EWCA Civ 1338, [2001] 2 FLR 1277 (Re H).

(3)   *Re S (A Child) (Residence Order: Condition)* [2001] EWCA Civ 847, [2001] 3 FCR 154 and [2002] EWCA Civ 1795, [2003] 1 FCR 138 (Re S (No 1) and Re S (No 2)).

(4)   *B v B (Residence: Condition Limiting Geographic Area)* [2004] 2 FLR 979 (B v B).

(5)   *Re H (Agreed Joint Residence: Mediation)* [2004] EWHC 2064 (Fam), [2005] 1 FLR 8 (which, for present purposes I propose to call *Re H (No 2)*).

(6)   *Re G (Contact)* [2006] EWCA Civ 1507, [2007] 1 FLR 1663.

(7)   *Re B (Prohibited Steps Order)* [2007] EWCA Civ 1055, [2008] 1 FLR 613 (*Re B*).

[13]   The 1989 Act, by s 8, defines a residence order as 'an order settling the arrangements to be made as to the person with whom a child is to live'. The shared residence order in the present case gives the father parental responsibility for L, although we were told at the Bar that he may well have already had it before the shared residence order was made.

[14]   *B v B* and *Re H (No 2)* are decisions at first instance. The remainder are decisions of this court. *Re E*, it seems to me, remains the leading case, and sets the tone for much of what followed. I propose, accordingly, to cite extensively from the leading judgment in the case, given by Butler-Sloss LJ (as she then was).

[15]   In *Re E* the judge at first instance had treated as separate issues the two questions: (1) with whom and; (2) where the children in question should live. He thus made a residence order in favour of the mother, but imposed a requirement under s 11(7) of the 1989 Act that the children should continue to reside at a named address unless otherwise ordered or agreed by the children's father. The mother wished to take the children to live with her in Blackpool: the father wanted the children to remain in London. On the mother's appeal, this court reversed that part of the judge's decision which imposed the s 11(7) requirement on the mother.

[16] Although not directly relevant to this appeal, it will, I think, make this judgment easier to follow if I set out s 11(7) of the 1989 Act, which reads as follows:

'A (residence order) order may—

(a) contain directions about how it is to be carried into effect;
(b) impose conditions which must be complied with by any person—
    (i) in which favour the order is made;
    (ii) who is a parent of the child concerned;
    (iii) who is not a parent of his but who has parental responsibility for him; or
    (iv) with whom the child is living, and to whom the conditions are expressed to apply;
(c) be made to have effect for a specific period, or contain provisions which are to have effect for a specified period;
(d) make such incidental, supplemental or consequential provision as the court thinks fit.'

[17] Giving the leading judgment in *Re E*, Butler-Sloss LJ said at 641–642:

'Section 11(7) applies to all four s 8 orders, including prohibited steps orders and specific issue orders. The wording of the subsection is wide enough to give the court the power to make an order restricting the right of residence to a specified place within the UK. But in my view a restriction upon the right of the carer of the child to choose where to live sits uneasily with the general understanding of what is meant by a residence order. In *Re D (Minors) (Residence: Imposition of Conditions)* [1996] 2 FLR 281, this court considered a similar condition placed on a residence order. In that case the mother had originally agreed that she would not bring the children into contact with the man with whom she had been living. On her subsequent application to discharge that condition this court held that a section 11(7) condition could not exclude another person from the mother's home, thereby interfering with her right to live with whom she liked. Ward LJ said:

"The court was not in a position to overrule her decision to live her life as she chose. What was before the court was the issue of whether she should have the children living with her."

That decision in my judgment applies with equal force to the issue in the present appeal.

A general imposition of conditions on residence orders was clearly not contemplated by Parliament and where the parent is entirely suitable and the court intends to make a residence order in favour of that parent, a condition of residence is in my view an unwarranted imposition upon the right of the parent to choose where he/she will live within the UK or with whom. There may be exceptional cases, for instance, where the court, in the private law context, has concerns about the ability of the parent to be granted a residence order to be a satisfactory carer but there is no better solution than to place the child with that parent. The court might consider it necessary to keep some control over the parent by way of conditions which include a condition of residence. Again, in public law cases involving local authorities, where a residence order may be made by the court in preference to a care order, section 11(7) conditions might be applied in somewhat different circumstances.

The correct approach is to look at the issue of where the children will live as one of the relevant factors in the context of the cross-applications for residence and not as a separate issue divorced from the question of residence. If the case is finely balanced between the respective advantages and disadvantages of the parents, the proposals put forward by each parent will assume considerable importance. If one parent's plan is to remove the children against their wishes to a part of the country less suitable for them, it is an important factor to be taken into account by the court and might persuade the court in some cases to make a residence order in favour of the other parent. But, on the facts of the present appeal, it is clear that the welfare of the children points firmly to their living with their mother, and the advantage of remaining in London is outweighed by the other factors leading to granting a residence order to the mother.'

[18]   In *Re H*, a father, in whose favour the judge had made a residence order, wished to relocate with the children concerned to Northern Ireland. The mother, who otherwise was the more suitable parent to care for the children, was disqualified from doing so by alcoholism. The judge made an order preventing the relocation, and the father's appeal to this court was dismissed. Applying s 1 of the 1989 Act to the facts of the case, this court took the view that the children's loss of contact with their mother would be akin to a bereavement; the effect on the mother would be devastating, as would the knock-on effect of her devastation on the children. Leading counsel for the father sought to rely on *Re E* as demonstrating that a condition against relocation was only to be imposed in exceptional circumstances which, it was argued, did not apply on the facts of the case. Giving the leading judgment, Thorpe LJ (at para [19]) said:

'The relocation within the United Kingdom may be highly problematic, as this case illustrates. The primary carer will invariably give notice, directly or indirectly, of an intended move. The court has power under section 8 to make a prohibited steps order or to impose a condition under section 11(7) to the residence order. Whilst the primary carer may not have an obligation to apply under section 13(1)(b), he will still have to defeat the challenge of an application for a prohibited steps order or for the imposition of a condition to the residence order. Perhaps the only certain constant is that, where there is a dispute between the parents, incapable of resolution by negotiations or mediation, it must be decided by the court. In making its decision the court must always apply the welfare test as paramount, whether the relocation is internal or external. The test, in the case of external relocation, is clearly laid down in *Payne v Payne* [2001] EWCA Civ 166, [2001] Fam 473.'

[19]   This judgment must, however, be read with Thorpe LJ's later commentary on it in *Re B*, as to which see para [33] below.

[20]   In *Re S (Nos 1 and 2)* the critical feature of the case was that the child in question was down syndrome, and thus not capable of understanding fully major changes in her life, including a reduction in her contact with her father. Her mother wished to relocate with her to Cornwall. The judge refused to allow her to do so, taking the view that he had a discretion to impose such a condition in an exceptional case. This court allowed the mother's appeal and remitted the matter to the judge for reconsideration.

[21] Giving the leading judgment in *Re S (No 1)* Thorpe LJ said:

'[16] The jurisprudence in those cases that are now caught by s 13(1)(b) had been established over the course of more than 30 years by decisions of this court which recognise the great importance of not imposing on primary carers' restrictions on their freedom to choose their preferred way of family life and their preferred place of residence for two good reasons. The first is that often the notion of such restrictions are simply contrary to good sense and, secondly, because the imposition of restrictions is likely to have an adverse effect on the welfare of the children indirectly through the emotional and psychological disturbance caused to the primary carer by denial of the freedom to exercise reasonable choice.

[17] This line of authority has recently been reconsidered by this court in the light of the arrival of the Human Rights Act 1998 in the case of *Payne v Payne*. It seems to me that it is necessary to have some consistency between that line of authority applying to s 13(1)(b) cases, and those in which a judge has to consider whether it is open to him to apply a condition under s 11(7) to a residence order that restricts the primary carer's place of residence. It is true that in the case of *Re E (minors) (residence: conditions)* Butler-Sloss LJ said:

"In my view, the principles set out in a long line of authorities relating to leave to remove permanently from the jurisdiction have no application to conditions proposed under s 11(7)."

[18] With that I am in complete agreement in the sense that it is not ordinarily necessary for primary carers who seek to make a local move to have to clear the various hurdles that confront an applicant for permission to move out of the United Kingdom. In such cases the applicant has to demonstrate that he or she has made a thorough research and exploration of the circumstances and conditions in the country to which he or she aspires to relocate and that the proposals are practical and reasonable. Such an applicant also has to meet whatever opposition there may be from the secondary carer on the front of reduction of contact or other suggested adverse consequences of relocation. Whatever tests are applied to the applicant under s 13(1)(b), they must inevitably be more stringent than the tests applied to the primary carer seeking a purely local relocation.'

[22] Thorpe LJ then turned to an examination of the judgment of Butler-Sloss LJ in *Re E* and concluded in this respect:

'[24] I am in no doubt that, in defining the possibility of exception, Butler-Sloss LJ was guarding against the danger of never saying never in family law litigation. The whole tenor of her judgment is plain to me, in that she was giving the clearest guide to courts of trial that, whereas it was not safe to say never in cases in which the imposition of such a condition would be justified, it would be highly exceptional and probably restricted to a case, as yet unforeseen and may be difficult to foresee, in which the ability of the primary carer to perform to a satisfactory level required the buttress of a s 11(7) order.

[25] Certainly, in my opinion, her judgment is not to be interpreted as giving trial judges a general latitude to strive for some sort of ideal over and above the rival proposals of the available primary carers. As is well argued in the appellant's skeleton, that approach could lead to quite unsustainable restrictions on ordinary adult liberties, extending even to the secondary carer's chosen way of life.'

[23] Clarke LJ (as he then was) whilst agreeing that the appeal should be allowed, took a somewhat different view of Butler-Sloss LJ's judgment in *Re E*. He said:

'[34] I do not read Butler-Sloss LJ as specifying precisely what cases would amount to exceptional cases and what would not. She simply gave some particular examples. I do not read her judgment as limiting the exceptional cases to the cases where the court was concerned about the capabilities of the primary carer. To my mind, it could scarcely do so given the words of the statute. However, I entirely accept the proposition that the court should not ordinarily dictate to the primary carer where he or she should live. Thus Butler-Sloss LJ made it clear, for example, that the court must not impose conditions simply because the proposals for the particular child are not ideal.

[35] I entirely agree with Thorpe LJ that the subsection should not be interpreted as giving trial judges a general discretion to strive for some ideal situation. A condition should only be imposed in genuinely exceptional cases.'

[24] *Re S* returned to this court after the circuit judge had reheard the case, and reached the same conclusion. Once again, the mother's appeal was dismissed. On this occasion the constitution comprised Dame Elizabeth Butler-Sloss P (as she had become) Waller and Laws LJJ. The former gave the leading judgment. She identified two conflicting principles:

(i) The appellate court, in accordance with the decision of the House of Lords in *G v G (Minors: Custody Appeal)* [1985] FLR 894; [1985] 1 WLR 647 ought not readily to interfere with the decision of a competent and conscientious judge who has taken into account the relevant factors and has exercised his discretion to arrive at his conclusion in favour of the child remaining in the London area.

(ii) The principle enunciated in *Re E* that the court ought not in other than exceptional circumstances to impose a condition on a Residence Order to a primary carer who is providing entirely appropriate care for the child.

[25] The President then conducted an examination of the previous authorities, and stated:

'[17] In accordance with the decisions which I set out above, the general principle is clear that a suitable parent entrusted with the primary care of a child by way of a residence order should be able to choose where he/she will live and with whom. It will be most unusual for a court to interfere with that general right of the primary carer. There will however be exceptional circumstances in which conditions will have, in order to protect the best interests of the child, to be imposed albeit those conditions will interfere with the general right to choose where to live within the United Kingdom. I did not intend in my judgment in *Re E* to exclude the possibility that an exceptional case might arise in which a parent against whom there is no complaint might nonetheless have to face some restriction of movement. Section 11(7) provides a safety net to allow for the exercise of discretion under the provisions of section 1 where the paramountcy of the welfare of the child exceptionally requires the court to impose restrictions upon the primary carer which otherwise would be unacceptable. I could not, as Clarke LJ pointed out in paragraph 34, in accordance with the wording of section 11(7) shut the door on the exceptional case. I respectfully agree with the interpretation given by Clarke LJ to that passage in my judgment.'

[26]   The President then conducted a full and careful review of the facts, at the end of which she concluded:

'[37] I am satisfied that the judge was entitled to treat this as an exceptional case. He was faced with an impossible task which he carried out carefully and conscientiously and with understanding of the conflicting emotions and issues which faced him. He considered and applied the principles set out in *Re E* and had regard to the rights of the parents under Article 8. He carried out the unusually difficult balancing exercise and came to a conclusion which in my view cannot be faulted. His exercise of discretion on the facts and on his view of the witnesses is not to be set aside by an appellate court without very good grounds to do so. It is not for the Court of Appeal to substitute its own view of the outcome where the judge has heard all the relevant witnesses and has the inestimable advantage of getting the feel of the case unless the judge has failed to direct himself correctly or has otherwise come to an obviously wrong conclusion. There is no obviously correct decision in this exceptionally difficult case which turns on the assessment of future risk to the emotional wellbeing of a delightful but seriously disadvantaged child. This is pre-eminently a case in which *G v G* should apply and the exercise of discretion by the judge should not be set aside by the appellate court. For these reasons, in my judgment, this court was right to uphold the decision of the trial judge.'

[27]   I note, in passing, that Laws LJ added:

'[39] The jurisprudence shows that the imposition, under Section 11(7), of conditions upon a residence order is something to be contemplated only in exceptional circumstances. However, to borrow a phrase from another area of the law, the categories of what is exceptional are not closed; nor was my Lady suggesting in *E* that they were. Indeed they could not be: to formulate a definition of exceptional circumstances, whether inclusive or exclusive, would be to transform a broad principle into a hard-edged rule. But hard-edged rules are made if at all by the statute, not by the courts.

[40] Here, applying the general principle, the Judge was in my view wholly entitled to treat the case as exceptional. The combination of this little girl's disability and

medical problems, the limits of her understanding, her foreshortened life expectancy, and the practicalities of travel between south London and Cornwall amply suffice to produce that result.'

[Wall LJ then quoted from *B v B (Residence: Condition Limiting Geographic Area)* [2004] 2 FLR 979 (FD), which is extracted in Appendix 4.1 and continued:]

[29]   *Re H (No 2)* is a decision of Baron J. It is the only reported case in which there was a joint residence order. The father wished to relocate to Devon in order to ensure his earning capacity and employment security. The parties were agreed that they would like a joint residence order and had agreed a schedule of contact for the parent with whom the child did not have his main home, but were unable to reach agreement as to which parent that should be.

[30]   Once again, I think it sufficient to cite the relevant part of the headnote of the case as reported:

'Applying the welfare principle and checklist, it was in the child's best interests to move to Devon with his father. The child's primary attachment was to his father. The special bond created in the period immediately following the separation had never been broken despite the fact that the mother had increased her role since that time. The child had never expressed any opposition to the move. The child would face disruption whichever parent he was with.'

[31]   I have included *Re G* for completeness, but I do not think it takes the matter any further. This court refused to implement an Australian order when there had been a number of changes of circumstances.

[32]   Finally, *Re B* was another Northern Irish case in which, in this instance, the judge had refused to allow the mother to relocate with the child, notwithstanding that she was plainly the 'primary carer'. This court allowed the mother's appeal and ordered a re-hearing.

[33]   Thorpe LJ, giving the leading judgment, reviewed his previous decision in *Re H*:

'[7] The judgment that I gave in the case of *Re H* does not, on reconsideration, sufficiently reflect the fact that the imposition of a condition to a residence order restricting the primary carer's right to choose his or her place of residence is a truly exceptional order. The case of *Re H* included an endeavour on my part to rationalise the interface between the true relocation cases governed by the decision of this court in *Payne v Payne* and the internal relocation cases governed by the decision of this court in *Re E*. At the conclusion of the passage, I questioned the rationalisation for a different test to be applied to an application to relocate to Belfast as opposed to, say, an application to relocate to Dublin, and having posed the question I continued:

"All that the court can do is to remember that in each and every case the decision must rest on the paramount principle of child welfare."

[8] I see that the Recorder, reading that passage, did not have his attention sufficiently directed to the earlier case of *Re E*. In my reasoning for upholding the imposition of a condition preventing the relocation in the case of *Re H*, I did not perhaps sufficiently clearly state that the circumstances (particularly the impact upon the mother of a refusal of the condition, fully established by mental health evidence) clearly took the case into the exceptional category identified Butler-Sloss LJ in *Re E*.

[9] By way of conclusion I would only endorse the treatment of this topic by Professor Lowe and his co-authors in *International Movement of Children* (Jordan Publishing Ltd, 2004). He, at page 90, considers movement of children within the UK, and reviewing the cases, concludes that a primary carer faced with an application for a prohibited steps order or the imposition of conditions on a residence order, will not, save in an exceptional case, be restrained by the court, because for the court so to do would be an unsustainable restriction on adult liberties and would be likely to have an adverse effect on the welfare of the child by denying the primary carer reasonable freedom of choice. Professor Lowe takes that proposition from the decision in *Re E* and in para 6.4 he states:

> 'The correct approach, therefore, is to look at the issue of where the children will live as one of the relevant factors in the context of the cross-applications for residence, and not as a separate issue divorced from the question of residence. If the case is finely balanced between the respective advantages and disadvantages of the parents, the proposals put forward by each parent will assume considerable importance. If one parent's plan is to remove the children against their wishes to a part of the country less suitable for them, it is an important factor to be taken into account by the court and might persuade the court in some cases to make a residence order in favour of the other parent.'

He then considers what might constitute an exceptional case and in particular refers to the decision of this court in *Re S (No 2)*.

What principles can be gathered from the authorities, and should there be a different approach in cases where there is a shared residence order?

[34]   In my judgment, the propositions which emerge from the authorities are well summarised in the citations from the judgment of Butler-Sloss LJ in Re E and from Thorpe LJ's judgment in *Re B* which I have set out in paras [17] and [33] above. Should there be any difference in approach where there is a shared residence order?

[35]   In my judgment, a shared residence order is, self-evidently, a species of residence order under s 8 of the 1989 Act. It settles the arrangements to be made as to the persons with whom a child is to live. In some, albeit rare cases, such *A v A (Shared Residence)* [2004] EWHC 142 (Fam), [2004] 1 FLR 1195 an equal division of the children's time between their parents is appropriate, but there is no doubt that a shared residence order can properly be made where there is a substantial geographical distance between the parties: – see, for example, the decision of this court *Re F (Shared Residence Order)* [2003]

EWCA Civ 592, [2003] 2 FLR 397, in which the mother was planning to relocate to Edinburgh, a considerable distance from where the father lived.

[36]   In my judgment, therefore, it is wrong in principle to apply different criteria to the question of internal relocation simply because there is a shared residence order. Plainly, the fact of such an order is an important factor in the welfare equation, but I respectfully agree with counsel that it is not, in effect, a trump card preventing relocation. In each case what the court has to do is to examine the underlying factual matrix, and to decide in all the circumstances of the case whether or not it is in the child's interest to relocate with the parent who wishes to move.

Discussion

[51]   [The trial judge] was wrong to distinguish this case from the authorities cited to him on the basis that they dealt with sole residence orders, whereas he was dealing with a shared residence order. This is not, in my judgment, a narrow legalistic point. For the reasons which I have given in para [36] above, the correct approach, in my view, is not to distinguish the case but to look at the underlying factual substratum in welfare terms, bearing in mind the tension which may well exist between the freedom to relocate which any parent must enjoy against the welfare of the child which may militate against relocation. In my judgment, it is this balance which is critical, and the danger of distinguishing the case as a matter of law is that the court will either lose sight of, or give insufficient weight to the former consideration.

[52]   In particular, a shared residence order must not, in my judgment, be seen as an automatic bar to relocation, or, as [counsel for the mother] put it, a trump card against relocation. There may be cases in which it is determinative of welfare, but there will be others where it will plainly be in the best interests of the child to relocate, notwithstanding the existence of a shared residence order. Simply to distinguish the case on the basis of a shared residence order is, in my judgment, to run the risk of making it determinative in all cases and of distorting the welfare balancing exercise.

4.3

RE F (INTERNAL RELOCATION)
[2010] EWCA CIV 1428, [2011] 1 FLR 1382

A4.2

Court of Appeal

Wilson, Rimer and Black LJJ

WILSON LJ:

[1]   A mother appeals against the refusal of Mr Recorder Bullock, sitting as if in the Middlesbrough County Court on 30 July 2010, to grant her application for a specific issue order. The order which she sought was that, as the primary carer of four children, she should be permitted to move their home within the UK, namely from their present home with her in a town in Cleveland to the island of Stronsay, which is one of the Orkney Islands. The father of the children, who also lives in the town in Cleveland, opposed her application. In that, however, the mother has at all times made clear that, were her application to be refused, she would continue to provide the home for the children in Cleveland, there was no question of any move by the children to the home of the father.

. . .

[4]   The mother and the father both appear to be excellent parents. Ever since their separation they have sought to co-operate in relation to arrangements for the children and, in particular, for the father's contact with them. The only major issue occurred in 2009 when, in court proceedings, the mother successfully objected to a holiday abroad which the father proposed to take with the children. For several years the pattern has been for the children to stay with the father on Wednesday evenings, at all alternate weekends and for longer periods during school holidays. Sadly, however, for reasons which the parents have not explained and perhaps cannot entirely explain, R, the only daughter, has in recent years chosen to go only rarely to the father on contact periods. The three boys in no way share her reluctance to go.

[7]   In March 2010 the mother and her husband were offered employment in the form of a job-share and they accepted it. The offer was that, jointly, they should act as the GP on the island of Stronsay, which is one of the northern Orkney Islands and has a population of 350, and that they should also act in this capacity on the neighbouring island of Eday, which has a population of

150. The main island of the Orkneys is called 'Mainland' and its capital is Kirkwall. Travel from Stronsay to Kirkwall is achieved by ferry, which takes 80 minutes, or by air, which takes 15 minutes.

[8]   The wish of the mother and her husband to move to Stronsay is deeply held and is the product not only of their very substantial connections with Scotland, including the Orkneys, but also of their conviction that life for the four children would be in every sense healthier and more fulfilled than the life which they are leading, and would be likely to continue to lead, in Cleveland.

[22]   I confess that I have not previously had occasion to study these authorities [on internal relocation] myself. For the purposes of today's appeal however I have studied them carefully and, in that regard, I have been greatly assisted by the full survey of them recently conducted by Wall LJ (as he then was) in *Re L (Residence Order)* [2009] EWCA Civ 20, [2009] 1 FLR 1157, at [11] to [33]. But I remain puzzled by three features of the authorities.

[23]   The first feature does not arise in the present case and therefore I offer only a passing view about it. In the present case it was the parent who aspired to relocate ('the aspiring parent') who wisely took the initiative by issue of legal proceedings. It is plain that she issued the correct form of application, namely an application for a specific issue order which would determine whether she might take the children to reside with her in the Orkneys. It is in circumstances in which the initiative to place the matter before the court is to be taken by the parent who objects to the relocation ('the objecting parent') that the authorities seem to me to give rise to confusion. To be specific, is the proper course for the objecting parent to apply, in a case where the aspiring parent already has a residence order, for the imposition upon it of a condition against the relocation pursuant to s 11(7)(b) of the Children Act 1989 ('the Act') or even to apply, in a case where the aspiring parent does not already have a residence order, for a residence order somehow to be foisted upon that parent and then for the imposition upon it of the same condition? Or should the objecting parent apply for a prohibited steps order which would in terms prohibit the relocation? Were the necessary result to be achieved by making a residence order, including in my view a residence order subject to a condition, it would not be open to the objecting parent to apply for a prohibited steps order: see s 9(5) of the Act. My provisional view is, however, that the necessary result cannot properly be achieved by the imposition upon a residence order of a condition. What the objecting parent seeks to secure is an express, enforceable prohibition, not merely a situation in which, if the aspiring parent breaches the condition, the only effect is that no residence order subsists in relation to the child. Thus I am of the view, which accords with an observation of Thorpe LJ in *Re B (Prohibited Steps Order)* [2007] EWCA Civ 1055, [2008] 1 FLR 613, at [4], that the relief appropriately to be sought by the objecting parent is a prohibited steps order.

[24]   The second feature relates to the interface between the respective principles which govern applications in respect of external relocation, on the

one hand, and those in respect of internal relocation on the other. In the first reported decision of this court in relation to internal relocation, namely *Re E (Residence: Imposition of Conditions)* [1997] 2 FLR 638, Butler-Sloss LJ said, at 643A:

'In my view the principles set out in a long line of authorities relating to leave to remove permanently from the jurisdiction have no application to conditions proposed under section 11(7).'

Is it so obvious, however, that there should be a complete dichotomy between the principles apt to each of the two types of determination? In the first of the decisions of this court in relation to the child, S, namely *Re S (A Child) (Residence Order: Condition)* [2001] EWCA Civ 847, [2001] 3 FCR 154, Thorpe LJ, at [17], and Clarke LJ, at [36], both observed that it was desirable to have some consistency between the two sets of principles. Two months later, in *Re H (Children) (Residence Order: Condition)* [2001] EWCA Civ 1338, [2001] 2 FLR 1277, Thorpe LJ said at [20]:

'What is the rationalisation for a different test to be applied to an application to relocate to Belfast, as opposed to, say, an application to relocate from Gloucester to Dublin? All that the court can do is to remember that in each and every case the decision must rest on the paramount principle of child welfare.'

The answer given by Thorpe LJ shows in my view that he found his question difficult. I do not mean to suggest, particularly in the light of the current controversy surrounding the aptness of the principles which have been developed in this court in relation to the determination of applications in respect of external relocation, that, as they stand, they should – or can – be applied to cases of internal relocation. Nevertheless, even if, for example, the effect upon the aspiring parent, and thus indirectly upon the child, of a refusal of permission to remove was one day to be considered to have been afforded too great an emphasis in our principles governing external relocation, I would expect our principles governing internal relocation to allow at any rate for some weight to be attributed to that factor. Indeed in that regard I note that in *Re L* above Wall LJ, at [56], expressly accepted that the effect on the aspiring parent of the refusal of permission to effect an internal relocation would be likely to be relevant. In the present case I am sure that the effect of the recorder's decision, if upheld, would be extremely negative for the mother and that, at any rate in that specific regard, the children might suffer, indirectly, to some extent. But such was not a point pressed upon the recorder on the mother's behalf in the written opening of Mr Myers; scarcely referred to by Mr Myers at the hearing before the recorder; not referred to in the judgment; and not included in the grounds of appeal. In the event, for reasons which I will explain, the point, whatever its precise degree of force, would in my view never have secured, or have helped to secure, the outcome for which the mother has contended.

[25] The third feature relates to the early insinuation into the principles governing internal relocation of a test of exceptionality. The development of

the case-law in this regard offers an interesting insight into the way in which law is made, perhaps not always satisfactorily. No one could quarrel with a proposition that it would rarely be in the interests of a child for the residential parent to be prevented from moving home with the child within the UK. The way in which, in *Re E* above, Butler-Sloss LJ chose to express that proposition was to turn it round and to say, at 642D, that 'there may be exceptional cases' which justified refusal. Thus were the seeds of a new test sown. In the first of the decisions in *Re S* above, Thorpe LJ, at [24], described the cases in which refusal would be legitimate as 'highly exceptional' and Clarke LJ, at [35], described them as 'genuinely exceptional'. By the time of this court's second decision in relation to S, namely *Re S (A Child) (Residence Order: Condition) (No 2)* [2002] EWCA Civ 1795, [2003] 1 FCR 138, exceptionality had become part of 'the principle'. For Butler-Sloss LJ, at [9][ii], referred to:

> '... the principle enunciated in *Re E* ... that the court ought not in other than exceptional circumstances to impose a condition on a residence order to a primary carer who is providing entirely appropriate care for the child'.

[26] In two entirely different contexts I have previously had occasion to refer to the danger that a decision-maker's attempt to explain his decision in terms which include reference to exceptionality gives rise to the subsequent elevation of a concept of exceptionality as the governing criterion: see *Currey v Currey (No 2)* [2006] EWCA Civ 1338, [2007] 1 FLR 946, at [19], and *R (M) v Haringey Independent Appeal Panel and Another* [2010] EWCA Civ 1103, [2010] ELR 823, at [29]. It is too late for it to be permissible for this court to rule that, in internal relocation cases, the analysis of the child's welfare, informed by consideration of the matters specified in s 1(3) of the Act, should not be conducted through the prism of whether the circumstances are exceptional. The recorder thus rightly asked himself whether the circumstances were exceptional; his answer was that they were; and the main thrust of the appeal is that he was plainly wrong so to have concluded. But, for the reasons given, I believe that, had I not felt bound by authority, I might have wished to suggest that a test of exceptionality was an impermissible gloss on the inquiry mandated by s 1(1) and (3) of the Act.

[27] Only half way through his short judgment the Recorder said:

> 'What the mother is proposing can be properly described as 'truly exceptional'. It is as close ... to a case of removal from the jurisdiction as one could possibly get. Stronsay must be one of the most remote inhabited places in the United Kingdom.'

[28] [Counsel for the mother] submits that the proper reading of the Recorder's judgment is that he found 'true exceptionality' in one feature which did not, of itself, justify the finding, namely that the move would be to Stronsay. In my view, however, although of course the Recorder was exercised by the fact that the proposed move was to be to Stronsay and was thus exercised by its effects, for example on the father's contact, the recorder was

finding exceptionality in the combination of circumstances to which he had already referred or was about to refer . . .

[29]   The Recorder proceeded to refer, albeit briefly, to the mother's proposals for contact. He said that they involved 'ferries, overnight ferries, flights, further flights, train journeys and ... car travel [of] up to seven hours.' The Recorder did not offer a view whether, in the light of the length and complexity of the journeys, it was realistic to consider that contact could be maintained at the level set out in the schedule without undue exhaustion, dislocation and frustration for the children.

[30]   Nor did the Recorder in terms address the depth of the likely upheaval for all four children in leaving their home, their schools, their friends and their out of school activities, and, in particular for T, the damage to the close ties with the father's stepson, E.

[31]   The Recorder did however make a relatively full reference to [the CAFCASS] report.

[32]   Then the Recorder expressed his conclusion. He said that the move would create 'huge emotional strain' for the children; that the mother was 'sailing into entirely untested waters'; and that, although obviously no physical harm would come to the children, there would be 'emotional harm'.

[33]   Such were the circumstances in which the Recorder announced the refusal of the mother's application.

[34]   In an attractively economical yet powerful presentation [counsel for the mother] submits to us today that there is nothing exceptional about the circumstances of this case; that it was irrelevant for the Recorder to draw a parallel with applications in respect of external relocation; that, as the mother stressed in oral evidence, the boys' comments, at any rate to her, about the move varied to some extent from day to day; that R's consistent and profound wish to move had not been afforded proper weight; and that, in the absence of expert evidence, it was improper for the recorder to have concluded that the move would generate emotional harm for the children.

[35]   In my view, even prior to service of [the CAFCASS report, which opposed the relocation], the mother's application was fraught with difficulty. All four children had been born and brought up throughout their lives in the town in Cleveland and could not have been more firmly rooted there. Their contact, or at any rate that of the boys, with the father on a frequent basis was patently important for them; and the tortuous nature of their proposed journeys to Cleveland and back to Stronsay placed an obvious question-mark against the very sustainability of the arrangements for contact which both parents had ultimately agreed to be in principle in the interests of the children. Even as it stood prior to service of the report, the evidence in my view clearly militated against a conclusion that it would be in the interests of the children to

make the move. Once, however, [the CAFCASS] report came to hand, the application in my view became almost unarguable. Of course when mature, intelligent children have conflicting views, it is as impossible for the court as it is for parents to accommodate all of them. But regard had to be paid to the strength of views articulated not only by R in favour of the move but also by T against it; it had to be paid to the mature ambivalence rather movingly articulated by A; and it had to be paid, in my view in particular, to the views of G. In the light of his particular needs for support, stability, routine and paternal contact, his views, expressed with such vehemence to Ms Bailey, were in my view even more in need of consideration than those of the others.

[36]   In the light of the gross upheaval which the move would precipitate for the children and of the fact that, in the case of G and T and to a lesser extent of A, the mother would be imposing upon the children, even at their relatively advanced ages, permanent living arrangements entirely contrary to their own wishes, the recorder was in my view entitled to forecast emotional strain and indeed harm for them.

[37]   In that the Recorder was vested with a discretion, it would be usual for this court, if minded to dismiss the appeal, to say simply that there was no error in the way in which he had exercised it. But such words, however legally appropriate, would fail to reflect my view of the matter, which is that the welfare of these children required the dismissal of the mother's application. Since that conclusion has to be expressed as a conclusion that the case was exceptional, so be it.

Appendix 5

SAMPLE APPLICATION AND RESPONSE MATERIALS

SAMPLE C100 APPLICATION FORM RELATING TO THE CASE STUDY IN CHAPTER 4

C100	**To be completed by the court**
Application under the Children Act 1989 for a residence, contact, prohibited steps, specific issue section 8 order or to vary or discharge a section 8 order	Name of court
	Date issued
	Case number

Before completing this form please read the leaflet **'CB1 – Making an application – Children and the Family Courts'**. You can get a copy of from your local court or at www.justice.gov.uk.

- Failure to complete every question or state if it does not apply, could delay the case, as the court will have to ask you to provide the additional information required.
- If there is not enough space please attach separate sheets, clearly showing the details of the children, parties, question and page number they refer to.
- Cafcass/CAFCASS CYMRU will carry out checks as it considers necessary. See Section J of leaflet CB1 for more information about Cafcass and CAFCASS CYMRU.

1. Summary of application

Some people need permission to apply - See Section C of the leaflet CB1 for details on who needs permission and how to get permission

Have you applied to the court for permission to make this application? ☐ Yes ☑ Permission not required

Your name (the applicant(s)) | SUSAN BROWN

The respondent's name(s)
See Sections G and H of the booklet CB1. | PETER BROWN

Please list the name(s) of the child(ren) and the type(s) of order you are applying for, starting with the oldest. To understand which order to apply for read the booklet CB1 Section D.

Child 1 - Full name of child	Date of birth	Gender	Order(s) applied for
CHARLES BROWN	1 0 / 1 1 / 2 0 0 2	☑ Male ☐ Female	RESIDENCE AND LEAVE TO REMOVE
Relationship to applicant(s)		Relationship to respondent(s)	
SON		SON	

Child 2 - Full name of child	Date of birth	Gender	Order(s) applied for
CAMILLA BROWN	2 0 / 0 7 / 2 0 0 5	☐ Male ☑ Female	RESIDENCE AND LEAVE TO REMOVE
Relationship to applicant(s)		Relationship to respondent(s)	
DAUGHTER		DAUGHTER	

Child 3 - Full name of child	Date of birth	Gender	Order(s) applied for
FREDERIC BROWN	3 0 / 0 3 / 2 0 0 9	☑ Male ☐ Female	RESIDENCE AND LEAVE TO REMOVE
Relationship to applicant(s)		Relationship to respondent(s)	
SON		SON	

C100 Application under the Children Act 1989 for a residence, contact, prohibited steps, specific issue section 8 order or to vary or discharge a section 8 order (04.12)

© Crown copyright 2012

2. About you (the applicant(s)))

	Applicant 1 (You)	Applicant 2 (if applicable)
Full names	SUSAN BROWN	
Previous names (if any)	FARMER	
Gender	☐ Male ☑ Female	☐ Male ☐ Female
Date of birth (If under 18 read section R of leaflet CB1)	D D / M M / Y Y Y Y	D D / M M / Y Y Y Y
Place of birth (town/county/country)	LONDON	

If you do not wish your address to be made known to the respondent, leave the details below blank and complete Confidential contact details Form C8.

	Applicant 1	Applicant 2
Address	6 THE GREEN, EPSOM, SURREY	
	Postcode	Postcode
Home telephone number	[INSERT]	
Mobile telephone number	[INSERT]	
Email address	[INSERT]	
Have you lived at this address for more than 5 years?	☑ Yes ☐ No	☐ Yes ☐ No

If No, please provide details of all previous addresses you have lived at for the last 5 years.

	Applicant 1	Applicant 2
If you do not wish your contact details to be made known to the Respondent, leave the details blank and complete Confidential contact details Form C8		

2

3. The respondents

Sections G and H of the the booklet **'CB1 - Making an application - Children and the Family Courts'** explain who a respondent is.

If there are more than 2 respondents please continue on a separate sheet.

	Respondent 1	Respondent 2
Full names	PETER BROWN	
Previous names (if known)		
Gender	✓ Male ☐ Female	☐ Male ☐ Female
Date of birth (If party under 18 read section R of leaflet CB1)	D D / M M / Y Y Y Y	D D / M M / Y Y Y Y
Place of birth (town/county/country)	MANCHESTER	
Address (to which documents relating to this application should be sent)	FLAT 2, THE MILL, EPSOM, SURREY	
	Postcode ☐☐☐☐ ☐☐☐☐	Postcode ☐☐☐☐ ☐☐☐☐
Home telephone number	[INSERT]	
Mobile telephone number	[INSERT]	
Email address	[INSERT]	
Have they lived at this address for more than 5 years?	☐ Yes ✓ No ☐ Don't know	☐ Yes ☐ No ☐ Don't know

If No, please provide details of all previous addresses for the last 5 years below (if known, including the dates and starting with the most recent)

6 THE GREEN, EPSOM, SURREY	

3

4. Others who should be given notice

There may be other people who should be notified of your application, for example, someone who cares for the child but is not a parent. Sections G and I of the the booklet **'CB1 - Making an application - Children and the Family Courts'** explain who others are.

	Person1	Person 2
Full names	N/A	
Previous names (if known)		
Gender	☐ Male ☐ Female	☐ Male ☐ Female
Date of birth	D D / M M / Y Y Y Y	D D / M M / Y Y Y Y
Address		
	Postcode	Postcode
Please state their relationship to the children listed on page 1. If their relationship is not the same to each child please state their relationship to each child.		

4

5. Solicitors details

Do you have a solicitor acting for you? ☑ Yes ☐ No   If No, see section R of leaflet CB1 for more information

If Yes, please give the following details

Your solicitor's name [INSERT]

Name of firm [INSERT]

Address [INSERT]

Postcode ☐☐☐☐ ☐☐☐☐

Telephone number [INSERT]

Fax number [INSERT]

DX number [INSERT]

Solicitor's Reference [INSERT]

Email address [INSERT]

6. The child(ren)

Are any of the children known to the local authority children's services?	☐ Yes ☑ No	☐ Don't know

If Yes please state which child and the name of the Local Authority and Social worker (if known)

Are any of the children the subject of a child protection plan	☐ Yes ☑ No	☐ Don't know

Do all the children share the same parents?	☑ Yes ☐ No

If Yes, what are the names of the parents?

If No, please give details of each parent and their children involved in this application

Please state everyone who has parental responsibility for each child and how they have parental responsibility (e.g. 'child's mother', 'child's father and was married to the mother when the child was born' etc.)
(See Section E of leaflet CB1 for more information)

SUSAN BROWN – CHILDREN'S MOTHER
PETER BROWN – CHILDREN'S FATHER

Who do the children currently live with?	☑ Applicant(s)	☐ Respondent(s) ☐ Other

If other, please give the full address of the child, the names of any adults living with the children and their relationship to or involvement with the child.

If you do not wish this information to be made known to the Respondent, leave the details blank and complete Confidential contact details Form C8

6

7. Why are you making this application?

Please give brief details:

- any previous agreements (formal or informal), and how they have broken down
- your reasons for bringing this application to the court
- what you want the court to do
- reasons given by the respondent(s) for their actions in relation to this application.

Do not give a full statement, please provide a summary of any relevant grounds and reasons. You may be asked to provide a full statement later.

The Respondent and I divorced approximately 14 months ago. Since our divorce, I have formed a new relationship with a gentleman who lives and works in Cape Town, South Africa. I wish to relocate with the children to Cape Town in time for the children to start at international schools there in September 2013. I plan for the children and me to live with my partner in his large apartment in central Cape Town. I have discussed my plans for relocation with the Respondent but we have unfortunately been unable to reach an agreement. The children have always had good relationships with the Respondent and spend time regularly with him. I will continue to promote the children's relationships with the Respondent and facilitate the children spending time with the Respondent in South Africa and in the UK.

I will be able to provide full details of my plans in a statement if necessary.

8. Agreements about residence and/or contact

Have you received a copy of the 'Parenting Plan: Putting your children first: A guide for separating parents' booklet?

☑ Yes   ☐ No

If No, you can get a copy free of charge from your local court or you can download a copy from the website www.tso.co.uk

Have you attended a mediation information/assessment meeting as suggested in the pre-action protocol and/or attached form FM1?

☑ Yes   ☐ No

You can find your nearest family mediation service by visiting the government's website DirectGov (www.direct.gov.uk) and search using the words 'family mediation'. You will find a database of accredited family mediation services on the website.

If you did not use mediation or attend a mediation information/assessment meeting please explain why:

7

9. Risk

Do you believe that the child(ren) named at Section 1 have experienced or are at risk of experiencing harm from any of the following by any person who has had contact with the child?

	Yes	No
any form of domestic abuse/violence	☐	☑
child abduction	☐	☑
child abuse	☐	☑
drugs, alcohol or substance abuse	☐	☑
other safety or welfare concerns	☐	☑

If you answered Yes to any of the above, please complete form C1A (Supplemental information form).

10. Other court cases which concern the child(ren) listed on page 1

Are you aware of any other court cases now, or at any time in the past, which concern any of the child(ren) at Section 1?

☐ Yes   If Yes, please attach a copy of any relevant order, and complete the details of the Cafcass/CAFCASS CYMRU officer and child's solicitor below. If you do not have a copy of the order please complete all the additional details below.

☑ No   If No, please **go to Section 11**

Additional details

Name of child(ren)

Name of the court where proceedings heard

Case no.

Date/year (if known)

Name and office (if known) of Cafcass/CAFCASS CYMRU officer

Name and address of child's solicitor, if known

Postcode ☐☐☐☐ ☐☐☐☐

If the above details are different for each child please provide details on additional sheets.

Please tick if additional sheets are attached. ☐

8

11. Attending the court

Section N of the the booklet **'CB1 - Making an application - Children and the Family Courts'** provides information about attending court.

If you require an interpreter, you must tell the court now so that one can be arranged.

Do you or any of the parties need an interpreter at court?

☐ Yes   ☑ No

If Yes, please specify the language and dialect:

If attending the court, do you or any of the parties involved have a disability for which you require special assistance or special facilities?

☐ Yes   ☑ No

If Yes, please say what the needs are

Please say whether the court needs to make any special arrangements for you to attend court (e.g. providing you with a separate waiting room from the respondent or other security provisions).

N/A

Court staff may get in touch with you about the requirements

12. Statement of truth

*delete as appropriate

*[I believe] [The applicant/respondent believes] that the facts stated in this application are true.

*I am duly authorised by the applicant/respondent to sign this statement.

Print full name

Name of applicant solicitors firm

Signed

Dated ☐☐/☐☐/☐☐☐☐

(Applicant) (Applicant's solicitor)

Position or office held
(If signing on behalf of firm or company)

Proceedings for contempt of court may be brought against a person who makes or causes to be made, a false statement in a document verified by a statement of truth.

continued over the page ⇨

9

Information for completing form C100

A copy of this application will be provided to Cafcass upon issue of proceedings. The information contained in the form C100 enables Cafcass to conduct enquiries prior to the first court hearing, without it they cannot conduct their initial safeguarding checks and enquiries.

Whilst every question in this form should be completed or stated that information is not available the following **essential** information is required by Cafcass/CAFCASS CYMRU and failure to provide this information could lead to unnecessary delays to proceedings:

Page 1

- ☐ Whether permission is required
- ☐ The full name(s) of the child(ren) in the proceedings
- ☐ Their date(s) of birth
- ☐ Their gender
- ☐ The applicants relationship to the child(ren)
- ☐ The respondents relationship to the child(ren)

Page 2

- ☐ Your/the applicant's full name
- ☐ Any previous names
- ☐ Your/the applicant's gender and date of birth
- ☐ Your/the applicant's address, including the postcode
    Note: if you/the applicant does not wish the address to be made known it should be included in an accompanying form C8.
- ☐ Your/the applicant's telephone number and if applicable, mobile telephone
    Note: if you/the applicant does not wish the number to be made known it should be included in an accompanying form C8.

Page 3

- ☐ The respondent's full name
- ☐ Previous surnames (if known)
- ☐ The respondent's gender and date of birth
- ☐ The respondent's address, including the postcode
- ☐ The respondent's telephone number and if applicable, mobile telephone

Page 5

- ☐ Solicitor details (if applicable), including a telephone number

Page 6

- ☐ The names of the child(ren)'s parents
- ☐ If the child(ren) is/are not living with either the Applicant or Respondent you must give:
    - the child(ren)'s current address
    - the full names of the adults living with them and their relationship or involvement with the child(ren)

Page 7

- ☐ The nature of the application for each child

Page 8

- ☐ Have the child(ren) suffered or are at risk of suffering harm

Page 9

- ☐ Check you have completed and signed section 12

What to do now

- ☐ Check you have attached copies of any **relevant orders** (as per Section 10).

- ☐ You must provide a **copy** of the application and attached documents for each of the respondents and one for the Children and Family Court Advisory and Support Service (Cafcass or CAFCASS CYMRU).

- ☐ Is form C1A attached (if applicable)?

- ☐ Is form FM1 attached?

- ☐ Are any additional sheets attached?

- ☐ If you have included additional sheets you must add the names of the parties and children at the top of the page and details of the questions and page number the additional sheets relate to.

- ☐ Check you have attached the correct fee. The leaflet 'EX50 County court fees' provides information about court fees you will have to pay.

Now take or send your application with the correct fee and correct number of copies to the court.

Court fees

You may be exempt from paying all or part of the fee. The combined booklet and application form 'EX160A Court Fees - Do you have to pay them' gives more information. You can get a copy from the court or download a copy from our website at www.justice.gov.uk

5.2

SAMPLE C2 CROSS-APPLICATION RESPONSE FORM RELATING TO THE CASE STUDY IN CHAPTER 4

	To be completed by the court
C2	
Application	Name of court
• For permission to start proceedings	
• For an order or directions in existing proceedings	Date issued
• To be joined as, or cease to be, a party in existing family proceedings under the Children Act 1989	Case number

Before completing this form please read the leaflet **'CB1 – Making an application – Children and the Family Courts'**. You can get a copy of from your local court or at www.justice.gov.uk.

- Failure to complete every question or state if it does not apply, could delay the case, as the court will have to ask you to provide the additional information required.
- If there is not enough space please attach separate sheets.
- Cafcass/CAFCASS CYMRU will carry out checks as it considers necessary. See Section J of leaflet CB1 for more information about Cafcass and CAFCASS CYMRU.

1. Summary of application

Your name (the applicant(s))

PETER BROWN

The respondent's name(s)
See Sections G and H of the booklet CB1.

SUSAN BROWN

Some people need permission to apply - See Section C of the leaflet CB1

Are you applying for permission to issue an application?

☐ Yes, and I attach a completed form C100
☐ Permission not required   ☐ Permission already granted

If you are making an application in existing proceedings, please give the existing case number(s).

FD2013

Please list the name(s) of the child(ren) and the type(s) of order you are applying for, starting with the oldest. To understand which order to apply for read the booklet CB1 Section D.

Child 1 - Full name of child	Date of birth	Gender	Order(s) applied for
CHARLES BROWN	1 0 / 1 1 / 2 0 0 2	☑ Male ☐ Female	RESIDENCE, SHARED RESIDENCE AND/OR CONTACT
Relationship to applicant(s)		Relationship to respondent(s)	
SON		SON	

Child 2 - Full name of child	Date of birth	Gender	Order(s) applied for
CAMILLA BROWN	2 0 / 0 7 / 2 0 0 5	☐ Male ☑ Female	RESIDENCE, SHARED RESIDENCE AND/OR CONTACT
Relationship to applicant(s)		Relationship to respondent(s)	
DAUGHTER		DAUGHTER	

Child 3 - Full name of child	Date of birth	Gender	Order(s) applied for
FREDERIC BROWN	3 0 / 0 3 / 2 0 0 9	☑ Male ☐ Female	RESIDENCE, SHARED RESIDENCE AND/OR CONTACT
Relationship to applicant(s)		Relationship to respondent(s)	
SON		SON	

C2 Application (04.11)   © Crown copyright 2011

2. About you (the applicant(s))

	Applicant 1 (You)	Applicant 2 (if applicable)
Full names	PETER BROWN	
Previous names (if any)		
Gender	☑ Male ☐ Female	☐ Male ☐ Female
Date of birth (If under 18 read section R of leaflet CB1)	D D / M M / Y Y Y Y	D D / M M / Y Y Y Y
Place of birth (town/county/country)	MANCHESTER	

If you do not wish your address to be made known to the respondent, leave the details below blank and complete Confidential contact details Form C8.

Address	FLAT 2, THE MILL, EPSOM, SURREY	
	Postcode ☐☐☐☐ ☐☐☐☐	Postcode ☐☐☐☐ ☐☐☐☐
Home telephone number	[INSERT]	
Mobile telephone number	[INSERT]	
Email address		
Have you lived at this address for more than 5 years?	☐ Yes ☑ No	☐ Yes ☐ No

If No, please provide details of all previous addresses you have lived at for the last 5 years.

If you do not wish your contact details to be made known to the Respondent, leave the details blank and complete Confidential contact details Form C8	6 THE GREEN, EPSOM, SURREY	

2

3. The respondents

Sections G and H of the the booklet **'CB1 - Making an application - Children and the Family Courts'** explain who a respondent is.

If there are more than 2 respondents please continue on a separate sheet.

	Respondent 1	**Respondent 2**
Full names	SUSAN BROWN	N/A
Previous names (if known)	FARMER	
Gender	☐ Male ☑ Female	☐ Male ☐ Female
Date of birth (If party under 18 read section R of leaflet CB1)	D D / M M / Y Y Y Y	D D / M M / Y Y Y Y
Place of birth (town/county/country)	LONDON	
Address	6 THE GREEN, EPSOM, SURREY	
	Postcode ☐☐☐☐ ☐☐☐☐	Postcode ☐☐☐☐ ☐☐☐☐
Home telephone number	[INSERT]	
Mobile telephone number	[INSERT]	
Email address	[INSERT]	
Have they lived at this address for more than 5 years?	☑ Yes ☐ No ☐ Don't know	☐ Yes ☐ No ☐ Don't know

If No, please provide details of all previous addresses they have lived at for the last 5 years.

3

4. Others who should be given notice

There may be other people who should be notified of your application, for example, someone who cares for the child but is not a parent. Sections G and I of the the booklet **'CB1 - Making an application - Children and the Family Courts'** explain who others are.

	Person1	Person 2
Full names	N/A	
Previous names (if known)		
Gender	☐ Male ☐ Female	☐ Male ☐ Female
Date of birth	D D / M M / Y Y Y Y	D D / M M / Y Y Y Y
Address		
	Postcode	Postcode
Please state their relationship to the children listed on page 1. If their relationship is not the same to each child please state their relationship to each child		

4

5. Solicitors details

Do you have a solicitor acting for you?	☑ Yes ☐ No If No, see section R of leaflet CB1 for more information
	If Yes, please give the following details
Your solicitor's name	[INSERT]
Name of firm	[INSERT]
Address	[INSERT] Postcode ☐☐☐☐ ☐☐☐
Telephone number	[INSERT]
Fax number	[INSERT]
DX number	[INSERT]
Solicitor's Reference	[INSERT]
Email address	[INSERT]

6. Details of application

Please give brief details about what you are applying for and your reasons for making the application.

My former wife has formed a new relationship with a gentleman who lives and works in Cape Town, South Africa and wishes to remove our three children from this jurisdiction to live with her in Cape Town. I have tried to persuade my former wife to reconsider and to stay here but she has refused to do so. I do not believe it would be in the children's best interests to relocate to South Africa. I have always made a significant contribution to the children's care and all of the children will suffer a significant reduction in the time they spend with me. Charles (Charlie) will lose the opportunity of moving to the grammar school where he has been offered a place on a scholarship. I am very concerned about how my relationship with Frederic (Freddie) in particular will be maintained in view of his young age and the lack of progression in the time he spends with me.

I believe that it will be best for the children that they stay living in this country. If my former wife insists on relocating, I would like the children to live with me, and will seek a Residence Order in my favour and a Contact Order defining when the children are to have contact with my former wife. If she agrees to stay here, I consider it will be best that the children live with my former wife and me under a Shared Residence Order.

7. Attending the court

Section N of the the booklet **'CB1 - Making an application - Children and the Family Courts'** provides information about attending court.

If you require an interpreter, you must tell the court now so that one can be arranged.

Do you or any of the parties need an interpreter at court?

☐ Yes ☑ No

If Yes, please specify the language and dialect:

If attending the court, do you or any of the parties involved have a disability for which you require special assistance or special facilities?

☐ Yes ☑ No

If Yes, please say what the needs are

Please say whether the court needs to make any special arrangements for you to attend court (e.g. providing you with a separate waiting room from the respondent or other security provisions).

N/A

Court staff may get in touch with you about the requirements

8. Statement of truth

*delete as appropriate

*[I believe] [The applicant/respondent believes] that the facts stated in this application are true.

*I am duly authorised by the applicant/respondent to sign this statement.

Print full name

Name of applicant solicitors firm

Signed

Dated [D][D]/[M][M]/[Y][Y][Y][Y]

(Applicant) (Applicant's solicitor)

Position or office held (If signing on behalf of firm or company)

Proceedings for contempt of court may be brought against a person who makes or causes to be made, a false statement in a document verified by a statement of truth.

continued over the page ⇨

6

What to do now

If you are applying for permission to issue an application

☐ Check you have attached copies of the form C100 application and form C1A if appropriate

☐ Check any necessary documents are attached to the form C100 application

For all applications

☐ Check you have completed and signed Section 8 of this form

☐ Check you have attached the correct fee. The leaflet 'EX50 County court fees' provides information about court fees you will have to pay.

Now take or send your application with the correct fee and correct number of copies (one copy for the court, one copy for Cafcass/CAFCASS CYMRU and one for each party or other person) to the court.

Court fees

You may be exempt from paying all or part of the fee. The combined booklet and application form 'EX160A Court Fees - Do you have to pay them' gives more information. You can get a copy from the court or download a copy from our website at www.justice.gov.uk

Appendix 6

SIGNATORIES TO THE 1980 AND 1996 HAGUE CONVENTIONS

6.1

LIST OF CONTRACTING STATES OF THE HAGUE CONVENTION ON THE CIVIL ASPECTS OF INTERNATIONAL CHILD ABDUCTION 1980

R: Ratification
A: Accession
A*: Accession giving rise to an acceptance procedure
C: Continuation
Su: Succession

Albania	A*
Andorra	A*
Argentina	R
Armenia	A*
Australia	R
Austria	R
Bahamas	A*
Belarus	A*
Belgium	R
Belize	A*
Bosnia and Herzegovina	Su
Brazil	A*
Bulgaria	A*
Burkina Faso	A*
Canada	R
Chile	A*

China, People's Republic of	C
Colombia	A*
Costa Rica	A*
Croatia	Su
Cyprus	A*
Czech Republic	R
Denmark	R
Dominican Republic	A*
Ecuador	A*
El Salvador	A*
Estonia	A*
Fiji	A*
Finland	R
France	R
Gabon	A*
Georgia	A*
Germany	R
Greece	R
Guatemala	A*
Guinea	A*
Honduras	A*
Hungary	A*
Iceland	A*
Ireland	R
Israel	R
Italy	R

Korea, Republic of	A*
Latvia	A*
Lesotho	A*
Lithuania	A*
Luxembourg	R
Macedonia, Former Yugoslav Republic of	Su
Malta	A*
Mauritius	A*
Mexico	A*
Moldova, Republic of	A*
Monaco	A*
Montenegro	Su
Morocco	A*
Netherlands	R
New Zealand	A*
Nicaragua	A*
Norway	R
Panama	A*
Paraguay	A*
Peru	A*
Poland	A*
Portugal	R
Romania	A*
Russian Federation	A*
Saint Kitts and Nevis	A*
San Marino	A*

Serbia	Su
Seychelles	A*
Singapore	A*
Slovakia	R
Slovenia	A*
South Africa	A*
Spain	R
Sri Lanka	A*
Sweden	R
Switzerland	R
Thailand	A*
Trinidad and Tobago	A*
Turkey	R
Turkmenistan	A*
Ukraine	A*
United Kingdom of Great Britain and Northern Ireland	R
United States of America	R
Uruguay	A*
Uzbekistan	A*
Venezuela	R
Zimbabwe	A*

6.2

LIST OF CONTRACTING STATES OF THE HAGUE CONVENTION ON JURISDICTION, APPLICABLE LAW, RECOGNITION, ENFORCEMENT AND CO-OPERATION IN RESPECT OF PARENTAL RESPONSIBILITY AND MEASURES FOR THE PROTECTION OF CHILDREN 1996

R: Ratification
A: Accession
A*: Accession giving rise to an acceptance procedure
C: Continuation
Su: Succession

Albania	A*
Armenia	A*
Australia	R
Austria	R
Belgium	
Bulgaria	A
Croatia	R
Cyprus	R
Czech Republic	R
Denmark	R
Dominican Republic	A*
Ecuador	A*
Estonia	A

Finland	R
France	R
Germany	R
Greece	R
Hungary	R
Ireland	R
Italy	
Latvia	R
Lesotho	A
Lithuania	A
Luxembourg	R
Malta	A
Monaco	R
Montenegro	A
Morocco	R
Netherlands	R
Poland	R
Portugal	R
Romania	R
Russian Federation	A
Slovakia	R
Slovenia	R
Spain	R
Sweden	R
Switzerland	R
Ukraine	A*

United Kingdom of Great Britain and Northern Ireland	R
United States of America	
Uruguay	R

BIBLIOGRAPHY

Behrens, J, 'U v U: The High Court on Relocation' *Melbourne University Law Review* 572

Boele-Woelki, K and González Beilfuss, C (eds), *Brussels II Bis: Its Impact and Application in the Member States* (Cambridge, Intersentia, 2007)

Boyd, S, 'Gendering the Best Interests Principle: Custody, Access and Relocation in a Mobile Society' in Niman, H, and Sadvari, G, (eds), *Family Law: 'The Best Interests of the Child'* (Ottawa, Law Soc of Upper Canada, 2000)

Brasse, G, 'The Payne Threshold: Leaving the Jurisdiction' [2005] *Family Law* 780

Council of Europe, *Prevention and Resolution of Parental Disputes (Relocation of Children)*, (The Hague, Document CDCJ(2013)1, 10 January 2013)

Eekelaar, J, Maclean, M and Beinart, S, *Family Lawyers: The Divorce Work of Solicitors* (Oxford, Hart Publishing, 2000)

Freeman, M, 'Relocation: The Reunite Research' (London, Reunite, 2009)

Geekie QC, C, 'Relocation and Shared Residence: One Route or Two?' [2008] *Family Law* 446

George, R, 'Changing Names, Changing Places: Reconsidering Section 13 of the Children Act 1989' [2008] *Family Law* 1121

——, *Ideas and Debates in Family Law* (Oxford, Hart Publishing, 2012)

——, 'International Relocation, Care Arrangements and Case Taxonomy' [2012] *Family Law* 1478

——, 'Practitioners' Views on Children's Welfare in Relocation Disputes: Comparing Approaches in England and New Zealand' [2011] *Child and Family Law Quarterly* 178

——, 'Re F (Internal Relocation) [2010] EWCA Civ 1428' (casenote) [2011] *Journal of Social Welfare and Family Law* 169

——, 'Re L (Internal Relocation: Shared Residence Order) [2009] EWCA Civ 20, [2009] 1 FLR 1157' (casenote) [2010] *Journal of Social Welfare and Family Law* 71

——, *Relocation Disputes: Law and Practice in England and New Zealand* (Oxford, Hart Publishing, 2013)

——, 'Relocation Research: Early Ideas from Ten County Court Cases' [2012] *Family Law* 700

——, 'Reviewing Relocation? *Re W (Relocation: Removal Outside Jurisdiction)* [2011] EWCA Civ 345 and *K v K (Relocation Shared Care Arrangement)* [2011] EWCA Civ 793' [2012] *Child and Family Law Quarterly* 110

——, 'The International Relocation Debate' [2012] *Journal of Social Welfare and Family Law* 141

Gilmore, S, 'The *Payne* Saga: Precedent and Family Law Cases' [2011] *Family Law* 970

Hayes, M, 'Relocation Cases: Is the Court of Appeal Applying the Correct Principles?' [2006] *Child and Family Law Quarterly* 351

Henaghan, M, 'Relocation Cases: The Rhetoric and the Reality of a Child's Best Interests: A View from the Bottom of the World' [2011] *Child and Family Law Quarterly* 226

Herring, J and Taylor, R, 'Relocating Relocation' [2006] *Child and Family Law Quarterly* 517

Hetherington, M and Kelly, J, *For Better or For Worse: Divorce Reconsidered* (New York, Norton, 2001)

Judd QC, F and George, R, 'International Relocation: Do We Stand Alone?' [2010] *Family Law* 63

Kaspiew, R, Behrens, J and Smyth, B, 'Relocation Disputes in Separated Families Prior to the 2006 Reforms: An Empirical Study' (2011) 86 *Family Matters* 72

Lowe, N and Douglas, G, *Bromley's Family Law*, 10th edn (Oxford, Oxford University Press, 2007)

Lowe, N, Everall QC, M and Nicholls, M, *International Movement of Children: Law Practice and Procedure* (Bristol, Jordan Publishing, 2004)

——, *The New Brussels II Regulation: A Supplement to International Movement of Children* (Bristol, Jordan Publishing, 2005)

Lowe, N, and Nicholls QC, M, *The 1996 Hague Convention on the Protection of Children* (Bristol, Jordan Publishing, 2012)

Maclean, M and Eekelaar, J, *Family Law Advocacy: How Barristers Help the Victims of Family Failure* (Oxford, Hart Publishing, 2009)

Parkinson, P, 'Freedom of Movement in an Era of Shared Parenting: The Differences in Judicial Approaches to Relocation' (2008) 36 *Federal Law Review* 145

Permanent Bureau of the Hague Conference on Private International Law, Preliminary Note on International Family Relocation, Preliminary Document No 11 of January 2012, online at www.hcch.net/upload/wop/abduct2012pd11e. pdf

Pressdee, P, 'Relocation, Relocation, Relocation: Rigorous Scrutiny Revisited' [2008] *Family Law* 220

Renton, C, 'Rethinking Relocation' [2010] *New Law Journal* 958

Taylor, N, Gollop, M and Henaghan, M, *Relocation Following Parental Separation: The Welfare and Best Interests of Children* (Dunedin, Centre for Research on Children and Families, 2010)

Taylor, R, 'Poels Apart: Fixed Principles and Shifting Values in Relocation Law' in Gilmore, S, Herring, J and Probert, R (eds), *Landmark Cases in Family Law* (Oxford, Hart Publishing, 2011)

Worwood, A, 'International Relocation – The Debate' [2005] *Family Law* 621

Young, L, 'Resolving Relocation Disputes: The "Interventionist" Approach in Australia' [2011] *Child and Family Law Quarterly* 203

INDEX

References are to paragraph numbers.